BOULDER CITY LIBRARY
3 1432 00183 7358

D0952589

HOW TO BE MARRIED

FICTION BY JO PIAZZA

The Knockoff: A Novel (with Lucy Sykes)

Love Rehab: A Novel in Twelve Steps

NONFICTION BY JO PIAZZA

If Nuns Ruled the World: Ten Sisters on a Mission

Celebrity, Inc.: How Famous People Make Money

HOW TO BE

MARRIED

What I Learned from Real Women on Five Continents About Surviving My First (Really Hard) Year of Marriage

JO PIAZZA

HARMONY
BOOKS • NEW YORK

This is a work of nonfiction. Nonetheless, some of the names and personal characteristics of the individuals involved have been changed in order to disguise their identities. Any resulting resemblance to persons living or dead is entirely coincidental and unintentional.

Published in the United States by Harmony Books, an imprint of the Crown Publishing Group, a division of Penguin Random House LLC, New York.
crownpublishing.com

Harmony Books is a registered trademark, and the Circle colophon is a trademark of Penguin Random House LLC.

Library of Congress Cataloging-in-Publication Data
Names: Piazza, Jo, author.
Title: How to be married : what I learned from real women on five continents about surviving my first (really hard) year of marriage / Jo Piazza.
Description: New York : Harmony Books, [2017] | Includes bibliographical references.
Identifiers: LCCN 2016036609 | ISBN 9780451495556
Subjects: LCSH: Piazza, Jo—Marriage. | Authors, American—21st century—Biography. | Newlyweds—Biography. | Marriage—Cross-cultural studies.
Classification: LCC HQ759 .P5222 2017 | DDC 306.81—dc23
LC record available at https://lccn.loc.gov/2016036609

ISBN 978-0-451-49555-6
Ebook ISBN 978-0-451-49556-3

Printed in the United States of America

Jacket design by Jenny Carrow
Jacket photograph by Christopher Silas Neal

1 3 5 7 9 10 8 6 4 2

First Edition

FOR NICK

You make my world make sense.

Contents

The problem with marriage is that it ends every night after making love, and it must be rebuilt every morning before breakfast.

—Gabriel García Márquez

Longed for him. Got him. Shit.

—Margaret Atwood

Author's Note

After many years spent wandering the world for both work and pleasure, I well know that you can't witness the truth of any country or culture in a single visit, or even in many. I'm a traveler and a journalist, not an anthropologist, psychologist, or historian. In these brief pages, I can't possibly describe the many nuances of marriage and partnership as they exist in every country I visited. The story of a voyage or a marriage will never be complete. No outsider can understand a culture any better than a mere bystander can understand the inner workings of someone else's marriage. I went on this journey searching for advice, for tangible things I could bring back home that would be useful in my own partnership—and hopefully yours. No doubt there are many things I missed along the way.

Talking about marriage, really talking about it, is like taking a shower with another person. You need to be vulnerable and fearless. Because marriage can be a sensitive topic, particularly in countries where women have much less freedom than in the United States, some names have been changed and some characters have been turned into composites.

In many countries I relied on translators to help me ask questions and to relay answers. I also relied on my own memory for descriptions of situations in which I was unable to take notes or make recordings. Both memory and translators found on Craigslist are fallible, but I've done my best in both situations to re-create the scenes in this book as they actually occurred. Everything that takes place in this book happened during the period right before my wedding and first anniversary. The text goes in a mostly chronological order, except for a few exceptions to make the narrative flow more smoothly and prevent reader fatigue.

My goal in writing *How to Be Married* is to start a dialogue about partnership, sex, love, marriage, fidelity, monogamy, polygamy, money, power, equality, kids, men and women, and how all of these things fit together in a world that's changing faster than most of us ever thought possible.

So, let's do this. Let's talk about marriage.

HOW TO BE MARRIED

1

San Francisco

After Happily Ever After

"You could leave me. Divorce me. Seriously. You could." I said to Nick, my husband of just four months. I slumped lower on the sofa and stared down at the blurry outline of a red wine stain on the orange cushion. "I mean it. You didn't sign up for this. Find someone else. Find a healthy wife."

"You're ridiculous," Nick stated with his trademark midwestern certainty, sitting beside me and placing one of his giant bear-paw hands on my lower back. His default is calm and cool, while mine leans toward hysterics and dramatic declarations. I narrowed my eyes, wanting to be mean and to be comforted at the same time. I slid away from him, adding physical space between us in case he took me up on my offer.

"I'm honest. I'm being honest. This isn't what you signed up for!" Why was I saying this? *Stop*, I thought. *Just stop.* But I couldn't. My eyes stung, my voice shook, and my heart slammed into my throat as I buried my face in the sofa we'd bought together. We'd decided it was cheerful and cozy, but also durable enough to withstand destruction from our big gross dog and, one day, our kids.

Hours earlier, following a routine checkup with my doctor, a genetics counselor named Violet, with a strangely chirpy upbeat tone, told me I had a good chance of developing the disease that was slowly killing my father—muscular dystrophy. For most of my life, my parents and doctors told me I couldn't inherit his condition, but they were wrong. Violet went on to explain that this particular kind of muscular dystrophy could strike at any time in my late thirties (I was thirty-five). Once it starts, there's no reversing its course. Your muscles, particularly in your legs, back, and face, stop working. Many people with the disease end up in a wheelchair and need assistance from a machine to breathe.

"It's a fifty-fifty chance you have this disease."

"Excuse me?"

"Fifty-fifty you have it. You'll do a genetic test and we'll need to check. Do you want to know or not? Some people don't want to know. By the way, I meant to ask you, are you planning on having kids?" Violet said all of this in the casual tone someone might use to ask if you're planning on watching the new season of *The Bachelor.*

My father showed symptoms before he turned forty and the progression of the disease was long, slow, and excruciating. By the time Violet delivered her news to me, my dad was confined to a hospital bed in the living room of my parents' house, unable to walk, to stand, or breathe on his own.

For my mother, the lines between wife, caretaker, and servant became invisible, a fact that eroded their marriage as well as her own mental and physical health. My mother's life, one of a dutiful but miserable caretaker, wasn't something I wanted for Nick—not now, not ever. I was trying to be humane, or maybe I thought that by creating a different awful situation I could make the current awful situation go away.

That's why I told my new husband—a man who loved riding bikes, hiking, skiing, climbing things, and doing anything with a strong set of two legs—to divorce me, I felt ruined, damaged, and powerless. I didn't want to ruin his life.

....

But let me back up a little. I set out to write this book six months before I heard from Violet. That was a happier time. And I promise this book isn't all doom and gloom and crying on couches. I was in the middle of planning my wedding and after months of receiving unsolicited advice about "the big day," I realized I had no idea what happened when the wedding was over. I had no idea *how to be married.*

Sure, there are plenty of books about fixing a bad marriage, but mine wasn't broken yet—it hadn't even started. Besides, none of them spoke to me. With their pastel covers emblazoned with flowers, sunrises, and couples who had perfect hair, those books were talking to someone more mature, someone more refined, someone who already owned napkin rings and didn't kill houseplants.

As my friend Jessica put it, "There are lots of books on how to be married, but they're awful." Speaking at a conference in 2011, the Facebook COO Sheryl Sandberg told the crowd that the most important career choice a woman can make is to marry well. But there was no guidebook on how to be well married.

My other conundrum was that I loved my life. Before Nick. Adding him to it was wonderful, but I didn't want being married to become the most important thing about me. I felt all tangled up inside when my engagement received more Facebook likes than that time I got a great job, or when I sold my first book, or made that excellent meme of Liz Lemon eating French fries with Leslie Knope. Everything else I'd ever done paled in comparison to the fact that I. Was. Getting. Married.

I'm not alone in finding my hard-won accomplishments outshone by a ring. During the 2016 Summer Olympics in Rio, the Chinese diver He Zi did something none of us could ever dream of doing when she won a silver medal. Her boyfriend proposed immediately afterward. The BBC article celebrating Zi read:

"Chinese diver He Zi had just received a silver medal for the women's three-metre springboard at the Rio Olympics on Sunday. But she ended up with an *even bigger* prize when her boyfriend Qin Kai, in front of a global TV audience, went down on one knee." Emphasis mine.

Just as a ring can overshadow a woman's achievements, personality, and identity, marriage itself can be completely eclipsed by the "twelve hours that change everything." No matter how progressive we think we've become in America, we're still a society obsessed with weddings. The *New York Times* allots premium real estate to dozens of wedding announcements in its top-selling issue of the week. Millions of viewers tune in to the *Bachelor* franchises, reality shows that toy with the viewer's fear of not finding "the one" before forcing two panicked and inebriated strangers into an engagement ceremony on top of a precariously windy seaside cliff. And even though it has long been hailed for breaking television's glass ceiling by portraying strong, independent women, three of the four heroines on *Sex and the City* were brides before the show's conclusion.

Nearly every romantic comedy ever made ends with the wedding and leaves out the most interesting part—the marriage.

As a culture, we're less interested in the machinery of a marriage, the quotidian challenges, the joys, pitfalls, irritations, surprises, and intimacies. No one would click on the headline: "Beyoncé Annoyed Jay Finished Watching *Game of Thrones* Without Her" or "Kanye Wishes Kim Would Stop Texting at the Dinner Table" or "Justin HATES That Jen Forgets to Put the Cap Back on the Shampoo." Although all of these things are definitely true.

If the wedding is the fairy-tale ending then what is the marriage? A sequel? What do we actually do after "I do"?

....

I have to be honest. My own marriage *was* the "fairy-tale ending" in the mad cap romantic comedy that had been my life for thirty-four years. I'd long been in the habit of selecting all the wrong men, gotten myself into hilarious misunderstandings, kissed all the frogs, and drunk all the pinot grigio with all the gay best friends. In my early thirties, I was the last woman standing among my girlfriends from college . . . the spinster, the one who would have cats and affairs with other people's husbands. And then, when I least expected it, I found my prince on a sightseeing boat during a business trip to the Galápagos Islands.

Yeah. I know.

I was working as the managing editor for Yahoo!'s travel Web site. Nick also worked in journalism, the serious business kind that sent him to the Galápagos to write about the stability of Ecuador's tourism plans. I was there to write about how to take wonderful selfies with baby sea lions. Nick quickly became my favorite person on the boat. We'd each brought our own tattered copy of Kurt Vonnegut's *Galápagos* to the Galápagos. When we went snorkeling, he grabbed my hand and showed me midget penguins swimming beneath the surface. He had none of the arrogant bullshit that oozed from the boys in New York City. And even though I'd shown up on this ecocruise with no makeup, no agenda, and not a single adorable outfit, he kissed me on our last night at sea. Either that kiss was going to be the start of something wonderful or I'd never see him again.

When we said good-bye at the airport in Ecuador he looked so sad, like a Labrador retriever who'd misplaced his favorite ball.

"I want to see you again," he murmured as we exited the security line to fly to our homes on opposite sides of the country.

"Maybe I'll see you on Tinder," I joked to make the moment less awkward.

"Can I call you?"

"Don't you even want to play a little hard to get?" Who was this guy.

He shrugged. "What's the point?"

I thought about it for a second, carefully considering my reply. "In a couple of weeks, I'll be in Palm Springs for a conference. I could come early. We could go to Joshua Tree. I've never been."

"I'll take you camping!" he exclaimed with glee, kissed me, and ran to catch his flight.

As soon as I got back on the Internet, I Google and Facebook stalked him to ensure that he wasn't a serial killer.

Nick promised to meet me in the parking lot of LAX, but I surprised him at baggage claim instead. I wasn't sure how I'd feel about seeing this near stranger again. But when he turned around, grinned, and enveloped me in an enormous hug with a full kiss on the lips, I knew I was a goner. He'd brought along a tent, a grill, two sleeping bags, and a first aid kit that included a foil blanket in case I got hypothermia.

"I also have iodine pills in case we need to purify water," he said matter-of-factly. "They taste like crap, but you won't get sick."

This was someone who was ready for anything. Nick Aster was clearly a man who could fix my broken garbage disposal with his bare hands, one who would know how to keep houseplants alive.

He was also handsome and clever and funny. When I asked him to help me with things, he said, "As you wish." This was particularly attractive to a girl whose first sexual fantasy was about Cary Elwes in *The Princess Bride*. But he wasn't the kind of guy I usually dated. Nick is very, very outdoorsy. He had long hair, rode his bike everywhere, wore hiking sandals, and once, while backpacking in Colorado, was chased and almost killed by a mountain lion. I always dated guys who were indoorsy—bankery types who drank overpriced vodka and would rather have dated supermodels than me.

Soon after we met, I lamented to my shrink, Jen, that Nick wasn't my type. She made a face like she'd swallowed a bad oyster.

"Your type isn't working for you!" she shouted and rolled her eyes. She was right, of course, and I was smitten, and that was all there was to it. To misquote F. Scott Fitzgerald, we slipped briskly into an intimacy from which we never recovered.

We were engaged just three months after we met.

"I couldn't wait to propose to you. The world makes sense to me with you in it," Nick declared as he pulled out a slender gold band spiraled in very delicate (fair trade, conflict-free) diamonds.

"Gahhhhhhhhhhhh!" I yelled. "What? SERIOUSLY?" Then I remembered I was supposed to say yes.

By falling in love with Nick I learned all of the clichés are true. *When you know, you know. When it's right, it's easy. Love happens when you least expect it.* When I was single I thought the people who said those things were liars. I knew the truth. The truth was you dated someone for two to three years and then tricked them into marrying you. But I was the one who was wrong all along.

It took a while to sink in that I was actually getting married. It still hadn't hit me in July, three months later, when I packed my yellow Fiat, no bigger than a golf cart, with all of the detritus of my single life. I was leaving New York, my home of thirteen years, the only place I'd ever lived as an adult, for San Francisco to live with Nick before our wedding. No matter how difficult life could be in New York, it was complicated and strange in a way that I understood and had grown used to, like Buddhism or *New Yorker* cartoons. Leaving terrified me.

Nick couldn't get out of work for the week, so my friend Glynnis drove the 2,906 miles with me and my giant dog, Lady Piazza. Our journey would take seven ten-hour days. We'd be like Thelma and Louise without the sex with Brad Pitt, the murder, or the drive off the cliff, but with the red lipstick. There was something incredibly empowering about telling your almost-husband that you didn't need him to drive with you across the country. I liked being able to say: I've got this.

I patted Lady Piazza on the head as I took a final look around my city and swiped at the sweat trickling down the back of my neck. I wouldn't miss the smell of Manhattan during a hundred-degree day, that was for sure.

"You're a good girl. We'll like it in San Francisco," I whispered to the dog. I looked over at Glynnis. "I'm moving across the country," I said, in shock.

"Yeah, you are," she answered as she fiddled with the radio and used her other hand to expertly apply a second coat of lipstick.

"And I'm getting married," I added, staring at the traffic of New York City one last time.

Glynnis landed on a Taylor Swift song and turned to look at me. The sun caught her wild curls, illuminating them into a halo of flames. "Babe, is this just sinking in for you?" It was.

Now that I had my movie-perfect happy ending, I projected the face of a happy and confident bride-to-be, but on the inside I was terrified. I was terrified I'd lose my identity and my independence by joining my life to another person. I was terrified I would fail—that Nick and I wouldn't work and I would lose him. This made it all the more important not to lose myself in the process. The media tells us over and over again that half of all marriages in America end in failure. No matter how special and unique I believed my bond with Nick to be, I knew the road ahead was going to be difficult to navigate.

My worries hit me in waves as Glynnis and I lazily drove across the country. Starting in Wyoming, at a dude ranch called Paradise, I began to have nightmares. In those dreams, Nick was gone. Just gone. I knew I *had* been in love. I knew I *had* been with someone special. But it didn't last, didn't stick, and I didn't know why. Then there was the opposite dream. Nick was still there, we were married, and we were miserable. We'd morphed into my parents—needy, codependent, and violently dysfunctional.

My parents have had a long but miserable marriage, the kind where they fought and screamed and threatened to leave each other every day during my formative years but didn't, out of a sense of obligation to me and a misguided notion that staying in an unhappy marriage equalled success and divorce equalled failure. Women used to be able to model how to behave in their marriage on their mothers, but that just isn't the case for many of us. I couldn't do that.

For most of human history there have been real economic and societal imperatives for a woman to find a husband. Marriage was both destiny and social imperative for my grandmother Carolyn, who met her husband Merwin as a fourteen-year-old farm girl in Rockford, Illinois, desperate for a better life. When he got a football scholarship to the University of Colorado she told him to put a ring on it and get her the hell out of there. She was barely sixteen. When he graduated she became a *Mad Men*–era housewife. Around the time Betty Friedan's *The Feminine Mystique* came out in 1963, Carolyn was the dissatisfied woman who "made the beds, shopped for groceries, matched slipcover material, ate peanut butter sandwiches with her children, chauffeured Cub Scouts and Brownies," and was "afraid to ask even of herself the silent question—'Is this all?'" Three decades later, once my grandfather passed away, she traded in her Marilyn Monroe bottle-blond hair for a chic brown bob, began collecting abstract art, and never married again.

My own mother, who came of age during the second wave of feminism, told me she went to college with the intention of marrying a doctor or a lawyer. She wanted her "MRS." She met my law-student father on her first night of college and married him when she was twenty-one years old. For her and many of her peers in 1976 this was not unusual.

I was the first woman in my family who didn't feel like she had to get married.

I talked about this evolution of marriage with the academic and author Stephanie Coontz, who wrote the book on modern marriage, literally, in *Marriage, a History*.

"Marriage is no longer about making alliances to further your parents' interest or about linking a dependent female to a dominant male. Now both women and men can say they want to marry someone with similar ideals, talents, aspirations, and qualities. We want equals," Coontz told me. Of course, that comes with its own downsides.

"It creates new tensions when each person in a marriage has the ability to just walk away," Coontz added.

I could walk away from my marriage at any time. I could support myself, protect myself, feed myself, buy my own property, and even make a baby alone with the help of a very expensive doctor and a turkey baster.

I also asked Erica Jong, the inimitable feminist writer of *Fear of Flying*, why she still believed in marriage in a world where women no longer need to be married. Erica's been married four times, the last time for twenty-seven years and they're still going strong. Three failed marriages didn't scare her away from tying the knot a fourth time.

"It's both essential and nice to have one best friend in a hostile world," she told me.

When I told Erica I was working on a book about marriage, I didn't know what she'd say, and I was a little surprised that she was all for it. "Good! It's up to us to create a new form of marriage, a new way of being married, one where both partners feel fulfilled, one where nobody's work is more important than the other's, one where you are both caretakers. The template doesn't exist yet."

....

In the months leading up to my own wedding, my job as a travel editor had me constantly on the move, regularly waking up in a strange new hotel and opening the curtains to remember where I was. I found myself asking all strangers with wedding rings what makes a successful marriage. Not for any assignment, but for me. I asked Jamaican hairdressers, Malaysian street food vendors, Maldivian scuba guides, and even the conservative Muslim Qatari who took me on a 4x4 off-road adventure near the border with Saudi Arabia.

"Marriage is very, very hard," my guide grumbled as he steered our Land Rover into a giant mountain of sand at speeds that seemed above one hundred miles an hour. He was wearing a white *thobe*, a loose robe that reminded me how much I missed wearing caftans, and a red-checked *ghutrah* around his head. His enthusiastic mustache reminded me of an early Tom Selleck.

"I have just one woman; I do not want another wife. I love my wife and more wives means more headaches. I don't need another headache. I have advice for your husband! I make myself listen to my wife even when my mind is somewhere else. Tell him that."

He paused for a moment and raised his binoculars to what he told me was a security checkpoint on the border with Saudi Arabia.

"Those guys are always messing with us," he spat about the Saudis, adding over the blaring Emirati pop rock on the radio, "Seriously. You tell your husband to listen to you. Your marriage will fail otherwise. You want to drive over there and freak those guys out?"

"No, thank you." I replied with all the diplomacy I could muster. "Let's leave the Saudis alone."

I called Nick that night and mentioned, casually, that he should listen to me more. "My Qatari dune-bashing guide suggested I tell you that when we drove down to the border of Saudi Arabia."

Nick grew quiet. "I always listen to you. Get back safe. Okay? Don't go to Saudi Arabia."

With few exceptions, the answers I got about how to be married were strikingly similar. I made lists of them on napkins and the backs of boarding passes.

Never stop talking

Talk about things that make you feel uncomfortable and itchy and happy and sad and strange

Talk in person, on the phone, over text, via emoji; just keep talking

Shut the door when you pee

You do you

Complaining is contagious; don't start the complaining or you'll never stop

Buy sexy new underwear once a month

Walk naked around the house, but don't lie around in sweatpants … ever.

A prostitute in Amsterdam told me that a wife needs to be strong and must "remain the captain of her own ship."

Plenty of men and women admitted to struggling in their own marriages. Still others had irritatingly perfect unions filled with happiness, date nights, and unicorns.

As my ramblings grew to ten pages and then twenty, I realized I was sitting on a treasure trove of wisdom from around the world. I had no idea how to be married, but what if, like Lin Manuel Miranda's Alexander Hamilton, I could write my way out of my conundrum.

Marriage experts call the first year of marriage "the wet cement year," because it's the time when both members of a couple are figuring out how to exist as partners without getting stuck in the murk, without being trapped by bad habits. It's a time to set and test boundaries and create good habits that will continue for the rest of your marriage.

"In that first year of marriage we create the momentum for the rest of the marriage. We decide whether we'll be a team or whether we'll take the other one for granted. That year sets the stage for how we deal with everything life throws at us during a marriage, and a lot of it isn't pretty," Dr. Peter Pearson, a marriage therapist and the founder of the Couples Institute, told me when I explained my mad cap experiment.

What if Nick and I could spend our wet cement year searching the globe for insight into marriage, love, and partnership and trying to implement it in our own marriage?

Growing pains grow faster on the road and hard conversations can't be avoided. Research suggests that couples who travel together end up more satisfied with their partnership. It leads to better sex, pushes your buttons, and takes you out of your comfort zone. There's this TED talk by the psychotherapist and relationship guru Esther Perel about sustaining desire and passion in a long-term relationship. I must have listened to it a dozen times while I researched this book, particularly the part where she explains that both men and women have a strong need "for adventure, for novelty, for mystery, for risk, for danger, for the unknown, for the unexpected, surprise, for journey, for travel." Nick and I could spend the first twelve months of our marriage binge-watching Netflix, or we could take a journey into the unknown, getting into and out of uncomfortable situations together while we figured out how to be married.

In the months leading up to our wedding, as we pored over venues and catering details, we spent as many nights looking at maps and airline routes. There were so many interesting models for marriage—polygamy in Kenya, arranged marriage in India, open marriage in France. And there were so many questions to be answered. Why were marriages on the decline in northern Europe? Did French marriages succeed because everyone was having an affair? I found a couples' therapist running a practice in the middle of the Mexican jungle who was said to be able to save any marriage worth saving. We needed to meet that guy!

I lined up reporting trips, and even our honeymoon, to take us to cultures that would have interesting things to say about marriage and commitment. Nick runs his own Web site, so he was often able to come with me and work from the road. My husband is also a hoarder of frequent-flier miles, which subsidized what should have been a cost-prohibitive endeavor.

In researching this book I've interviewed hundreds of men and women around the world—ordinary people as well as experts—to find out what makes a modern, and sometimes not so modern, marriage work. Many of the things I learned were surprising. The truth is that marriage is evolving everywhere and most people our age, from cosmopolitan Paris to rural India, are also trying to figure out how to be a husband or a wife in wildly changing times.

I didn't find *the* answer, but I did get plenty of remedies, suggestions, and advice. There were some key things I heard over and over again: patience, good communication, a healthy sex life, teamwork, having a strong community of peers, gratitude, equality, having similar views on raising kids, being on the same page about personal finance, keeping a sense of adventure, compromise. I slowly began to form a portrait of what it meant to be a good partner.

This book also traces our own wet cement year from start to finish—the wonderful, the bad, the strange, and the sometimes surprising. As I share stories of my travels, both alone and with my new husband, I'm also telling the story of how I dug into my heart, my guts, and my fears to figure out how to make this marriage thing work.

....

I should tell you the most important thing I've learned, even if it means you aren't going to keep reading past this introduction. The most important thing I've discovered is that a good marriage isn't about shit always going right. It's about the times when shit goes wrong, very wrong, and two people coming out the other side and saying, "Okay. We're still in this together. I still want you to be here when I wake up in the morning." I didn't expect our first year of marriage to be filled with loss, death, drama, and illness. I thought the hardest thing we'd have to face would be deciding what color to paint the living room and whether the dog could sleep in the bed.

But life happened.

What I've learned along the way is figuring out how to be married is an actual journey, a different one for everyone. What matters is being willing to take that journey together.

....

As we were lying in bed the night after I talked to Violet about the muscular dystrophy, after I'd told my still-new husband to divorce me, Nick kissed my shoulder and nudged the back of my calf with his big toe until I rolled to look at him. I wasn't asleep, just staring at the numbers on the alarm clock as they ticked closer to dawn.

"I need you to know this changes nothing between the two of us. Our marriage is exactly the same as it was yesterday. If I have to push you around in a wheelchair, we'll get you a lovely wheelchair with cup holders and room for a cheese plate."

For the first time since we'd been married, I understood how it felt to face obstacles and adversity with another human by my side, how it felt to share both the good things and the bad things life throws at you. It was nice to have a friend in this hostile world.

We'd figure this out. Together. That's what this story is really about.

2

Chile

Surrender?

> A long marriage is two people trying to dance a duet and two solos at the same time.
>
> —Anne Taylor Fleming

When I was single I wondered what made being married so different from dating, so much harder. Was it the fact that it was more difficult to walk away from a marriage? That it was legally binding? That the commitment was more intense? That the stakes were higher? Was it the fact that you now had to take another person into consideration all of the time? To constantly worry about their needs, their wants, and their feelings?

Plenty of people gave me unsolicited advice about getting married, including my gynecologist, Amy.

"It's a lot of work," she said, her arm wrist deep in my pelvis and her voice slightly muffled by my vagina. "But no one tells you what kind of work you have to do. That's not fair. Sometimes I think it would be easier to be alone."

"Really? That's a big bomb to drop on someone right before they walk down the aisle," I said, scooching my butt closer to the end of the metal table. She was too distracted by her inspection of my cervix to answer.

Ben Affleck also told us marriage was hard. Remember that? It was right before he ran away with the nanny and got the kind of tattoo that appeals to teenage boys who work at gas stations.

The hard part for me was learning to live in tandem with another human being. For a long time I was the captain of my own ship—the boss. I'd spent fifteen years taking care of one person—me. I was good at it. I reveled in my solitude and independence. While the cliché tells us it's the man in a relationship who "needs more space," in my relationships, it was me. I delighted in stretching out alone in my queen-size bed. I loved taking myself out for Chinese food and a matinee. I even preferred dancing alone. I was always the girl on wedding dance floors fist pumping and doing the lawn mower solo while couples bobbed and weaved their heads and hips in tandem.

Well before I'd met Nick on a boat in the middle of the Pacific Ocean, I'd gotten it in my head that dancing well as a pair was an important asset for a successful long-term relationship. I'd just never found anyone I wanted to dance with. When I first moved to New York after college, my neighbors were a Chilean couple in their sixties who were approaching their fortieth wedding anniversary. The wife wore long gypsy skirts that rustled when she walked on four-inch heels down the hallway, always carrying their feeble terrier in her arms like a baby. The husband was smaller and quieter with an interesting mustache. They leaned in close to each other whenever they spoke, their heads touching. They didn't have kids. It was just the two of them and a sequence of ever-daintier dogs, but they were both kind and nurturing to me, a broke kid new in the city. They'd often have me over for drinks that turned into meals so large I wouldn't need to eat for another twenty-four hours. This was welcome during a time in my life when I survived on appetizers passed at parties and drinks paid for by dates. When I broke up with my lousy college boyfriend and began lusting after someone equally unsuitable, I asked them the secret to their long marriage.

The woman threw her head back and laughed straight from her fleshy belly.

"We dance together every week," she said. "We've been dancing for forty years. When we dance we become one. He sees me, and I see him. Everything I know about him, I learned while dancing."

Many years later, I still had my ex-neighbors' advice rattling around in my brain when I was given a reporting assignment in Chile at the end of August—four weeks before our wedding day—entitled "Skiing in SUMMER? Head South of the Border!" Besides the prospect of hitting the slopes, Chile was enticing as a launchpad for writing about marriage. The South American country has one of the lowest divorce rates in the world, mainly because in 2004 it was one of the last countries in the Western Hemisphere to legalize divorce. But more important, Chile was a country where Nick and I could learn to dance together.

Dancing successfully with a partner is all about patience and anticipating what the other person is going to do. It demands communication without speaking. These three skills are also cornerstones of a successful marriage. A bit of research also informed me that dancing has been proven to boost general happiness and improve emotional well-being. The novelist Vicki Baum once wrote, "There are shortcuts to happiness and dancing is one of them!" In a study conducted at the University of Derby in England, depressed patients were given salsa-dancing lessons. Their moods improved significantly after only nine weeks of hip swiveling. Researchers attributed the improvement to the endorphin boost from exercise and the increased self-confidence brought about by learning a new skill.

There also happens to be a good amount of scientific research that couples who dance well together tend to feel more emotionally and psychologically connected. I have no idea if this is complete bullshit, but it certainly worked for my former neighbors.

Following soccer, dancing is pretty much the national pastime in

Chile, and most Chilean couples perform an elaborate dance at their own weddings, often involving a particular style called the *cueca*, an intricate, multipart dance of seduction, love, and attracting your soulmate.

"We have to learn this dance for our wedding," I insisted to Nick before we headed to Chile.

"I thought you wanted to dance to 'Crazy Love' by Van Morrison," he said as we tried to narrow down our wedding guest list one final time.

"We'll do both!" I replied. "The people won't care. We have an open bar."

Nick waggled his bushy eyebrows, snapped his fingers, and threw an arm over his head.

"*Olé!*"

....

Tall and narrow like a supermodel, Chile stretches as long as the North American coastline from Alaska to Mexico. To reach Santiago from San Francisco took two flights and an entire day of flying with a brief pit stop in the Dallas airport for barbecue. Somewhere above Mexico, Nick and I began holding hands. We hold hands a lot, something new for me. On the plane ride to South America the turbulence made me clutch his hand tighter than usual, so that I could feel his bones with my fingertips. He assured me the turbulence wouldn't continue much longer, due to our altitude, the weather, and the topography of the region. Nick always checks a plane's flight path and which side of the plane will have the best views throughout the flight. Prior to check-in, he will change our airplane seats many, many times to ensure optimal views and a row of seats to ourselves.

Nick loves everything about planes and flying. When we board them, he knocks on the outside of the jet for luck and then his face lights up with the frenetic energy of a child who has been given ice cream for the first time. "We're going to fly!" he will cheer.

No matter where we are in the stratosphere, I can point out the plane window and ask, "Where are we now?" and Nick will know. I get such a kick out of it, I do it a dozen times on each flight.

"Since we're on the left side of the plane, we'll be able to see Aconcagua as we land," Nick explained as we descended into Chile. I nodded to let him know he could tell me more. "It's the highest peak in the Southern Hemisphere at almost twenty-three thousand feet."

We were arriving in Chile, less than a month before the actual wedding, with no vows written and no idea how to dance together. And first, we had to ski.

....

The skiing in the small mountain village of Portillo is hands down some of the best in the world, but most Americans, outside of the national ski team, have never heard about it. Surrounded by towering, rocky peaks with skies a shade of blue you can't even conjure on Instagram, the place is a little slice of heaven.

Nine feet of snow had dumped on the Andes mountains two days before we arrived, a gift from the gods or El Niño. We spent long days gliding down the steep valleys. Together we conquered one of the most complicated ski lifts in the entire world, the Va et Vient (French for "comes and goes"), a gonzo invention that drags four or five people up a sheer mountain face and then slingshots them backward onto black-diamond and double-black-diamond ski slopes. Some call it the "slingshot to heaven"; others refer to it with a trail of expletives.

When we reached the top of the Va et Vient, I refused to take Nick's hand, certain I could conquer this devil lift on my own. I fell flat on my face into a pile of powder, sliding ten feet down the mountain upside down, convinced I would plummet all the way into the Laguna del Inca lake below. As I tried to regain my ski legs and my dignity, the ski instructor told the story associated with the crystal blue waters of that lake. On full-moon nights the locals believe you can hear strange cries from within the water. Legend has it that the Inca princess Kora-Illé tragically fell from a cliff during a royal mountain banquet here. Her soulmate, the warrior Illi Yunqui, was shaken with grief and believed that no earthly grave could compare to the lake. Shrouded in white linen, she was lowered into its depths. From that moment the waters became tinted the color of her eyes, and Illi Yunqui stayed to mourn her forevermore.

"I don't want to die in that lake," I said to Nick when he skied down to help me up. "That's not my idea of romance."

Nick shrugged. "Then you should probably let me help you off the ski lift."

Let him help you, came one voice in my head. *Screw that. You don't need help. You're a badass independent woman,* came the other. The second belonged to the long-single girl who once scared off a potential mugger by brandishing a hairbrush like a handgun. I didn't know how to *be* if I wasn't the one taking care of myself. I was only just learning to include another person in all aspects of my life, just understanding what life was like when I couldn't decide to eat Thai food every night for four days or spend an entire Saturday watching only movies that starred Hugh Grant.

Maybe I was asserting my independence to buck the idea that I needed my almost-husband to help me do anything. Maybe it was a desperate assurance that becoming someone's wife wouldn't turn me into a dependent. Maybe I was being an arrogant asshole. I face-planted off that lift another six times before retiring to the lodge in search of a hot toddy.

In the resort's bar, we were swiftly informed salsa lessons would be held in the hotel gymnasium that very evening. When we arrived at the resort's indoor basketball court, I decided this was exactly like *Dirty Dancing*, if you replaced Johnny and Penny with two remarkably sexy Chileans. The female instructor resembled Shakira, except with a mod Vidal Sassoon haircut. Her lacy white bra peeked out from a tight pink tank top that did nothing to conceal the jiggle of her ample breasts as she shimmied across the slick wood floor. Her counterpart was a Chilean Jason Statham, bald, stoic, and hot.

"*¡Hola! ¡Bailamos!*" Nick greeted the instructors. His Spanish is quite good and since we boarded the plane in San Francisco, he'd been mouthing foreign words, silently practicing what to say next. "You look like a schizophrenic," I'd warned him, but I enjoyed watching him doing it anyway.

The entire time we were in Chile people kept complimenting him on his accent, which seems even more impressive given how incredibly apple-pie American Nick looks with his blond hair, blue eyes, and broad shoulders. When he began introducing me to people as his *novia*, which means "fiancée" in Spanish, everyone asked us about our plans for the wedding. When was it? How many people? What would we eat? Did we have a first dance? "That's what we're here to learn," I said, eliciting nods of approval from these complete strangers.

While his Spanish is legitimately terrific, Nick only *thinks* he is a wonderful dancer. One of his buddies told me he used to try to dance with all the Latina girls during his past trips to Mexico and South America and at salsa nights in the Mission Street bars in San Francisco. On most of those occasions he just confused the hell out of them.

"He does strange things with his hips," his friend Jeff told me. "And his arms. They move in funny directions. He once accidentally hit some poor girl in the nose. I think he broke it."

I had my own dancing baggage that included two left feet and an inability to actually enjoy myself. "I need to learn how to not lead," I whispered to Nick before the lesson began. "I've never been able to dance and let a man lead."

"Well, you just can't. It's forbidden," he replied with a teasing grin. Nick is more of a feminist than I am. He once pulled out dog-eared copies of my childhood Judy Blume books from boxes I'd brought from home and held them with great delight.

"I read these," he said, thumbing through a copy of *Blubber.*

"No, you didn't," came my automatic reply, grabbing the book back from his hand to return it to the box.

"I read all the Judy Blume books," he insisted. "They weren't all for girls. I read the ones for girls too, and *Are You There God? It's Me, Margaret* was a little confusing, but I remember being sad I didn't have anyone to talk to about it." This image of my fiancé as a tow-headed little boy reading about what it was like for a girl to get her period for the first time made my heart melt like a s'more.

But in Chile he was telling me that he was going to be in charge. And I didn't like it. "You'll have to stop. You need to let me lead." Easier said than done.

Salsa steps appear simple until you try to do them. You step backward. You step forward. You tap your foot. You tap your foot. When you get good, you wiggle your arms in a sexy way and move your hips like you're doing the hula hoop, without a hula hoop.

"*Uno, dos, tres,*" our instructor shouted, shaking her breasts like a Vitamix. "*Cuatro, cinco, seis . . . ¿Todo bien?*" She wanted us to give her a thumbs-up that we understood. I gave her the thumbs-up because I hadn't been paying attention.

As the sultry instructors counted the steps, I stumbled and mumbled under my breath, "Goddamn, son of a bitch," instead of "One, two, three, four, five." As I watched the instructors move in sync, I thought about swans, those pretentious, beautiful birds that mate for life. Floating across the water they appear calm and composed, but beneath the surface they paddle circles in perfect sync with their partners. Scientists believe that the synchronous movement tells potential romantic interlopers to bugger off. The same may be true for humans. According to William Michael Brown, PhD, a psychologist and dance researcher at Queen Mary University of London and the University of East London, humans who can dance well together signal that they are highly committed to each other. I wanted our physical movements to prove our commitment in case Nick was ever tempted, like Ben Affleck, to run off with the nanny and get a tramp stamp.

Nick and I began counting together, but somehow I stepped on his foot each time we reached *cuatro*. Was it my left foot or my right foot that went first? I didn't know. I was out of breath from the altitude and the exertion. "This is hard," I pouted. Sweat dribbled down my back. "It's harder than that chairlift!"

Nick kept swiveling his hips. "It's not hard. Six-year-olds can do it. Latin people do this, like, every day. It's why they're in great shape."

On the five count they wanted us to spin.

"*¡Gire, gire, gire!*" Shakira yelled.

"Ooooo, that's a new Spanish word for me. I didn't know that one," Nick said. "It means 'turn around.'"

Our spins were terrible. I stepped on his foot. He spun me too fast and I stumbled onto the floor.

"We're the worst," I cried.

"I'm good," Nick said.

Shakira did not think we were good. Her breasts cut in and began dancing with Nick. The second he danced with someone who wasn't me, his rhythm improved.

I huffed off into the bathroom. Shakira waited for me outside the door.

"Can I tell you a secret?" she whispered to me like we were two women in a tampon commercial. I nodded. "Let the man lead. Let him think he is in charge. If you decide to allow it, then you are the one in control." Over the next week I would hear this again and again from Chilean women, whether we were discussing dancing, driving, or daily life. South American men may radiate machismo, and a long history of patriarchy may still permeate daily life, but it's the women who rule the roost at home. They consistently told me that men's fragile egos demand a sense of control, and sometimes a wife needs to let her husband think he's the one calling the shots—even though she's influencing his behavior and decisions in more subtle ways. I couldn't help but be skeptical. Wasn't I a feminist? Didn't I believe that any form of submission took power away from women and handed it right on over to men?

To me this sounded like a way for women to delude themselves into believing they had control when they didn't, a lie they told to make the reality of male domination more bearable.

Yet I was consistently assured by women in South America that nurturing a male ego is not a sign of weakness. These women are astute anthropologists of male behavior, and they long ago learned how to operate within the constraints of a historically patriarchal society. They chose to behave in certain ways to preserve their self-worth in a system that was often stacked against them. And maybe "submission" is the wrong word to use here. It's more about reading cues and managing egos, regardless of gender, and there isn't a great word for that. It's more about control . . . and trust. By being sensitive to the male ego, the women I met in Chile ultimately remained in control of major decisions for their families, their finances, and their personal freedom. While the country still has a ways to go in terms of true gender equality, it's a place with strong female role models and one of the few countries in the world to have elected a female president. Nudge, America.

That's not to say times aren't changing. Young Chileans are putting off marriage well into their thirties (though they often still live in their parents' homes until they marry). Women my age are now pickier about choosing a husband, and when they do marry it's often for love instead of the security and protection sought by their mothers. They're more likely to work outside of the home and often become breadwinners in their families.

In the United States we don't talk about catering to the male ego or allowing a man to think he is in charge of a relationship, because the concept of submission is a controversial one. Our Internet pundits erupted in a furor in 2013 when the American volleyball superstar Gabby Reece wrote a book about her seventeen-year marriage to professional surfer Laird Hamilton (whom she describes as an alpha male) in which she explained that being submissive in a relationship is a sign of power rather than weakness. She emphasized that behaving submissively is not the same as being submissive. "Women have the ability to set the tone. . . . The ultimate strength . . . is creating that environment. I don't think it's a sign of weakness. I think it's a sign of strength," Reece said.

When the book came out, she was accused of setting women's causes back fifty years. I'd watched those attacks play out in the media and on Twitter, and I didn't know how to feel about them. Reece is a strong woman. Becoming a wife and a mother, the person responsible for the survival and happiness of other human beings, didn't come naturally to her all at once. I felt the same way in finally becoming someone's wife. What worked for Reece in being married to an alpha male was to take on some aspects of submissiveness, like being a little softer, a little more receptive. It was the first time I realized that we all have to adapt and make concessions in a marriage or long-term partnership. When Reece's book came out, I'd been dating a nice guy, a really nice guy. You know the guy I'm talking about, the one who was almost too nice. Because I could be, because it was so easy, because I was louder and more aggressive, I became the dominant one in that relationship. I made our dinner reservations and vacation plans. I bossed him around. I was critical and a little mean. I mocked him when he gained weight and grew man boobs and I paid for things for no other reason than I liked feeling in control. In hindsight I know one of the reasons our relationship turned sour was that I wouldn't let him do any of the things a man feels like he should do. It was a sign of utter disrespect on my part. I stripped him of every vestige of manliness, and the control I seized would have put off anyone, man or woman. In return, I eventually caught him carrying on a secret Internet affair with a stranger he'd met in a chat room (her handle was @FuzzyBunnyBaby) who boosted his ego in the ways I couldn't.

I had thought about that failed relationship a lot since meeting Nick.

Before we left for Chile, Nick and I were walking Lady Piazza through Golden Gate Park. Nick was concerned about work, about making sure his company was successful and growing.

"I want to be able to take care of you," he said, and I swear his chest began to puff out a little.

My entire body tightened and my response was short and clipped. "I don't need you to take care of me. I'm fine. I'm good. Did I ever tell you about the time I thwarted a would-be mugger with a hairbrush?" I rattled off a list of other reasons I was both fine and perfectly capable of taking care of my self.

My declaration made his chest slump, and it felt as though he'd drifted away. He grew quiet for several minutes while the dog lazily sniffed around the rose garden.

"It makes me feel good to be able to take care of you," he finally said. "Let me try?" It wasn't a command or a directive. It was a question, one that only I could answer.

"Can I lead this time, baby?" Nick asked me when I returned to the gymnasium to finish our salsa lesson. I relaxed my iron grip on his hand and nodded, allowing my almost-husband to pull me in the direction of his choosing and dervish me around as he liked. This time I stopped staring at my feet and looked directly into Nick's eyes—still smiling—having a groovy time. Then, a miracle happened. This time, neither of us stepped on the other one's feet; we glided like pros between the two basketball nets. Giving up some of my need for control, letting Nick call these shots, helped us move in sync.

"We're good," Nick said, looking down at me with unabashed tenderness, tipping me into a precarious dip. "Let's celebrate with a cocktail!"

The traditional Chilean drink is the pisco sour, a combination of cloudy distilled wine, sour mix, and frothy egg whites. Chile and neighboring Peru have been at war for a hundred years over who makes the better pisco sour and which country has the authority to claim it as their own national drink. It tastes cheerful and strong and only grows more so after the first one.

We retired to the dark wood-paneled bar and drank several of them, along with a glass of the local *vino tinto*, while enjoying a Swiss-style fondue. We struck up a conversation with an older gentleman named Keith from Minnesota who had been married for nearly fifty years. Keith was exactly the kind of guy I wanted to talk to. Fifty years! How do you stay married to the same person for five decades?

"So, Keith, tell me your advice for a happy marriage," I said, motioning to the waitress to bring another round, on us.

He considered it and looked at Nick. "Always say, 'Yes, dear,' to your wife." He chuckled in a way that made me question the sentiment, his jowly cheeks growing red from the pisco.

The candlelight at the table played on Nick's face as he grinned. "I'm starting to get my 'Yes, dear' down pat. Right, baby? I've been practicing it in Spanish, though: *Sí, cariño.*"

"He's doing okay. There's always room for improvement," I said.

This kind of advice is a favorite among older gentlemen who've been married for a long time. The problem with it is I can never tell if they mean it. Do they genuinely allow their wives to make all the decisions, in a way of submitting to them or, is it a way of ignoring and placating them? Maybe it's something that elderly men think makes them seem endearing to women half their age? It wasn't Keith's only advice. "When my son told me he was getting married, I asked him two questions: Does she ski and is she a Republican? Those are the things that really matter."

....

With the basics of salsa in place, we left Portillo and flew to the northern Chilean desert plateaus known as the Atacama. Our base was San Pedro, a tiny town of about four thousand people with a distinct hippie vibe. To get there we flew over broad, silvery swaths of alpine salt flats that Nick informed me were called *salares* in Spanish.

"That's where the flamingos typically congregate," he told me. The *salares* were so white the flamingos looked even more pink on top of them, creating the illusion of a vanilla cake dotted with strawberry frosting. "In the rocks there we might get to see a viscacha. It's a rodent that looks like a rabbit with a long tail. It's ridiculous.

We'll find some." Having dispensed this information, Nick returned to reading the in-flight emergency instruction manual in search of new Spanish words.

"Did you know the word for 'flotation slide' in Spanish is *tobagano*?"

We landed in the mining town of Calama and drove sixty miles west through an alien red dirt landscape. The road goes straight forever into a vast emptiness that vaguely resembles the American Southwest but is also truly unlike anything else on earth. A sign announced our location as "Patience Plain" as we crossed a vast expanse where the color of the sand slowly shifted from brown into yellow, then orange, then red, and finally a deep violet before rising into the snowy peaks of Andean volcanoes.

"This is a pretty place to reflect on patience," I said. Patience is derived from the Latin *patientia,* meaning "bearing, supporting, suffering, enduring, permitting." Was patience what I'd need to both dance with and wed my life to another person?

The desert has a different personality for each season. Some sections haven't had rain for more than four centuries, making them among the driest spots on the planet. Others remain dry and salty for most of the year before blossoming for a brief month into a floriated paradise where more than four hundred types of flowers of all shapes, colors, and sizes blanket the desert floor.

The terrace in the backyard of our hotel overlooked the Licancábur volcano, a somnolent giant waiting to be disturbed on the border with Bolivia, and our open-air shower allowed a view of the Milky Way, a sparkly curtain drawn across the sky, as I conditioned my hair. It reminded me of the top deck of that boat in the Galápagos where Nick and I had met. On the last night on that boat Nick and I stayed up much later than the rest of the passengers, stretching out on adjacent chaise longues and drinking warm Ecuadoran lager, trading life stories, each of us gathering the courage to make a first move. By strange coincidence we talked about Chile that night for at least an hour. Nick had once backpacked from Lima around Peru and all the way to the tip of Chile for six months in his twenties. During that trip he had come here to the Atacama, where he had been stranded overnight and lost in the Valle de la Luna with a bossy Israeli backpacker girl he'd met in a hostel. He hadn't even kissed me yet, and I was jealous of a girl who got to be marooned in a desert with this handsome near stranger. Maybe that's what compelled me to finally lean in close enough for him to kiss me for the very first time. I initiated the first move, and he closed the deal. It was a pretty equal division of labor.

I got my own chance to explore the Valle de la Luna with Nick the very next day during a horse trek through the jigsawed landscapes of red rocks and sand. As we galloped up precarious red sand dunes and bellowed into the canyons to hear our voices bounce back at us, I pried information about the country's low divorce rate, which still hovers around 3 percent, from our guide, Danielo, a sturdy thirty-seven-year-old who had come to the Atacama from Santiago on vacation fifteen years earlier and never left.

I explained to Danielo that we were in Chile researching a book about marriage and trying to learn how to dance properly together.

"We do have one of the lowest rates of divorce in the entire world," Danielo said with a shrug as if he were ticking off baseball statistics. "It's not something to be proud of."

Huh? I was confused.

He went on to explain that the actual rate didn't mean anything. For the past hundred years Chileans who had wanted to end their marriage had found ways to live apart from their spouse despite remaining legally married. And a lot of couples had just stayed in unhappy marriages. When divorce finally did become legal, the courts expected a rush for divorces, but that didn't happen. The couples who didn't want to stay together had already found a way around the law. The divorce rate is now ticking up higher and higher each year, but not with great intensity. The stigma around the concept of divorce will probably stick around for another generation. But something interesting is also happening. Civil unions, which were made legal in 2015 and allow for many of the same rights as marriage but are easier to legally dissolve, are increasingly popular among young Chileans, both hetero- and homosexual.

"More young people look at that as a better alternative to marriage," Danielo explained. "Like a contract they can renew if they continue to agree to the terms."

That was good. I liked that. There was something appealing about actively choosing your partner again and again.

Danielo paused for a moment before telling us that he was divorced. "And it was awful. I did get the PlayStation." As an afterthought he added, "And the kids."

"I'm sorry," I said.

He didn't pause this time.

"My wife and I *were* great dancers. That was the good part of our marriage, but it wasn't enough. You don't need to learn to dance. You need to learn to talk. Never stop communicating. The second anything feels weird, you talk about it. That's what went wrong with my marriage. We stopped talking. We stopped communicating. You need to talk about everything. You share a bed. You need to share everything else." This was progressive advice compared to "Yes, dear" and "Let the man lead." And even though it had nothing to do with learning to dance and it came from a divorcé, it was the best advice we'd gotten in Chile about how to make an actual marriage work.

Nick and I had only shared a bed full-time for two weeks. At night we still stayed up late asking each other questions, determined to make up for our abbreviated courtship. We discussed our hopes and goals, values and morals. We nattered on about how we'd raise our kids and what would happen if we needed to take care of a sick parent. We talked about religion and debt and about all of our ex-boyfriends and ex-girlfriends. We asked the big question: How are you crazy? Because every person is crazy and broken in their own way.

But, maybe we needed to dig even deeper about the everyday

things. For example, I hadn't yet told Nick how scared I was to be living in a strange new city where he was my only friend. I hadn't wanted to put a damper on the delight of moving in together and our approaching wedding. It was definitely something that made me feel strange. It was definitely something we *should* be talking about.

We rode on through the Martian landscape, up and over another sand dune, the wind kicking up and sprinkling the fine dust into my face and hair. That dust would find its way into every bodily crevice and our luggage and eventually travel with us around the world for the next year in our bags. Danielo's Chilean street dog named Pirate led the way, nipping our horses' heels when they moved too slow.

"My brother has a wonderful marriage," our guide continued without prompting. "He and his wife have a tradition. You two should do this. They go away on vacation alone for two weeks every year. She goes away with her friends and he goes on a real macho trip with his friends. Then they take a two-week vacation just the two of them, no kids. They're so in love. They say two weeks apart makes them miss one another . . . makes them long for one another."

Ovid, the Roman poet who lived during the time of Jesus and had three different wives, wrote something similar: "What makes men indifferent to their wives is that they can see them when they please. So shut your door and let your surly porter growl, 'There's no admittance here!' This will renew the slumbering fires of love." There was something to that. Since we'd met, I'd wondered whether Nick and I were infatuated with each other due to the long breaks forced on us by living on opposite coasts. I smiled back at Nick, who unsteadily bounced up and down in his saddle. He doesn't love riding horses. He does it because I love it.

"Will you get married again?" I asked Danielo as we trotted back to the stables.

He shook his head. "I don't know if I believe in marriage." He paused. "I do believe in love. I love love."

....

Back in town that night, we asked everyone we met to teach us to dance *cueca,* but they all refused. The folks at the hotel said no. The bartenders said no. No one would teach us this damn dance.

Even though most everyone in Chile knows about the *cueca*, has learned it, and has likely danced it, quite possibly at their own weddings, they're loath to teach it to a couple of gringos only down in their country for a week. One of the reasons is that the dance has a mixed history. It's believed to have local Indian and perhaps even African origins and dates back at least two hundred years. But when the dictator Augusto Pinochet seized power in 1973, he attempted to co-opt the *cueca* for his nationalist movement, demanding it be performed as the Chilean independence dance. In response, women began performing the dance alone, as a symbol of the men who disappeared during Pinochet's reign. Today the *cueca* has evolved. There's still the traditional *cueca*, which is often performed at weddings, but there's also the new *cueca brava*, the original dance mixed with street dancing. It remains an integral part of Chilean culture, but one that isn't readily shared with outsiders.

"We can teach ourselves this dance," Nick said over dinner. He was on his third glass of a Chilean cabernet he'd become quite fond of during this journey. "It's all on YouTube. Baby, we can do this."

Everyone should watch videos of the *cueca* on the Internet. There are hundreds, maybe thousands. There are instructional videos and competition videos, most of which consist of teenagers trying to win large cash prizes. The juvenile *cueca* competition in Chile is like *Dancing with the Stars*, but for indigenous towns and villages in South America. They're deadly serious about it, and the champions from each town are as famous as reality television stars. One video, "Campeones de la Cueca," has more than a half million views.

We watched a half dozen of the performances and read a detailed list of *cueca* instructions. It's a dance of flirtation, courtship, submission, and union condensed into seven minutes. All together there are eight steps. The first is referred to as "the invitation," during which the man offers his arm to the woman. Next he positions her in the middle of the dance floor and then moves a few meters opposite her. He claps with a mighty vigor and the dance begins. The dancers complete a full circle around the room, waving napkin-sized handkerchiefs in circles in the air. Next up is the pursuit. The man's steps become more aggressive as he dances closer to the woman. She retreats, barely escaping him each time he draws near. Suddenly the dancers move to opposite sides of the room. They each appear to "sweep" the floor with their feet in a metaphorical clearing of the past. Both of them stomp on the floor, the man forcefully and the woman ever so daintily. He reaches for her again. This time she accepts his arm. They finish the dance, locked together in an embrace.

After watching several videos, Nick felt confident. "Boom!! I've got this." He took a slug of his wine and grabbed two full-sized bath towels from inside the shower to use as handkerchiefs.

"Go into the bathroom," Nick said. "That way I can invite you to join me." He turned on *cueca* music we had also handily found on the Internet.

I stepped tentatively into the doorway of the bathroom. Nick gallantly bowed in my direction before prancing to the center of the room, waving his bath towel wildly.

I laughed with a snort before remembering this was a dance of flirtation. I raised my towel above my head as we circled each other. Nick attempted to lasso me with his towel.

Halfway into the dance my almost-husband grew more serious and began staring at me in a way that made me believe he was actually trying to seduce me. We each began to use the salsa steps we'd learned in the Portillo gymnasium, moving within inches of each other before backing away. I caught our reflections in the mirror. We began this dance looking ridiculous, but now we didn't look half bad. We wouldn't win even a juvenile Chilean *cueca* championship, but we looked like a couple who could dance with each other.

We finally touched as the dance came to an end. I twirled into Nick's arms and performed a *giro* that didn't end with my stepping on his toes, and when he dipped me, no one fell down.

"Do you think we're ready to dance at our wedding?" I asked as we fell back on our bed.

He leaned over to whisper in my ear, his breath warm on my neck. "Do you trust me enough to lead?" he asked.

I considered it for a moment.

"Sometimes."

....

Still, I tossed and turned that night mulling the question of whether anyone should "lead" in a relationship. Isn't equality between the two partners what we should strive for? Did equality have to mean that no one led in a relationship? Wasn't that a recipe for anarchy and chaos? Or could it mean taking turns, with each person leading in the things they were good at?

Unable to sleep, I walked out onto our patio to admire the giant moon, stretching my arms high up into the air, thinking back to the tragic cries of the Inca princess Kora-Illé mourning her lost love during the full moon. When I brought my arms back to waist level, my eye caught the light glinting off the gold of my engagement ring.

It's no secret that engagement rings have long been a way for men to mark their territory before marriage. Some historians believe a pagan caveman would bind his mate's ankles and wrists with braided grass to signify his control of her before they consecrated a relationship. Mythology claims the first engagement rings were used by the ancient Romans, rings with tiny keys attached to them that denoted a husband's ownership of his wife. In the Middle Ages a betrothal ring was often considered to be an insurance policy for the bride's virginity leading up to the wedding. Once diamonds were discovered en masse in South Africa, Tiffany & Co. introduced the classic six-prong ring setting in 1886. In 1947 De Beers, which controlled the majority of the world's diamond mines, introduced the greatest and perhaps most important marketing slogan of all time: "A diamond is forever." From then on it was the fate of American men to spend between one and three months' salary on a single piece of jewelry. These days engagement rings get even more attention as brides-to-be give them their very own Facebook posts, tacitly telling the world, *I'm taken.*

I'd surrendered my independence during the dance, but there was another way I could assert myself here in Chile to maintain a kind of cosmic balance. I could buy Nick his own engagement ring.

It isn't uncommon for a man in South America to wear a ring after he gets engaged. In Brazil and in Chile both the groom- and the bride-to-be wear a plain metal wedding band on their right ring fingers to mark their betrothal. Following the wedding, the band is moved to the left hand.

The tradition has made vague inroads in the United States. The *Atlantic* even published a story called "The Rise of the Man-gagement Ring," which claimed 5 percent of engaged American males now wear one. I don't personally know any. Naturally, American jewelry companies have done their damnedest to capture the male market in the same way that De Beers made a huge diamond engagement ring a must-have for women after World War II. In 1926 the department store Bamberger's, which would eventually become Macy's, tried to market a male engagement ring with over-the-top macho names like "The Pilot," "The Stag," and "The Master." Imagine walking up to the jewelry counter in a place with a name like Bamberger's and having the saleswoman ask you, "Is your husband more a Stag or a Master?"

The main reasons the man-gagement ring hasn't taken off in the United States are that American men are squeamish about jewelry in general and that we live in a culture that still promotes bachelorhood as continuing up until the wedding day itself. When we talk about bachelor parties, we still refer to them as the man's last stand, as if proposing marriage weren't an actual commitment. *The Playboy Guide to Bachelor Parties* has helpful sections like "How to Choose an Escort," "Strippers and Belly Dancers or Midgets and Fat Ladies?" and "To Lie or Not to Lie—What to Tell the Bride Afterward."

Nick didn't have a bachelor party, not really. The weekend I went away to my bachelorette party in Charleston with the goal of eating all of the food, Nick went out to the Russian River in Sonoma County with two of his buddies to drink beer and float on inner tubes down the river. Little did he know it was Lazy Bear Weekend, a gay party weekend frequented by chubby men with beards. The river was filled with large, hairy homosexuals drinking rosé, instead of escorts and midget strippers.

But many American men are still sent into marriage with a party filled with copious amounts of alcohol and sex workers. In the days before they walk down the aisle they use expressions like "the beginning of the end," "tied down," and "taking on the old ball and chain." There's no other event in a man's life that has so much negative bias attached to it before it even happens. It's no wonder most men don't want to wear a ring until the very last minute.

It didn't matter to me that our wedding was just weeks away. I liked the symbolism of Nick wearing his own engagement ring. It put the two of us on equal ground before we said our vows.

The next night, as Nick and I strolled down the main drag of San Pedro, dodging ebullient street dogs and backpackers with elaborate dreadlocks, I spied a shop with men's copper rings in the window.

While Nick picked out a llama wool scarf for his mother, I wandered alone into the warm jewelry shop carved out of an adobe row house. The ring I had my eye on was cool. Really cool. It was silver with three intricate braids of copper on the inside. I imagined all manner of scenarios for how I would propose. I could drop it into Nick's wineglass or hide it in a molten chocolate cake. I could wait until the sun began to rise over the volcano and drop to one knee on our terrace wearing very tiny underwear. For a moment I wondered if he could possibly say no, if my proposal would give him an "out" right before our wedding. I had been reading about a tribe called the Garos on the border of Tibet and Burma. In their society the groom is expected to run away, to actually flee from a bride's proposal of marriage. The bride's family then chases him down and drags him kicking and screaming back to their daughter. There was a very small chance that Nick could flee into the desert and I would never see him again. This foray into the unknown terrified and excited me. I bought the ring and slipped it into an innocuous paper bag.

A bitter chill had settled in the desert air and I shivered in my tank top and the pair of Nick's plaid boxer shorts I'd worn to jog into town. Nick wanted to walk back to the hotel because he thought it was silly to take a cab just a mile. He was certain he could navigate his way back to the hotel through the dark and unsafe streets. *Let him lead*, I thought. *You don't have to be in control all of the time.* Being able to get me home safely, powered only by his memory and our bodies, was clearly important to Nick.

We set out down an ominous dirt road back to the resort. Even if it hadn't been dark, there wouldn't have been much to see—a few grubby hostels, corrugated iron shacks, and crumbling adobe walls. Eight minutes into the walk I was chattering away about looking for meteorites in the desert when Nick paused in the center of the road.

"We're lost." He was clearly upset that his usually eerily accurate internal GPS had failed him.

"It's okay," I said, shivering. "If we turn right we'll hit the hotel." I hoped I was right.

We looked around. "Maybe we can cut across this field," Nick said, heading into a pasture of cows. An angry German shepherd leapt out at us, snarling and baring his teeth. We sprinted a quarter mile down the road getting even more lost. I needed to have faith that Nick would lead us to safety . . . eventually. It wasn't about being submissive. This was about learning to trust my partner. I had trusted Nick to lead when we danced and now I trusted him to rescue me from a rabid dog and death by freezing in the desert. He trusted me to tell him when he was wrong and maybe a little stubborn. We'd both need to figure out when to cede and when to take control. We hadn't known each other long enough to know all our strengths and weaknesses.

When we had been on our grand road trip to the West, Glynnis had astutely compared marriage itself to a kind of road trip. "Sometimes you're in the driver's seat, you know? And then, when you get tired, you need to let Nick switch and take over. That's not submission. It's an equal sharing of the road. I suspect the best marriages are when you're both submitting to each other and allowing the other person to feel safest during their most vulnerable moments, and shine at their best."

Shaken from the near dog attack, I stretched my arms wide and folded them around my shoulders in a pinched hug. In the past, with any other boyfriend, this would have been the moment I would have said, "I told you we should have taken a cab," and stomped back to town to hail my own taxi.

Instead I dropped down on one knee in the gnarly bushes, the rocks scratching my skin, dust billowing into my nose, exposed and cold.

Nick looked down, confusion flickering across his face.

"I *hate* getting lost," I said. "I hate it. It makes me nervous and angry and I'm freezing right now." I pulled more air into my lungs. "But I don't mind getting lost with you." My voice quavered. I finally understood why men get nervous when they propose. "I don't care that we suck at dancing together; I just like being the person you dance with. I don't even mind now when you take the lead. In fact, it's nice sometimes. I love you and I am going to love you for a hundred thousand years. Will you marry me?"

3

Mexico

Never Stop Talking

> Much unhappiness has come into the world because of bewilderment and things left unsaid.
>
> —Fyodor Dostoyevsky

We'd been married less than forty-eight hours when we landed at the Cancún airport—the only airport in the world, I have to note, that has a giant Corona bottle on the air traffic control tower. The start of our honeymoon should have been one of the happiest times of our life. Except absolutely everything was going wrong.

Wicked food poisoning hit me the second we landed in Mexico, the result of a late-night pizza binge in Philadelphia the night of our wedding. I'd hardly eaten a thing during our actual reception. How's a bride supposed to eat, with all the dancing, picture taking, hugging, champagne drinking, and remembering the names of new Wisconsin relatives? I'd needed something in my stomach, no matter how questionable, before we went to sleep.

But only an hour off the plane in Mexico, my belly began to convulse in the rental car.

"Do you need me to pull over?" Nick looked over at me in alarm. I nodded weakly as he maneuvered our cheap Mexican vehicle onto the side of the highway so his new wife could retch undigested pizza, coffee, and airplane peanuts onto the road outside the car. Nick's back pats were reassuring but timid. Meanwhile, I hung my head between my knees and moaned that I was almost certainly about to die.

"You're gonna be okay, Squeaky. We'll get there soon and I'll take care of you," Nick said. Like my old Irish grandmother, Nick has a menagerie of nonsensical nicknames for me—Squeaky, Lovebomb, Honeypie, Chauncey, Meerkat. I can count on one hand the number of times he's called me Jo.

I moved my head in a vertical motion to signal agreement as I stared at footprints in the gravel that included toes. Who would walk here without shoes? Inches from my face a used condom sat atop a broken beer bottle. Heat rose from the cement and I doubled over again.

Long before people admitted to having premarital sex, one of the reasons newlyweds went away on a honeymoon was to get to know each other's bodies. Now my body was betraying me, right in front of my brand-new husband, in the worst way possible. I'd assumed marriage would free me of my anxiety about trying to look and act perfect all the time, but I still felt terrible that Nick was seeing me with my hair matted in vomit.

We continued to the village of Tulum, a slice of Mexican paradise famous for bathwater-warm, crystalline water and sand as soft and white as confectioners' sugar. Once the purview of yogis and hippies with just enough money to catch a flight to Cancún, Tulum's beach shacks have been replaced by hipster hotels that serve $14 margaritas and $20 avocado toast. It had changed a lot, almost too much, from the first time I'd visited on a solo trip twelve years earlier. But it remained a special place for me and I wanted to share it with Nick.

I'd finished my first book here on another visit, furiously scribbling pages in a tree-house hotel overlooking the ocean that had cost me just $25 a night. Ancient myths promise that the waters surrounding Tulum and the entire Yucatán Peninsula contain something magical for the soul, and it was still one of the most romantic places I'd ever been, even though in the past I'd always visited alone.

I didn't know that in Tulum, September is the most off part of the off-season. When we arrived, the beach stank of decaying fish and the town's sewer system hadn't been cleaned in weeks. It literally smelled like shit.

I couldn't imagine being able to have sex. No one *could* possibly have had sex in the shape I was in. I'd always thought you were supposed to do it like monkeys on your honeymoon, but the first night we spent in Mexico, Nick snored next to me while I sweated out my illness, fended off mosquitoes, and attacked a colony of sand fleas I believed were breeding in my right foot. A tight panic began to squat in my stomach like a recalcitrant troll.

The only thing that made me feel better was remembering our wedding. Like an addict in the throes of withdrawal, I obsessively checked my social media accounts for more of our wedding posts from friends with the meticulous fervor of a heroin fiend tapping for a vein.

Too agitated for sleep, I replayed the past week in my mind.

Nick met my dad in person for the first time just a few days before we were set to walk down the aisle. John Piazza took a long look at my fiancé and announced, "I'm going to give you the number of my barber." Nick's hair was shaggy, nearly clearing his shoulders. My dad had married my mother almost forty years earlier with hair much longer than Nick's, which is why he got a kick out of teasing my almost-husband. He liked Nick.

Despite the fact that my dad's condition now made it impossible for him to even stand up, much less walk on his own, he made it to our wedding and parked his wheelchair and oxygen tank in the front row throughout the ceremony. I walked down the aisle alone to Pachelbel's *Canon* played by a bluegrass band. My floor-length veil nearly tripped me twice, but it still made me feel like a Disney princess. Glynnis officiated the ceremony in a stunning vintage Halston gown while my most hilarious friend Ben emceed. Together the pair were Fred Astaire and Ginger Rogers (or maybe Sonny and Cher) tap-dancing us into matrimony. The crowd loved them! Midway through the ceremony, they gave the floor over to my father. I clasped Nick's hand as my dad cleared his throat and strained to speak. John Piazza was once a strong and virile guy. He was the life of the party, the guy you'd want to sit next to in a bar, a jolly mixture of Sicilian and Irish blood combining a young Frank Sinatra, Tony Soprano, and Bob Dylan—a man constantly searching for his identity, but in such an elegant way that he still seemed completely comfortable in his own skin. Everyone wanted to be friends with my dad, men and women alike. He had the ability to command a room with a single word.

He began with "I wish I were in better shape for this," and the whole hall had tears in their eyes.

Our wedding was perfectly imperfect, and it was the greatest party I've ever been to. It rained that day. People like to tell you rain on your wedding day is good luck. When I was in middle school Alanis Morissette sang that it was ironic, but that made less sense to me than the fact that she once dated the guy from *Full House*. In Hindu traditions rain on the wedding day foretells a strong marriage, since a wet knot is more difficult to untie than a dry one. My friend Ras, who was once a practicing Bhakti Hindi monk, explained the logic behind the allegory. "Rain on your wedding day can throw an already stressful situation into disarray. If the couple weathers the stress together, that's a good indicator of a healthy marriage to come," he said. "Besides, you're preparing for a marriage, not just a wedding. Who cares about getting wet?"

Our original plan was to get married in the courtyard of the archaeology museum at the University of Pennsylvania, where I went to college. It's one of those grand, imposing stone courtyards with beautifully manicured gardens and a giant fountain. We would hang mason jars holding very tiny candles from the maple trees, just as I had seen in a half dozen BuzzFeed lists on how to have the greatest wedding of all time. As a lazy bride, I'm not even a little ashamed that I stole every single idea from "rustic barn," "vintage French country," and "eclectic but sustainable" wedding boards on Pinterest.

It turned out that the rain plan was even better than mason-jar candles in the courtyard, because it included an Egyptian tomb and a three-thousand-year-old Sphinx, both inside the museum. Nick first saw the Sphinx during our rehearsal the night before the ceremony and he gasped with delight. "There had better be a thunderstorm," he proclaimed. And there *was* a storm, complete with bellowing thunder and lightning and the kind of rain that soaks into your bones and melts a bride's carefully done hair. And yet it was the best thing that could have happened. Every hipster in Brooklyn gets married outdoors with a band dressed like Mumford & Sons, rustic barn benches, and mason jars hanging from trees. We got married in front of a three-thousand-year-old Egyptian god-cat.

We picked an assortment of our favorite traditions from different cultures. In the Quaker tradition, guests can say whatever they want during the actual ceremony. We had an open bar during the ceremony, which punctuated the speeches and readings with the popping of champagne corks. I liked my friend Matt's speech the best. Matt and I obsessively watched every episode of *Friends* in college. It was like comfort food during a strange time of change, uncertainty, and fear of sexually transmitted diseases. We'd stay up late and cuddle in bed together a decade before he came out of the closet. In his wedding speech Matt praised Nick for being the one to lock me down and reminisced about how he'd always dreamed of being the Ross to my Rachel. He ended his speech by saying he was pleased, in the end, to become the Will to my Grace.

Since Nick loves bikes, I'd arranged ahead of time to have thirty of the city's bike-share bikes delivered to the museum so that we could ride, with some of our guests, the mile and a half to the boathouse where we would have our reception. The rain cleared for a brief moment and everyone, Nick and I included, hopped onto the bikes in the misty evening. I pulled up my dress, pleased that Spanx offered the same support as bike shorts, and balanced my four-inch Badgley Mischka heels on the pedals. We screamed and hooted, shaking cowbells and tambourines as we tore through the streets of Philadelphia.

In the pictures everyone is smiling sloppily, stuffing their faces with pork sliders and Rice Krispies treats. Everyone, Nick and I included, drank too much, but it was a blur of love, strangers who are now family, compliments and congratulations. It was overwhelming and wonderful all at once.

Nick and I didn't make it to any of the after parties. (Instead we went out for that ill-fated pizza.) We hardly made it back to bed before we passed out, our wedding clothes in a crumpled heap on the floor. At 5:00 a.m., our heads pounding, we slugged water from the bathroom sink, took Advil, and consummated our marriage.

....

Now, on my honeymoon, I traced the moles on my new husband's back with my index finger and began to feel a strange melancholy.

Could it be possible that I had some form of postwedding depression? Was that even a thing?

Google "unhappy" and "honeymoon" and you're presented with a catalog of stories telling you your marriage is doomed. Google "miserable" and "honeymoon" and you learn Kim Kardashian and Kanye West were miserable on their Irish honeymoon. I took little comfort in this fact.

In 1886 the Reverend Edward John Hardy wrote a suspiciously titled treatise, *How to Be Happy, Though Married* (an alternate title was *Still Happy, Though Married*). In it he emphasized that a good start to a marriage was imperative for future marital happiness. "In matrimony, as in so many other things, a good beginning is half the battle," Hardy wrote. He went on to note the importance of the honeymoon. "The honeymoon certainly ought to be the happiest month in our lives; but it may, like every other good thing, be spoiled by mismanagement."

Shit.

That night, in the midst of my panic, I e-mailed an actual authority on marital neuroses, clinical psychologist and marriage counselor Laurie Sanford, the mother-in-law of Nick's best friend and the only person I didn't feel weird asking about how weird I felt.

"I'm so fucked . . . ," I started to write in my e-mail, then deleted it. Don't start with something negative. Just ask if what is happening is normal. I half expected Laurie to write back and tell me I *was* indeed fucked. She didn't.

"Of course there is such a thing as postwedding blues, honey," Sanford wrote back right away. She lives in Hawaii, so the time difference was in my favor. "There's a letdown after all the buildup, after all the expectations, focused effort, work, excitement, and stress. It's kind of like the way ocean waves work. The bigger the wave, the flatter the water is after the wave passes. There has to be a flattening out after such a huge buildup of emotion. This occurs despite the happiness you know you should feel. It's the way emotions work. It's normal to feel a depression, a sense of fatigue on the honeymoon. It's a natural emotional slump."

Phew.

So even though I was itching and sweating and puking and crying, what I felt was normal (well, not the food poisoning). Postwedding depression *is* a thing, and no one talks about it because no one wants to seem like an ungrateful twit right after everyone just shelled out a lot of money for those rustic barn benches no one got to sit on because of a thunderstorm. Research has even shown that one in ten spouses experiences what experts now refer to as "postwedding depression."

Maybe having the perfect honeymoon was too much to live up to. What are modern honeymoons anyway, besides the creation of clever marketing by resorts, cruise lines, and countries with beautiful beaches? It wasn't until relatively recently that the honeymoon was upheld as the *most* romantic, *most* perfect, and *most* Instagrammable vacation of all time.

The word "honeymoon" was first used in the sixteenth century when the poet Richard Huloet compared the first weeks of a marriage to the waning phases of the moon.

"Hony mone, a term proverbially applied to such as be newly married, which will not fall out at the first, but th'one loveth the other at the beginning exceedingly, the likelihood of their exceadinge love appearing to aswage, ye which time the vulgar people call the hony mone," Huloet wrote.

What he meant, I think, is that love was only going to wane, to grow less and less, after the actual wedding night. Through the 1700s, the "honey" part of "honeymoon" also referred to honey beer, which European couples drank for about a month after the wedding as they spent time getting intimately acquainted with each other's bodies for the first time. The intention was to make you good and loose the first time you attempted intercourse, like after the high school prom. Starting in the nineteenth century, fancy couples began embarking on what they called the "bridal tour," during which they visited family and friends who couldn't attend the actual wedding. Afterward the couple would take time for themselves, usually on the French Riviera or in the Tuscan countryside, to rest, recoup, and try to make a baby. From there the honeymoon became one of the first institutionalized forms of mass tourism. By the turn of the twentieth century, even the lower classes were starting to take a mini break after they got hitched.

Right before we got married I found a dusty old hardcover in a used-book store called *The Happy Family*. It was a prescriptive book written by medical doctor John Levy and his wife, Ruth, a psychologist, about how to create a happy marriage and family unit in 1938. Even though it was written during a time when most women weren't allowed to pursue higher education and most men didn't know how to find a clitoris, lots of things in *The Happy Family* are weirdly progressive. One bit I kept returning to was the chapter on the chimpanzee experiment.

The chimpanzee in said experiment is a perfectly happy primate who has a healthy, if boring, diet of lettuce. He likes lettuce, eats it all the time. He thinks lettuce is a good thing. One day the chimpanzee is sitting there scratching his bum and he sees the researcher place a banana under the box in front of him. This is new and exciting and different from lettuce. The chimpanzee is then led away and the banana is secretly replaced by lettuce. When the chimp returns and lifts up the box, he is furious. He expected that banana. He tears the lettuce into little pieces, throws it on the ground, and stomps on it to make his point clear. He was promised bananas and will not settle for lettuce!

According to the authors of *The Happy Family*, this has a lot to do with marriage. Married people "reject the good marriage we have because it is not the perfect marriage which, consciously or unconsciously, we are told we could be having. Our unconscious expectations are more dangerous than the naïve idealism we express. . . . The first step, then, toward permanent and satisfying marriage is disillusionment, the willingness to accept one's self and one's partner on the level of everyday living, to take the worse along with the better."

A better interpretation is that you should always expect lettuce and then you will be extra delighted when your marriage, or your honeymoon, gives you a banana. It also explains why looking at other people's happy-seeming marriages on social media can make some people feel so anxious and confused. I expected my honeymoon to be all banana and was depressed when there was a little bit of wilted lettuce. In his twilight years the German author Johann Wolfgang von Goethe put it well when he said, "Love is something ideal. Marriage is something real; and never with impunity do we exchange the ideal for the real." It doesn't get more real than vomiting for two days straight while your new husband holds back your hair.

A few hours of sleep did nothing to improve the situation. Clearly nervous his new wife was about to take her last breath in the Mexican jungle, Nick did his very best to nurse me back to health the next morning: He mopped the sweat off my forehead, force-fed me tortilla chips, and made me drink as much bottled fizzy water as my body could handle.

"If I die, will you take care of Lady Piazza?" I asked weakly. Lady Piazza is 110 pounds and suffers from an anxiety disorder. She was salvaged from a Brooklyn trash can when she was four weeks old, to which I attribute her sharing my attachment issues. She's been a patient of the top veterinary psychiatrists in New York and was at one point prescribed Xanax, Zoloft, and Valium.

Nick nodded without conviction. Lady Piazza also smells funny and sheds, and sometimes she bites. Nick isn't a dog person. Having Lady Piazza in his life was a bigger adjustment for him than having a wife.

"I'm serious. I'll be dead and you'll be this sexy widower with a full head of hair and a very sad story about how the love of your life perished in Mexico, the best years of her life ahead of her. The least you can do is take care of my sometimes-unfriendly large dog."

"Of course I will, Squeak."

....

By the third day of the honeymoon I'd morphed back into a full-fledged human. I knew this was true because I suddenly had a hankering for margaritas. Still, a piece of my depression and anxiety lingered. I kept trying to put it out of my head because we had an appointment with Bobby Klein, the greatest marriage therapist of all time, the man who was going to teach us the art of marital communication.

The advice we'd gotten from Danielo, our rugged Atacaman Indiana Jones, continued to rattle around in my head when we returned from Chile: Good communication is the key to any healthy relationship, particularly a marriage.

Before our wedding, a very well-off friend who made a career of traveling the globe to find "healers," "therapists," "shamans," and "gurus" told me we had to pay a visit at some point during the first year of our marriage to one Bobby Klein, a healer/therapist/shaman/guru based in the jungles of the Yucatán.

"He can make any couple communicate better." Her rose quartz crystals jangled against her collarbone. "Even couples who probably shouldn't be together. He saved my marriage. Also, don't forget to ask him about Jack Nicholson." With that she flounced off to text her psychic.

Bobby Klein *is* the most interesting man in the world. Devotees of the guru travel thousands of miles and pay $300 to speak to him for a single hour. Back in the sixties Bobby was a rock photographer who took some of the first publicity stills of the Doors, including heaps of pictures where Jim Morrison is staring directly into the camera like he wants to have sex with you. Next Bobby landed in the restaurant business with Jack Nicholson and opened the Black Rabbit Inn in West Hollywood, a natural-food restaurant during a time when most people were discovering TV dinners.

Then Bobby became one of the first acupuncturists in the United States and threw himself into traditional Chinese medicine and Eastern philosophy. That's when he realized he had intuitive abilities in medicine and healing, which led him to get a doctorate in clinical psychology and embark on a forty-year practice as a counselor and energy worker.

He's expensive, but then, so is divorce. This is what Bobby promises couples will get out of meeting with him for just an hour: "Couples are made to feel safe and are given the practical tools and processes that will bring truth and clarity to the forefront of their relationship. No matter the length of your union, clear communication is the key to achieving a healthy vibrant and loving bond. In these sessions both partners will be empowered as they recognize where and why obstacles may exist that cause misunderstanding and disconnect."

Everyone in Tulum knows Bobby. You don't even have to say his last name. "Where can I find Bobby?" you can holler at any of the boutique hotels or organic taquerias along the beachfront road. Everyone pointed us to his fancy Yaan wellness center in the middle of the jungle.

We were greeted there by a pretty young woman in a tight white tank top and equally snug striped miniskirt.

"We're here to see Bobby?" I said nervously.

"You have already paid?" she asked. I shook my head. Not knowing about the astronomical fee, Nick delivered her a goofy lopsided grin. She sized up the two of us, decided we probably wouldn't steal anything if she left us in the lobby on our own, and strode away to let Bobby know we'd arrived.

The unbearably cool lobby of Yaan sold all manner of unbearably cool things, like linen caftans for $250, artisanal aphrodisiac spray made in Brooklyn, and handcrafted leather man purses. I sat down to thumb through the spa menu as we waited.

"Oooh, they do a special kind of colonic here," I said to Nick.

"What does that do again? Clean out your ass?" Nick said.

I nodded. "I think so."

The pretty girl returned and looked at us, pitying two humans who had never enjoyed the pleasure of a proper colonic.

Nick looked over my shoulder at the menu of services.

"I hope all of these people are well paid," he said. "The prices here are as high as San Francisco prices, if not higher. I'll bet they pay next to nothing for rent, so I hope their employees are paid significantly higher than average."

"You're such a communist."

I could tell Nick wanted to inform me, as he had dozens of times, that I was confusing the meanings of "communism" and "socialism."

I'd tried to explain to Nick about Bobby Klein's crazy mixed-up path to becoming a healer, communication expert, and couples counselor in the jungle, but he had no idea what we were getting into until we were inside the guru's cozy hippie-chic office.

Wearing a loose-fitting orange shirt and linen pants and peppering his remarks with a refrain of "That's beautiful," Bobby looks and sounds more like a well-dressed Grateful Dead roadie than a healer or a marriage counselor. He walks with a slight swagger and his face has a healthy glow that makes him seem much younger than he is. Nick has the same youthful exuberance, and people are often surprised that he's seven years older than I am, which leads me to believe I should spend more time talking about Botox with my dermatologist. Bobby encouraged the two of us to sit back on his wide couch, take our shoes off, and get comfortable. He asked us to tell him an abbreviated version of our story—how we met, when we got married, etc.

Then he stared at the two of us in disconcerting silence for longer than a minute.

"This is a powerful time," he finally said. "The time right after you get married. I don't want to call it an exciting time. I would rather say it is a powerful time for a marriage."

We nodded, unsure if we were supposed to respond. Then Bobby cut right to the chase.

"People come to me right after they get married and they say, 'Now we're one.' That's bullshit. And it's a problem. You're not one. Becoming one is impossible."

This made me think about the fact that Nick and I were currently sharing the same electric toothbrush at home, and I made a mental note to order a second electric toothbrush.

From memory Bobby quoted the Lebanese poet Kahlil Gibran:

Let there be spaces in your togetherness,
And let the winds of the heavens dance between you . . .
And stand together, yet not too near together . . .

Most of the advice we'd been given up to this point, particularly in Chile, had been about how to successfully meld our lives into each other. I already felt like I was melting into Nick's life. Hadn't I moved across the country, far away from my family and friends, my professional contacts, and the city that I knew and loved? I depended on Nick so much more in San Francisco just to help me figure out how to get on the right bus, one that wouldn't take me across the Golden Gate Bridge. I made a silent vow to focus on building my own life in San Francisco, in addition to the one I'd build with Nick.

"Be a witness to each other's solitude, man," Bobby concluded in his best spiritual-adviser voice. "You each need to live your own lives. And you need to be able to communicate about that life to your partner."

And then Bobby told us about "Five Minutes"—or what I like to call the greatest thing to happen to our new marriage.

Every day for the next forty-five days, Bobby instructed us to try a ten-minute exercise during which we would each speak, uninterrupted by the other, for five consecutive minutes. These are the rules:

1. The other partner is not allowed to react or speak during the five minutes.
2. Whatever is mentioned in the five minutes can't become a source of contention later.
3. You can never bring something up that is more than three weeks old. Bobby told us we should never be fighting about *anything* that is more than three weeks old. The point of the five minutes is to resolve issues before they get old and begin to rot the base of our marriage.

"It's important to listen without trying to fix or comment. This way you will learn never to give your partner advice unless they ask you for it. That's the easiest way to breed resentment. Only tell the truth; don't lie about anything. You don't accomplish anything if you lie."

It reminded me of something the writer Erica Jong had told me the last time I'd interviewed her. I asked her specifically about why her last marriage ended up being her most successful.

"We have always been outspoken," she said. "We don't hold grudges or grievances. You have to speak up in a marriage about the things that bother you. Both members of the marriage have to do it, and it's hard!"

It was so simple, really. Too often we expect our partners to be mind readers, knowing what's happening in our brains without our telling them. That's insane, right? Of course the only way to know what another person is thinking is for them to actually tell us.

Bobby left us alone to give it a shot, closing the heavy wooden door behind him with a thud.

Nick and I both giggled at first. We understood the intention of Five Minutes, but it still felt like the kinds of icebreaker activities you're told to do on the first day of summer camp or confusing corporate retreats with your crazy coworkers.

"I'll start," I said. "I feel silly doing this, since I talk to you about all things all the time. I don't know what I'm doing. I want to be good at this. I don't want to be like my parents. I'm insecure as hell about a lot of things. Sometimes I don't know why you love me so much."

I sucked in a breath and looked toward the door. Why not say it? Say the thing I was afraid to admit. If there was any time to be vulnerable, wasn't it here, on our honeymoon, in the office of a rock-and-roll-photographer-turned-guru in the middle of the jungle? As Bobby said, the things we leave unsaid in a marriage are the things that rot away at us. In all relationships there are things you never say. What I was about to say could have been one of them.

"Sometimes I think you're too damn good for me." The second it came out of my mouth I realized how ridiculous it sounded. It had been one of those clinging doubts that stuck around after our first few dates, particularly after I met the army of Nick's ex-girlfriends. I've had ex-boyfriends describe me, in no particular order, as the love of their lives, a psychotic bitch, the one who got away, that chick I was fucking, and the kind of girl you date but don't marry. Nick's ex-girlfriends universally adore him and still cling to him like grapes on a vine, constantly emailing him for directions, life advice, and help with their frequent flier miles. They were fine, sweet even, except for their insistence that they knew Nick long before I did and perhaps better. I should have been happy that I'd married someone who inspired such loyalty in the women he'd broken up with, but it only served to remind me that Nick Aster is a *very good person.*

He's gracious and kind and wears his heart on his sleeve. He really can fix your garbage disposal with his bare hands and he will do it with glee. He's built a business on the premise that good people can change the world. He's genuinely nicer, kinder, more empathetic, and patient than I'll ever be. He would never tell someone they were a liar for bringing a fake service dog on a plane or yell at an Uber driver for blasting Megadeth all the way to the airport. These were among the many reasons I loved him.

And yet his goodness made me feel like I needed to work very hard to be a better person. I'd dated so many jerks in the past that the moral high ground came naturally to me. I reveled in being the "good one," the one who made all the plans, who didn't cheat, who had a job. With the tables turned I felt unmoored, like an egg balanced on it's skinny face, certain I'd topple, certain I'd crack.

"Sometimes I'm worried you'll run off with the kind of girl I think you should be with—one who likes roughing it outdoors with just a fishing pole and tarp, one who's single-handedly solving the world's water problem, one who's very calm and chill and likes jam bands and would never scream at an Uber driver." The words surprised me. Out loud they sounded silly, almost juvenile. I cribbed a line from Jack Nicholson from the movie *As Good as It Gets*. "But I think it's okay, because you make me want to be a better woman."

I went on like this for five straight minutes; my anxieties and tensions and neuroses poured out of my mouth. If I were still Catholic, I'd call it confession, a spilling of the soul without interruption.

Then it was Nick's turn.

"Oh, baby girl. How can you think you're not a good person? No one else would keep Lady Piazza. She's a bad, bad dog. But you love her so much! And that's just one of ten thousand and nine examples

I could give you. I'm as scared as you are. If I hadn't met you, there was a very real possibility I'd end up a creepy single old man with a beard talking to himself on the streets of San Francisco.

"I fear that I'll fail you in some way or fail myself. I worry about not being good enough too. I worry you'll leave me for some corporate lawyer who makes piles of money. You're the most dynamic and driven person I've ever met. You push me and challenge me. I worry that I don't challenge you. What if I can't make you happy?"

Nick kept talking. He said he was generally nervous about not being the only one in control of his own life. He was scared about making the next big steps, buying a house and having kids. But what I couldn't stop thinking about was the fact that he'd said he thought *he* wasn't good enough for *me*. That thing that I didn't want to talk about, that I was scared to say out loud? My husband felt that thing too. Now that we'd both said it, it felt like a much smaller thing. Communication for the win.

Nick later told me that he appreciated the challenge of learning to simply listen and not react. He found it relaxing and refreshing to just say whatever came to mind. I agreed. The willingness to listen really shows the other person that you're trying to understand them better. It also allows time to work things out when you're cool and calm, before things get heated and your minds begin to race.

The honeymoon was supposed to be a time when we got better acquainted with each other's bodies, but we were spending just as much time getting intimate with the inner workings of the other person's mind.

You'll probably be as surprised as I was to learn that one of the most poignant quotes about the importance of maintaining conversation in your marriage comes from Friedrich Nietzsche, the prolific German philosopher and maybe father of fascism. In one of his earlier works, *Human, All Too Human*, Nietzsche emphasized the importance of husbands and wives talking to each other: "Marriage is a long conversation," Nietzsche said. "When entering into a marriage one ought to ask oneself: do you believe you are going to enjoy talking with this woman up into your old age? Everything else in marriage is transitory."

Our gray-haired guru was knocking on the door before we knew it. Bobby Klein placed his hands on our shoulders and I thought for a brief moment that he might try to kiss us on the mouth, but he just imparted one last nugget of wisdom before we left to pay our bill.

"Let go of all your crap. Get rid of what happened before. Enjoy each other. Talk to each other. Listen. Really listen. Don't just pretend to listen. Embrace your life together. It's beautiful."

....

Bobby said to let go of our crap. That was how I convinced Nick that in the midst of our Mexican honeymoon we should try a traditional Mayan *temazcal* ceremony, a kind of sweat lodge that would cleanse us and purify us for our new marriage.

"What crap do you need to get rid of?" Nick asked me. "Didn't we talk about all the crap? There's more?"

I delivered the knowing gaze I'd perfected by watching Mariska Hargitay talk to victims on *Law & Order: Special Victims Unit*. "There's always more."

He agreed to do the *temazcal* ceremony if I would agree to go visit the Chichén Itzá ruins the following day. Marriage, I was learning, is about compromise.

Temazcal translates loosely into English as "medicine house." It could just as easily translate into "really hot hut." Mexican Aztecs, Mayans, and some native North American tribes have used these sweat lodges in a variety of ways for centuries, but often to purify a couple right before or after their marriage ceremony.

Most of the high-end resorts along the Riviera Maya offer some tourist version of the *temazcal* ceremony for visitors, gouging outsiders for as much as $1,000 for a private couple's ceremony. We laughed at the idea of paying a good portion of our monthly rent to sweat in a tent, but serendipity intervened during a stop at an organic juice shop, where the barista promised that for just $100 total she could score us a sweat lodge session that included a shaman named Julio and two shots of locally made artisanal tequila.

I have no idea how to tell if someone is truly a shaman or if tequila is artisanal, except to take the word of an organic juice barista.

Just past sundown we met our shaman in the dense jungle behind the juice store. He was fairly obvious, the guy mixing up a pot of herbs and wearing a loincloth who reminded me of the dude my friends bought weed from back in high school. He had a lady friend with him, a bright-eyed and beautiful Argentinean girl named Gisele who smiled at us and wiggled her fingers in a trifling wave, her twentysomething skin glistening with sweat, sand, and seawater.

"She's here to balance the masculine and feminine energy in the ceremony," Julio said.

All I could think was *She'd better not take her top off in the temazcal.*

I asked Julio how long we'd be in the sweat tent. He gazed past me into the fire and muttered in a thick Mexican accent, "Who can tell? Only the rocks will know." Was he on drugs?

"Do the rocks think we'll be out in time to grab a late dinner or maybe just nachos before bed?"

This time Julio pretended not to understand my English.

The *temazcal* ritual usually involves spending five hours in a very hot tent or stone hut while a shaman or other religious practitioner uses scorching volcanic rocks doused with healing waters to bring the temperature inside above 170 degrees. The shaman leads the group in chanting ancient prayers that are supposed to unveil traumas, fears, and emotional stress trapped within the body and mind—all of the crap. The ancient Mayans believed that spending time in the *temazcal* represented a return to the womb, a place where you can be freed of past troubles and worries.

"The process is hard. It takes patience," Julio explained. "You're forced to suffer together." I remembered that the word "patience" was born of the word for "suffering." "And afterwards you're reborn as a pair of warriors, bonded for life. You will be on the same team . . . like the New York Giants."

The ceremony began simply enough. Julio's shaman assistant, Miguel, shoveled the volcanic rocks into a claustrophobic hut constructed of sticks and blankets. I likened it to a yurt, even though I wasn't entirely sure what a yurt should look like. Nick would know what a yurt looked like, but I didn't want to ask about it, for fear of compromising the illusion of my confidence in the ceremony.

The stones sparkled like pretty little stars as they came out of the fire.

"*Meteoritos*," Julio said, his smile revealing a row of crooked and tobacco-stained bottom teeth. Meteorites. The stones did glow like something from another planet. We crawled in the dirt on our hands and knees through the hut's tiny door. Inside we formed a circle around the fire as the temperature rose. Julio pounded on an oblong calfskin drum and chanted, encouraging us to repeat the half-Spanish, half-Mayan phrases. Nick's deep baritone singing voice surprised me.

It wasn't that I'd never heard my husband sing before. Nick sings all the time. He makes up silly little songs about everything from applying shampoo and conditioner to whether Lady Piazza needs a bath. He captivates neighborhood children with a three-chord guitar rhapsody about cheese puffs. But I'd never heard him seriously sing anything, and I was in love with his voice.

Before we knew what was happening, it got hot . . . really, really hot.

Sweat dripped over my eyelashes. Of course Gisele took off her bikini to reveal her Victoria Secret model perfect boobs. It was 150 degrees inside a hut that smelled like feet, and a sexy Argentinean woman had just taken off her top in front of my new husband. I had no idea how this would purify our marriage.

Time became completely irrelevant in the *temazcal*. Minutes could have been hours and hours could have been days. There was only the singing and the drums and the heat. Oh my God, that heat. Sometimes I felt closer to Nick than ever before as I wound my fingers through his and listened to his singing. Other times I hardly even knew he was there.

"Shed your fears, shed your anxiety. Give them up to the fire. Burn them away," Julio chanted in Mayan and then in broken English. He looked directly at me, the smoke blurring his face around the edges. "You don't trust happiness. You find comfort in the pain and fear you've known for so long. Embrace these good new things."

"I peed my pants," Nick whispered, breaking Julio's spell over me. He wasn't kidding. My husband, who has a very small bladder and who had drunk a gallon of water in anticipation of sweating for five hours, peed his pants in the Mayan hell yurt. What had I gotten us into? Why were we boiling in a hot box with a maybe shaman who came highly recommended by a girl who made juice, and his girlfriend with the tits of a porn star? I plotted escape routes. Nick curled into the fetal position. He might have passed out. I burrowed a hole through the sand and underneath the tent to stick my head outside to escape the smells of the tent saturated with pee, sweat, and body odor, desperate for a single breath of wonderfully cool, clean air.

"Give it all away!" Julio boomed as I brought my head back inside. "Sometimes you need to scream once in a while. Scream it all out. If you keep everything inside, you'll explode."

What did I want to give away? At this very moment I wanted to give away the few items of clothing still clinging to my body. I stripped my shirt off, dropping the sweat-drenched tank top into the fire.

I wanted to let go of my anger at my parents for not being better marital role models. I had to give away my insecurities about not being pretty enough or good enough or lovable enough. I wanted to be less selfish. I wanted to be better at considering Nick's needs before my own. I screamed these things into the fire. I yelled louder than I'd ever yelled before. I yelled until the back of my throat got tight and began to hurt. I saw myself rubbed raw.

Julio spit into the dirt, the moisture sizzling around his ankles. He shook a pole that sounded like the rain stick my kindergarten teacher at Greenwood Elementary used to make the kids be quiet and lie on their mats for nap time. "And now the newlyweds touch and be close," Julio said. "For the last of the rocks. The most powerful of the rocks. You shall seal your bond. You express your love and your gratitude."

Julio opened the hut's flap one last time to shovel more fiery rocks into the middle of our circle.

"No more," I whispered, but he didn't hear me.

We were spent. I lay down in front of Nick and pressed my body into his. Realizing I was too close to the heat rising off the rocks, he wordlessly moved in front of me to try to block me from the flames. I felt the air in front of me cool several degrees, like walking into a shadow on the street.

"Express your love for one another. Express your vows." I couldn't believe Julio was still talking.

In our handwritten wedding vows I'd vowed to love him, to nurture him, and to inspire him. He had vowed to support me, cherish me, give me back rubs, and strive to make me happy every day for the rest of our lives. We grasped hands and said these things to each other again in the yurt tent. But we also said other things. Nick promised to help calm my anxieties and insecurities, and I promised to let my guard down more often. He promised to be strong when I couldn't be, and I promised to be patient and supportive. This time the vows felt more real than when we said them in front of the Sphinx. This time we were saying them just for each other instead of for a crowd of people.

I rolled onto my belly and buried my face in the sand to cool it off.

"You will suffer," Julio said. "In a marriage you will suffer together. But together you will be warriors!"

My body went limp. I fell into a fugue state. Time passed.

And then it was over.

We crept out of the *temazcal* like weakened lambs who'd somehow escaped slaughter.

"Now we will cleanse in the healing waters of the sea."

Julio led us, barefoot, across the pockmarked street and onto the grounds of a nearby resort, paying no mind to signs that warned against trespassing. We weaved through a labyrinth of palm trees and chaise longues until we came upon the ocean.

In the sea Nick held me above the waves, my head tipped back to stare at the sky. "How do you feel?" he asked, his voice hoarse from bellowing into the fire.

"Lighter?" I said, more of a question than a statement. "I don't need to throw up anymore. I thought I was going to throw up most of the time we were in the hut. But now I feel good. Surprisingly good."

"Me too."

"That was hard."

Nick nodded. "Did you get rid of your crap?"

"I feel nice." I didn't know what to say except for that. I buried my nose into Nick's wet shoulder and inhaled his distinctive musky smell, a mix of sweat, heavier than usual tonight, and something vaguely sweet.

"Should we do Five Minutes?" Nick said, half teasing me.

"Here?"

"Why not? Here is as good a place as any."

"Okay. I'll start. Thank you for indulging me in trying all of these madcap rituals and ceremonies. Thank you for accepting me as I really am, even the parts of me that are broken and not perfect and sometimes strange. You make me happier than I ever could have imagined." I went on for the remaining four minutes and thirty seconds, expressing my gratitude and happiness.

Then Nick went, beginning with "You know that I think you are stronger and braver than you think you are." I stuck my tongue out at him.

"You just want to have honeymoon sex."

Nick began to laugh as we treaded water. "We've been married a week."

"What a one-week anniversary, Mr. Aster!"

"I daresay I liked it, Mrs. Aster."

"Want to go another week?"

"Yeah. Then we'll check in and see if we want to renew the contract for another."

"Do you feel like we're on the same team now?" I asked Nick as we walked down the starlit beach back to our *palapa*. "Like the New York Giants?"

He took so long considering it that I wasn't sure if he'd heard me. I nudged him and he nodded slowly. "We're getting there."

4

Maine

We're a Team?

Coming together is a beginning. Keeping together is progress. Working together is success.

—Henry Ford

"Don't drop your wife."

You just don't hear that enough. One of my drunk relatives said it to Nick in reference to carrying me over the threshold, but Uncle Jack wasn't in a position to give anyone advice about anything after all those Johnny Walker shots at our wedding.

It's good advice, in any case.

We heard it again a month after we got married, the day we signed up for the North American Wife Carrying Championship at Sunday River, Maine. The Wife Carrying Championship is like one of those Tough Mudder races, but shorter and scrappier, on a gonzo obstacle course where men carry their wives over logs and hurdles and through a pit of freezing-cold water. When we signed up over the phone, we asked the organizers of the race what we needed to do to win. They were blunt, relaying in a thick Mainer accent, "Don't droop yah woife and remembah to wok as a team."

Nick knew that if he dropped me I would post it on Facebook for all his friends, and his mother and her friends, to see. I knew this was the reason he was determined not to drop me. The second part of the advice was the trickier of the two. Working as a team wasn't something that came naturally to Nick or me, two humans who had been fiercely independent for most of their lives. But it was time to figure it out, the team thing. We were about to encounter the big-life-decision things that happen after you get back from a honeymoon. Not only were we going to compete in a wife-carrying competition, but we were about to buy our first home.

Every reputable expert on marriage and everyone who has ever bought a home will describe property buying as one of the most stressful things a couple can do together outside of having a baby. I believe that if the government made getting married as hard as banks make getting a mortgage, more people would say, "Let's just keep living in sin, because then I don't have to sign my name a hundred and twenty-seven times."

If buying a house just a month after planning a wedding sounds quick, well, it was.

We'd swiftly outgrown Nick's cramped, rent-controlled studio, a place where we could see each other no matter where we were sitting, with the exception of on the toilet (if we closed the door). When I moved in, the place was neat and clean, but it still smelled like boy. The walls were a matronly shade of peach, and when I remarked on them Nick just shrugged. "They were like this when I moved in." I'd expected some feminine decorating touches from his last girlfriend, a sweet girl who was into canning pickled vegetables, but all she left were a few old mason jars that smelled like cabbage. My things migrated around the apartment with no clear place for them, stacks of books beneath the couch, underwear and socks in the desk drawer. Lady Piazza was relegated to living under the bed. That made the bedroom, which was no bigger than the queen-sized bed, smell like a zoo. Renting a bigger place in San Francisco would have cost us a fortune and, oddly, it was more cost-effective for us to try to find something to buy. The owners of Nick's building also wanted to kick us out so they could increase the rent by 300 percent. I had a little bit of money from a book I'd sold the year before, and since I'd grown up surrounded by financial instability, buying a home represented something important, something solid. Nick didn't need anything besides me to feel stable. Left to his own devices my husband would be living in a van with a cooler filled with cheese, beer, and bananas. He'd catch his own fish, hunt his own dinner, purify his own water, and live happily ever after. Before we met, he and his friend Charlie used to go on excursions poetically named "burrito camping," which literally meant heading into the wilderness with a tarp, a fishing line, and a hunk of cheese. If it rained, they would roll up in the tarps . . . like burritos.

"I spent six dollars on that tarp and I had it for twenty years. It's the best investment I ever made," Nick argued when I suggested we might throw away the tarp to make room for other things, like towels.

Nick had told me in Bobby Klein's office that rushing into something huge like buying a home made him nervous. It was me that wanted to make the purchase and I know he agreed because he wanted me to be happy.

The housing market in San Francisco is typically a playground reserved for millionaires with an excess of money, time, and assistants. As working journalists, Nick and I had none of those things. Yet just a month after our wedding we stumbled onto an elegant two-bedroom condo in a prewar Edwardian building for sale in a neighborhood that real estate blogs kept saying was on the verge of being really interesting. Built in 1902, the house had survived two massive earthquakes and had a charming, if ill-kept, backyard and bay windows with narrow views of the actual bay if you looked out of them at the right angle. From our bedroom we could see the Transamerica building, and hummingbirds dancing along the fence posts. Some magical alignment of the stars placed it within our price range.

Few things teach you the necessity of teamwork and compromise in a marriage more than buying your first home together. Case in point: When the seller rejected our initial offer, I unilaterally told our real estate agent to increase our bid by $10,000 without even glancing at my new husband. We didn't exactly have thousands of dollars to spare, but it didn't feel like a big deal to me. When you're dealing with figures so astronomically high, it all feels like Monopoly money.

"Do it!" I yelled into the phone like James Cramer on CNBC.

I blame this knee-jerk reaction on the fact that when I was single I made all of the decisions about my life, from negotiating the price of my car to the terms of my leases and my salaries. But as soon as I said it, I knew I'd done something wrong.

Nick stood and walked the two steps from our couch to the kitchen sink to do the dishes. He tidies when he is upset, which is a sweet habit for a husband to have.

I followed him. "What's wrong?"

"Nothing," he lied.

He grabbed the broom and swept the dog hair off the living room floor. As he picked up a tuft of Lady Piazza's fur the size of a Chihuahua, he said simply and calmly, "I would've liked to be consulted. I would've liked you to at least say something to me before you spent ten thousand dollars more on the house." He wasn't wrong. And I felt dreadful that consulting him hadn't even occurred to me. There are all these bits of teamwork that you don't think about until you're part of a two-person team created both by choice and a legally binding vow.

There are other things too. For instance, if you're a team, you shouldn't open all of your wedding presents when your new spouse is away on a business trip.

Nick learned that one the hard way. "I really didn't think you gave a shit," he said when I informed him it would have been nice if he'd waited.

A good team member doesn't let the dog sleep in the bed, even when her husband is out of town, because he hates it and believes dogs should not sleep in beds.

Being a team means not eating all of the delicious chocolate the two of you bought on your honeymoon on your own in one go, even though you have your period and chocolate is the only thing that will stop you from wanting to kill someone.

It's about the big things as well. It's about sorting through the byzantine mortgage application process, applying for three new joint bank accounts to manage that application process, digging up years and years of personal finance history in order to send that history by fax to a mortgage broker who clearly still lived in 1998. Teamwork is telling your spouse that it's their turn to find a goddamn fax machine.

We'd been told time and again that acting together as a team is one of the most important things for new couples to learn. "It's not just important; teamwork is an imperative," Dr. Peter Pearson, the founder of the Couples Institute in Palo Alto, California, explained to me shortly after our honeymoon. Peter and his wife, Dr. Ellyn Bader, are pioneers in the field of couples therapy, having founded the institute more than twenty-seven years ago and counseled thousands of couples from around the world. They're the go-to marriage counselors for Silicon Valley bigwigs. If you're a Facebooker married to a Googler and can't figure out how to make your individual operating systems work together, they've got you covered.

They've also worked as psychologists for the San Francisco 49ers, so they know a few things about team dynamics.

Peter Pearson's acronym "TEAM" stands for "Together Each Accomplishes More."

"When you do something on your own, you aren't as successful," he said. "You and your partner need to have an agreement to coach one another, to tell one another what works for you and what doesn't work for you. When you start doing that, your relationship really starts to hum and the hidden capacities of the team start to surface." His advice was to find something neither of us had done before and try to conquer it together, preferably something fun that didn't involve draining our entire savings account, making the largest purchase of our lives, and taking on hundreds of thousands of dollars in debt.

Soon after we submitted all of our paperwork to find out if we were worthy of becoming homeowners, we found out about this batty wife-carrying race in New England.

The concept for the race didn't originate in Maine. It began in Finland, which made wife carrying (they call it *eukonkanto*) an actual sport in 1991. The grand prize of the competition is the wife's weight in beer. No joke. The idea for the obstacle course actually dates all the way back to a nineteenth-century legend about a robber named Ronkainen, who was the overseer of a large band of unsavory criminals. In order to figure out who would be a good robber, one who was adept at pillaging and destruction, Ronkainen made his recruits race through an obstacle course carrying a woman on their backs. A woman, you see, is about the same size and weight as a bag of stolen gold, jewels, and china; it was also a helpful tool for Ronkainen to assess whether his recruits could help him steal an actual woman.

We wouldn't be able to make it all the way to Finland. (Good lord, it was $2,000 a ticket!) But by a bizarre stroke of luck, the North American wife-carrying qualifying race happened to be taking place the very same weekend, and in the same state (Maine) as my friend Leah's wedding. How could we possibly say no?

The wedding was scheduled for the afternoon and the wife-carrying race would end by midday.

"We'll be cutting it close," I said to Nick.

"So what? We'll bring them your weight in beer!" Fair point.

It turns out that there are a lot of ways a man can carry his wife across the finish line in the sport of *eukonkanto*, but by far the most popular method for racing is the "Estonian carry," whereby the woman hangs upside down behind her husband with her legs thrown over his shoulders. It looks ridiculous, but it properly balances the woman's weight and allows the husband's hands to be free for climbing over logs and protecting himself when he falls on his face.

Of course there are rules. A wife has to weigh at least 108 pounds. If she weighs less, she has to carry a heavy rucksack to make up for it. Neither husband nor wife can wear any sort of "equipment." This means no harnesses, saddles, or ropes. If a contestant drops his wife, he is required to pick her up and continue carrying her to the finish line unless he is gravely injured.

The Finnish wife-carrying Web site offers wonderful tips for how to become a "master wife carrier" that may or may not have been written by the author of *Fifty Shades of Grey*:

> The wife carrying is an attitude toward life. The wives and the wife carriers are not afraid of challenges or burdens. They push their way persistently forward, holding tightly, generally with a twinkle in the eyes. . . . You can sense the excitement in the air during the wife-carrying competition. The core of the race is made of a woman, a man and their relationship. The wife carrying and eroticism have a lot in common. Intuitive understanding of the signals sent by the partner and becoming one with the partner are essential in both of them—sometimes also whipping.

Yes, whipping. A wife who is being carried is encouraged to smack her husband's ass like a jockey urging on a prize-winning steed.

We made our first practice run just a couple of days before the race. Nick squatted on the ground while I flung myself over his shoulders so that my own head hung down below his backside. I grasped his hips for dear life.

We teetered left and right and then toppled over.

"You've got to work with me," Nick said. "Get centered. Shift your weight." I shifted my weight, but nothing made it any less awkward. Working together as one physical unit is not the way humans are naturally built.

"Our limbic system—that ancient nerve network that controls our emotions, our desires, and our instincts, moods, and drives—is organized around immediate gratification and avoidance of pain and fear. That means that a lot of the time our bodies think about our own needs and we want our partner to adapt and bend to what we want to make everything easier," Peter Pearson explained to me about the challenges all humans face when trying to work in tandem. There was such an inertia to being single. We'd become so set in our ways. Nick and I were a classic example of two individuals calcified in our habits, our primordial limbic systems in tune with our individual survival, unaware that another team member even existed.

"Because more people are marrying later, they have a better sense of who they are. They are more fully formed in certain ways, and their ideas about how things should be and how life should go may be different from their partner's. A lot of people forget that they're going to have to compromise in lots of ways when they get married because they've lived autonomously for so long," Lori Gottlieb, a world-renowned couples therapist and *New York Times* best-selling author of *Marry Him: The Case for Settling for Mr. Good Enough*, told me. She added that women can be particularly averse to giving up freedoms because we've worked so hard to establish ourselves and our autonomy. Having to compromise in a marriage can often feel like a much bigger loss than it really is because of what it represents. According to the experts, there was no quick fix that would instantly make compromise come more naturally to the two of us. The only thing that would rewire our brains for teamwork was practice.

After years of perfecting the art of wife carrying, the Finns also realized that working as a team does not come naturally to many human beings. That's why they warn potential wife-carrying participants that finding a mutually beneficial groove is crucial for the winning team.

> It is of great importance to find a mutual rhythm. If the wife on the man's back is rocking out of time, the speed slows down. When the rhythm is good, the wife and the carrier become one in accompanying the motions of each other. It is advisable to practice in order to find the mutual rhythm before the competition.

This is as true in marriage as it is in a race where the husband carries his wife upside down on his shoulders.

Lori Gottlieb told me that many of the couples she sees are adamant about treating marital teamwork like work teamwork. "They divide everything fifty-fifty. Half the time one person does the laundry; the other half of the time the other person does the laundry. They split the bills down the middle and the child care down the middle," Gottlieb said. "You can't treat a relationship like a spreadsheet. It has to be more organic than that. Each couple needs to find their own rhythm, where each person is participating in a way that makes you both feel like you're getting a good deal."

It was hard to say who was getting the worse deal when it came to wife carrying. Was it Nick for having to carry a person around on his shoulders, or was it me for having to dangle upside down with my head just below my husband's butt cheeks?

Nick and I attempted a second practice run. This time he was able to straighten his legs and I was able to balance on his shoulders. Then, without warning, Nick took off running a lap around the park.

"I'm going over a bench," Nick yelled.

"What? No. You aren't going over a bench. Do not go over that bench."

He was already going over the bench. He climbed onto the seat and then up onto the back as I dangled, helpless.

"Keep your head up."

"*Put me down!*"

"Let's try going over this log."

"*Seriously. Put me down!*"

"Just one log."

"Screw you."

After two more logs, I hated my husband.

When Nick finally chose to stop, I was able to awkwardly unwrap myself from his body by doing a handstand and tumbling to the ground. I made my way to a park bench to rub my bruised tailbone and thought about a quote one of my creepy athletic coaches from high school used to tell our team before a big game: "Coming together is a beginning. Keeping together is progress. Working together is success."

We were not a success.

The originator of the quote was not my pervy athletics coach, but Henry Ford (who was talking about building cars), but the quote can easily be applied to high school lacrosse, wife carrying, and building the solid foundation for a marriage.

....

"Could your wife step on the scale?" the race coordinator asked Nick when we went to pick up our wife-carrying race packets at the rustic ski lodge at Sunday River.

"That's not necessary," I said in what I believed to be an adorable singsong voice. "I weigh a hundred and thirty pounds."

"You'll have to get on the scale if you want to compete," the no-nonsense Mainer replied.

One hundred and forty pounds.

"More beer for you!" Nick and I high-fived.

It wasn't until we arrived at the race that we realized just how serious the people who participate in wife-carrying competitions really are about wife-carrying competitions. The other couples had arrived hours earlier, much closer to dawn, and were already practicing in the chill morning air as we lazily sipped our lattes.

"That's a steep-ass hill," Nick said, gazing up at the ski slope.

The other men leaped over log hurdles like gazelles or Namibians, their petite wives balanced delicately on their shoulders.

"All of these people look *very* athletic," Nick said, staring them down. "We are not *very* athletic."

"Let's do a practice run," I said, rubbing his shoulders. "It's cool. We've got this. We're a team."

We attempted a hurdle. Nick lost his balance and I fell on my head.

"*Sonofabitch!*" Rubbing my head and glaring up at my husband from the ground, I began to think that a marriage is like a long and difficult race . . . or an obstacle course where you carry your wife up a mountain and through a pond of muck and sometimes, albeit by accident, drop her on her face. You can't expect to glide through it. There will be obstacles and pain and incredible highs and terrible lows, and you need to keep moving through it together. I told my sentimental thoughts to Nick, but he was preoccupied.

"Did you see that guy's biceps?" he said about a wife-carrying challenger with upper arms the size of chubby babies.

It was clear we were the least prepared couple to arrive in Sunday River.

Contenders began to gather at the base of the ski slope, sizing one another up with elevator eyes and inappropriate questions.

"What's your wife weigh?"

"How much did you eat for dinner last night?"

"Are you flexible?"

There were all sorts of couples competing. There was the Alpha Couple. They were the ones doing synchronized jumping jacks while emitting low, intimidating grunts. There was the drunk couple who kept crushing beer cans on the ground and chest bumping each other. You'd think they might be less prepared than we were, but they clearly felt no pain of any kind. There were the couples in matching costumes. Nick and I wore a motley mismatched mixture of yoga clothes and pajamas from the night before.

There were the strangely swift older couple in their sixties and a pregnant couple who moved like a pair of cheetahs. The husband on that team was wearing a shirt that said, "I'm carrying two." The wife wore a shirt that said, "I'm carrying one." She was two and a half months along.

"The doctor said it was fine as long as he didn't drop me," she said.

There were the Russells, who were about our age but had their four kids with them, each of them adorably outfitted in his or her own Team Russell T-shirt. I loved the Russells. I wanted to put the Russells on *our* Christmas card and send it out to family and friends.

"We almost didn't make it," Mama Russell told me before the race began. "But we wanted to make sure to do this together. Not much else bonds a couple like this. The key to a happy marriage, even after four kids, is to never stop adventuring," she told me. Mama Russell was wiser than she knew. Scientists have long insisted that maintaining novelty in a marriage contributes to a couple's general well-being, their happiness, and the success of the partnership. New experiences activate the brain's reward system, flooding it with dopamine and norepinephrine, the same chemicals that are released in the brain in the early throes of romantic love (and also incidentally when you do a lot of cocaine). Continuing to adventure and try new things helps remind a couple of the feelings that made them fall in love in the first place.

Researchers from the State University of New York at Stony Brook recruited fifty-three middle-aged couples to test this theory. One group was sent out on a pleasant but run-of-the-mill date night once a week. The second was sent off to do something completely new and "exciting." The couples who engaged in the "exciting" evening showed a much greater increase in marital satisfaction than the group that simply had a "pleasant" date night. The wife-carrying competition was definitely not a pleasant date night, but it did qualify as a new and exciting experience. More than a year later we'd still show pictures of us in the Estonian position to friends at dinner parties.

As we walked away from the Russells I asked Nick, "Honey, can we bring our kids here one day?"

"Yes, Squeaky . . . if we survive." We had entered this race with the intent to win. Now we just wanted to cross the finish line intact.

As we approached the start line for our heat, we realized we were racing against Alpha Couple—last year's wife-carrying champions. As Alpha Husband limbered up, he lunged from side to side, giant thigh muscles pulsing beneath spandex. Alpha Wife leaped into the air like a nimble little bunny.

"This won't be humiliating at all," Nick said. My husband likes to be very, very good at things, and when he isn't very, very good at things, he is mortified. He also hates showing weakness in front of strangers. This competition could be the perfect storm of awfulness for him. And I'd be on his back the whole time.

"A lopsided contest always makes for a better story," I said with a small smile. I'd heard that somewhere, but I didn't really believe it.

"Saddle up!" cried the announcer. I stepped in front of Nick and gave him a brief peck on the lips.

"We've got this!" I lied.

Nick heaved me onto his shoulders and we were off.

Alpha Couple sped up the hill and became tiny specks in the distance within seconds. We moved forward slowly and steadily. Unable to see anything, I had to trust Nick to tell me when we were about to climb over a log or risk smacking my face into the obstacle. He had learned his lesson from our tempestuous practice runs in San Francisco and this time around warned me about obstacles in plenty of time.

"Log comin'!" he'd shout.

"We've got a hole in the ground! Watch your head."

All I could see were his feet, moving slower and slower. The crowd cheered and shouted encouragement, which I worried was embarrassing Nick even more.

"Smack his backside," they hollered. "*Smack his ass!*"

I did my best to balance my weight equally between his front and back, striving to make myself as easy as possible to carry, trying to breath in rhythm with his steps. A sense of impotence came over me. What else could *I* be doing to make this easier for Nick?

I could be his biggest cheerleader or, as Peter Pearson had suggested, his coach.

"You're the best! Don't drop me. I love you. Don't drop me. I love you. You are the greatest husband in the history of husbands! Don't drop me. I love you. Don't drop me," I hooted, high on adrenaline. "*I love you so much, baby!*"

And he didn't drop me. We crossed the finish line in two minutes and twenty seconds, the longest race time of any team that hadn't dropped a wife. Yes, several wives were dropped. Nick was out of breath, muddy, and freezing.

"This is the first major hurdle we've gotten over as a couple. I kinda can't believe we did it. We agreed to do this crazy-ass thing together and then, you know, we did it," Nick babbled on, in possible shock. He wrapped me in an enormous hug. "You know, Squeaky, this taught me a lot about having a sense of humor about setting expectations for things. I'm just happy I didn't drop you. Also I think I threw out my back."

I posted pictures on Facebook of us slogging through the muddy pit with the caption "We may not have won the North American Wife Carrying Championships, but at least Nick didn't drop me." My friend Matt pointed out, rightly so, that "Nick Aster isn't just not dropping you. He's holding you up!"

And he was.

Soon after we made it home from the race and the wedding, we learned we'd been approved for our mortgage, which opened the door for even more paperwork and appointments. I don't want to give all the credit to the wife-carrying competition, but it felt like we were in a better place to handle it all together, trusting each other to work in our team's best interest. I took care of the inspection process. He fought with the bank to lower our interest rate while I negotiated the lowest price possible with a moving company that may have been run by the Mob. We divided and conquered, and our newfound commitment to teamwork kept us from wanting to kill each other through the process.

"It wasn't so bad," Nick said, once it was all over and we'd forgotten how many times we had to search the city for fax machines.

"It was terrible," I disagreed, taking one final look at Nick's bachelor apartment. "We're never buying a home again."

"Yeah, you're right. I'd rather run up a ski slope with you on my back thirty more times than get another mortgage. It looks like we'll have to live in the new place forever. I hope you really like it there."

5

Denmark

Make Your House a Home

The ache for home lives in all of us, the safe place where we can go as we are and not be questioned.

—Maya Angelou

We bought a home. We own a home. We're homeowners.

Gahhhh! What next?

After all the buildup, the paperwork, the meetings, the fretting, the faxing, we had done it. We closed, a verb I still didn't fully understand, on our own very small part of the American dream.

This colossal marker of adulthood felt almost more significant to our marriage than the wedding.

I don't know what I expected—a party, balloons, someone to welcome us into our new place with a banner that read YOU'RE REAL GROWN-UPS NOW? Someone to hand us cloth napkins with napkin rings, stamps, and Tupperware containers with matching lids?

The day of our closing our real estate agent met us after work, shook our hands, and handed us a plastic bag filled with two dozen unmarked keys. No one congratulated us. There was no banner, no parade, just two people squinting in the last light of the day, smiling dopily despite their new burden of gigantic debt.

"Good luck," the agent said and drove off, her job with us complete, her commission paid. She'd seen every bank statement I'd had since college, helped me sign away my life savings, and held my hand at the title office, but our brief intimacy had come to an end. It took Nick and I an hour to figure out which key unlocked the front door.

Soon after, one Saturday morning, we sat in a tableless dining room eating off the two plates we kept washing and reusing until we'd located their mates. I assured Nick I was going to get all of this new-apartment chaos under control. "I'm going to learn how to take care of the house. I'm going to be a homemaker," I announced.

"Okay, Sugar. Just don't burn the place down," my husband said with a mixture of skepticism and curiosity. He walked into the kitchen to turn off the toaster I'd left on and then opened a window to let out the smoke.

When we got married, the problem wasn't just that I didn't know how to properly take care of another person. The problem was I hardly knew how to take care of myself. For a long time New York City fulfilled the duties of being my spouse. In the city that never sleeps there's always someone who can do anything for you. When I first moved to New York, I lived with two roommates in a one-bedroom apartment I could barely afford. I ate all of my meals at work events, filling up on passed appetizers and champagne, wrapping bite-sized brownies in napkins and hiding them in my purse. We never set foot in a grocery store.

As I grew into jobs with higher salaries and more responsibilities, I worked late and got cheap takeout from Seamless, ordered in the back of a cab on my way home and delivered warm, ready, and delicious to my door before I went upstairs. I dropped a bag of laundry off every Monday morning and picked it up, clean and folded, on Tuesday. I let the apartment get messy. This was the check and balance on my love life. Did a guy like me enough to wade through an ocean of dirty underwear just to get to my couch or my unmade bed after a date? Once a month a wonderful woman named Wencess came to clean my apartment. She scrubbed the bathrooms, mopped the floors, changed the sheets, and left me lovely notes reminding me to thank Jesus. I *did* thank Jesus many times for Wencess. My trash disappeared down a chute at the end of the hallway and someone even washed my windows twice a year. Like a 1950s working husband, I didn't have a care in the world when it came to home economics.

"And how do you plan to do this?" Nick kissed me on the cheek and nibbled the black bits on his burned toast.

"I don't know yet," I said and shuffled off to sit on the couch with my laptop to figure out how to bake a chicken.

One of my personal heroes, the writer Nora Ephron, wrote: "Whenever I get married [Ephron was married three times], I start buying *Gourmet* magazine. I think of it as my own personal bride's disease." That's exactly how I feel about Pinterest. I never looked at the site until the months leading up to my own wedding. But now I consider the Web site to be my own personal bride's disease, a place where I can ask, without shame, the most basic of homemaking questions.

How do I get the duvet on the comforter without climbing inside of it?

The burrito method. Lay the duvet on top of the comforter. Safety-pin the corners. Roll it like a burrito. Invert the duvet cover on itself. Roll it back. (This changed my life.)

What is a lemon zester and what do I do with zest?

It's like a cheese grater, and you use bits of the lemon rind as garnish on desserts and in cocktails.

How do I keep Christmas lights from getting tangled when I store them?

Wrap them around a wire hanger and hang them in your closet for next year.

How do I bake the best chicken ever?
Panko crumbs, butter, Parmesan cheese, and ranch dressing.

What should I do if my towels start to smell funny?
Baking soda and vinegar in the washing machine.

How do I tie my husband's tie?
Cross, behind, over, through.

What do I do with leftover wine besides drink all of it?
Braise short ribs.

How do I get pet fur off all of the furniture?
Use a car squeegee.

But it wasn't enough.

....

"We should go to Denmark," I said to Nick later that week. While researching a story on the evolution of modern Scandinavian cuisine, I'd also learned that the Danish are a people who are particularly adept at creating a cozy and happy home.

Maybe it's because the country is enveloped in cold and darkness for the majority of the year and making a cozy home is fundamental to not going insane. Maybe they just know something we don't about being happy humans. Regardless, it's a place where the concept of household coziness is so ingrained in culture and daily life that they have their own term for it—*hygge*, a word confusing to the American tongue that vaguely sounds like "whoo-gah" and involves an enthusiastic clearing of one's throat. Its roots come from the Germanic word *hyggja*, which translates loosely into "feeling satisfied."

"We don't need to go all the way to Denmark. I can make anything hoog-hah," Nick said. "Remember our second date?"

I did. After I'd been blown away by Nick's Eagle Scout level of preparedness at LAX, we'd trekked to Joshua Tree National Park for my very first camping trip. On the second night a thunderstorm triggered flash-flood warnings in the park. We scrambled to pack our supplies and find shelter at a hotel for the night. Keen to impress me with his camping skills, in or out of doors, Nick went foraging for sticks in the posh Palm Springs resort's garden wearing only the hotel's terry-cloth bathrobe. He lit the gas fireplace and candles, poured two glasses of wine, and roasted s'mores for me over the fake flames. They were the best s'mores I'd ever tasted. I ate three in succession. "I think I might throw up," I said that night. "But I don't care. I want another three."

"I live hoog-hah, pretty girl," Nick said to me as he recalled the memory months after we'd gotten married. "I know what I'm doing."

We ended up making it to Denmark anyway when Nick was invited to speak at a pair of conferences in Scandinavia. When I told friends I was going to explore the Danish concepts of homemaking and happiness, they scratched their heads.

"You're going to Amsterdam?" they said.

"No," I responded. "They're totally different people, the Danish and the Dutch. The Danes come from Denmark. They're Scandinavian, like Vikings."

The truth is that even though I was a longtime travel editor, I was nearly as clueless about Denmark as most of my friends. I knew little except that it was the country where Hamlet lost his mind and that its capital city, Copenhagen, was home to the best restaurant in the world, Noma. Wikipedia informed me that Denmark is the smallest of the four Scandinavian countries, the farthest south, and is an archipelago that sticks out of the top of Germany like a lobster's claw.

Of course, the Netherlands and Denmark do have some striking similarities. Gender equality is very normalized in the two countries, the social safety net is strong, and both nations prioritize family, quality time, and personal happiness over billable hours at work.

Denmark was the first country to legalize gay marriage and the first to allow gender changes without sterilization. They elected a female prime minister, Helle Thorning-Schmidt, in 2011, and one of the country's most popular television shows, *Borgen*, is popular for depicting the life of a strong and independent female politician. The Danes' love of gays, women, classy design, and delicious food won me over before we'd even left San Francisco.

"They're a very smart people, the Danes," Nick said once we'd landed in Copenhagen. "The Danish are very organized, like the Germans, but with a much better sense of humor."

Denmark is most often named the happiest country in the world by the kinds of studies and stories that rank such things. They came in first in the United Nations' World Happiness Report in 2013, 2014, and 2016.

Based on my limited knowledge of the Danes and their headline-making joy, I expected to be greeted by shiny, happy people milling around streets of gold and smiling like Moonies. But on first impression, after we landed in Copenhagen's spotless airport, I wouldn't have known these were the most blissful people in the world.

To start, they wear a lot of black, which is the color I associate with looking thin but not the color I associate with delight and joyfulness. On weekdays the city bustles with the same frenetic activity as any American city. The Danes are efficient and aggressive bike commuters. During rush hour and around midnight, when the bars close, Copenhagen's bike lanes are more crowded than its car lanes.

But here's the difference between Copenhagen and any busy American city: A normal workweek for the Danes averages about thirty-seven hours, and most Danish employees get five weeks of vacation a year. While Americans usually spend a disproportionate number of waking hours in their offices, Danes spend more quality time in their homes bonding with family and friends. Perhaps that's where their focus on creating a cozy home comes from. They simply spend more time in their houses than they do in their offices, which is the complete opposite of how too many of us live our lives in the States. It was definitely the reverse of how Nick and I lived. We stared at the blank white walls of our respective workplaces for far more hours than we spent in our new apartment.

....

Our Danish adventure began splendidly. We'd been informed by fellow travelers that Copenhagen was one of the most expensive cities in the world, but Nick and I were surprised and delighted to learn the current exchange rates were in our favor. Nick ran the calculations in the first bar we stopped into, a charming dive called Escobar with pleasant graffiti on the wall that read, "Let all your pain be champagne," where patrons as old as my grandmother sipped giant beers while wearing black twinsets. We invented our own system for figuring out how to convert the Danish krone into a dollar. We divided the amount by ten and cut it in half.

"These beers were, like, three dollars," Nick said, plunking two generous mugs in front of us. Coming from San Francisco, where the average beer now cost ten dollars, this was a bargain. "It's an exciting city, isn't it, Squeak?" Nick said. "Doesn't everyone look like they're doing something interesting?" We clinked glasses and looked around at the Danes happily letting off steam after their thirty-seven-hour workweek, all crowded around candlelit tables or spilling out of the bar to drink their tall cans of Carlsberg on the street.

At dinner that night our entrées, a wild elk burger and arctic char, were just $10 and a taxi home $5. We were a happy (and wealthy!) couple in the happiest country on earth.

The next morning, my head cloudy from so much Danish beer, I woke to an e-mail alert from our bank.

"Shit! Honey, what did you say the exchange rate was again?" I asked Nick. He rolled over in bed and put the pillow over his face. I looked at the totals from the night before one more time.

"I think it may go the other way from what we were doing. We need to divide by ten and then triple it." Those delicious Danish beers had cost closer to $16 a beer and the entrées had been $40.

No wonder the Danish were so happy. They were making a mint off confused foreign tourists.

That afternoon, wiser and poorer, we decided to take a walk around the city (because it was free), which is how we found ourselves admiring the Københavns Rådhus, the city hall.

Before I knew what was happening, I became a wedding photographer.

Weddings in Denmark tend to be low-key affairs that take place at the town hall. Danes marry on the later side, thirty-five for men and thirty-two for women. The country has the fourth-highest divorce rate in Europe, 42.7 percent, which is about the same as the United States, but the divorces are almost as low-key as the weddings. Divorces are cheap (under $100) and relatively painless. You can even file for them online. Danes explained to me that because female employment is so high and the social safety net is so strong, a Danish divorce is less likely to become a nasty battle over money, which can make the entire process much less filled with hate. Because divorces don't tend to be acrimonious, there isn't as huge a stigma attached to them. Many Danes who do get divorced tend to get married again *and* stay friends with their ex-wife or ex-husband. Some of them even celebrate their "divorce-aversary" together over beers and a well-cooked meal of elk and arctic char with their new partners.

And instead of paying thousands of dollars for a wedding photographer, the Danes just hand their iPhones over to foreign strangers, like me.

I snapped a photo of a handsome gay couple, both of them in matching blue blazers, one in perfectly pressed jeans and the other in khakis, with thirty of their family members smiling broadly behind them. "That was nice," I said to Nick as we began to walk away. But then I was asked by a second couple to take their photo, and another and another after that. I was the most popular girl in the Rådhus. In the space of a half hour we saw more than twenty wedding parties (half of which I was now a member of) gathering on benches or in corners of the building, laughing and drinking champagne out of plastic cups. Some brides wore formal princess gowns while others wore jeans and white T-shirts.

Guests stuffed their faces with *rådhuspandekager*, the famous town hall pancakes, made in the hall restaurant and served on paper plates. The top secret recipe for the butter-fried pancakes covered in soft vanilla ice cream and apricot jam is kept locked in the town hall safe, and it isn't unusual to see flower girls wandering around the hall with whipped cream mustaches before they hand the bride her bouquet. (Imagine serving pancakes at your wedding reception. I had relatives who were aghast that I served macaroni and cheese.) After they've made the marriage legal and signed all the paperwork, Danes will have an intimate party in a café or a picnic along one of the city's many canals. It's sweet and civilized. It was warm that day for Copenhagen (in the high sixties), and it seemed as though the entire city had come out to revel on the cement banks around the canals, filling picnic blankets with bottles of wine, bricks of cheese, and large round loaves of bread.

"Let's get married again," Nick said, caught up in the merriment and the smell of top secret pancakes. "Seriously. I'll marry you again right now."

....

Our plan for the rest of the day was to get some *hygge*. That's how the Danes described it to me, as if *hygge* were something you could fetch from the market like eggs or deodorant. But before we ran around Copenhagen trying to get it, I wanted to better understand what "it" was. *Hygge* has no translation in English. It's supposed to encompass the concepts of coziness, contentment, comfort, and companionship all in one word. It's about good living, happy living, and living with really well-designed chairs. At its core, *hygge* is about creating a pleasant life, consciously thinking about comfort and happiness in everything from what you eat to how you design your home to how you work and how you treat your spouse.

"It's about taking pleasure in gentle and soothing things. Dinner with close friends is *hygge*. Large family dinners are *hygge*. It just plays into every aspect of Danish life. It's about being kind to yourself and those close to you, and that also helps make you a better partner," explained Helen Russell, the author of *The Year of Living Danishly*. Helen is a former magazine editor (just like me) who'd worked the grind in an incredibly stressful job that she loved (just like me) and gone off to search for advice and happiness in a different part of the world (the similarities were uncanny). She was a Brit who had moved to Denmark a few years earlier when her husband landed his dream job at LEGO. She'd promised she would give their Danish experiment a year, but now they'd been living there for three. Before they moved, Helen was working her ass off in London, and it took a toll on her family. For two years she'd been unable to get pregnant, enduring fertility treatment after fertility treatment. Just six months into "living Danishly," relaxing into the happiest culture on the planet and getting some *hygge*, Helen discovered she was pregnant.

"*Hygge* can be anything, really. It's about finding the happiness in small things." In her book Helen talks about finding *hygge* by decorating her home with beautifully designed Danish chairs and deliciously scented candles. But it was even more personal than that. "For me, *hygge* is about being nicer to myself and I'll be nicer to the people around me. You find yourself being less spiky to your partner," Helen said, adding that one key aspect of getting *hygge* at the beginning of her Danish experiment was eating as many Danish pastries (with the Harry Potter–sounding name *snegles*) as possible.

Maybe that was how Nick and I would start getting our *hygge*—through Danish food. I'd only recently shown any interest in food preparation whatsoever. Determined to be a master homemaker, I'd been pushing myself to prepare two meals (breakfast and dinner) a day to cut down on the number of times we were eating out during the week. It was just one of the ways I was trying to save money as we tried to pay off our mortgage. It was also much healthier, and to be honest, we'd both been getting chubby since the wedding.

When we got married I could cook two things—pasta and eggs. I believed nachos were an acceptable dinner. My new strategy was to find dishes that looked pretty on Pinterest and attempt to re-create them using food-preparation videos on YouTube. If only the housewives of the 1950s knew the tools I now had at my disposal.

There were some successes (a particularly tasty Jerusalem artichoke soup, surprisingly airy scones) and plenty of failures (that time I melted a plastic bowl in the oven and the neighbors called the fire department). I wasn't what you'd call a joyous chef. I'd developed a cultural bias against cooking and household duties as something inherently antifeminist. To be honest doing all those things made me feel slightly guilty. I felt like I was letting down all the sisters who came before me if I didn't work one-hundred-hour weeks and eat tuna from a tin. I wanted to be good at cooking, but I felt guilty enjoying it.

There's no way to properly convey just how delicious the cuisine in Denmark is. Sure, the city was home to the best restaurant in the world, but I can't tell you anything about it because we aren't Beyoncé and Jay so we couldn't get a reservation there. It didn't matter. Everywhere Nick and I ate, from the most modest coffee shops to the fanciest Michelin-starred restaurants, served food that blew our minds. Even the takeaway *smushi* (a combination of Denmark's *smørrebrød* open-faced sandwiches and raw fish) was spectacular.

Going out to eat together, having date nights, can be considered a form of *hygge*, at least according to Danish psychotherapist and family counselor Iben Sandahl.

"When building up the relationship, you´ll find *hygge*-moments everywhere; candlelight dinners, walking in the parks, movie nights, and a lot of focused attention. Continuing to embrace *hygge* is a fantastic way to nurture your marriage," Sandahl told us. "We all know the feeling of stressful days with very little time and energy to remember love for each other. *Hygge* can help you to find that again. If you want to *hygge* more with your partner, it means that you have to put the drama of everyday life to one side for a moment."

Sandahl has even created a "*hygge* oath" that includes things like:

1. Turn off phones and iPads.
2. Leave drama at the door.
3. Share fun and uplifting stories.
4. Do not complain unnecessarily.
5. Make a conscious effort to enjoy the food and drinks.
6. Light candles if you are inside.
7. Do not brag.
8. Tell funny and uplifting stories. Retell those stories again and again.
9. Make a conscious effort to feel gratitude and love.

The oath could also be called "How to Have an Enjoyable and Mutually Beneficial Date Night with Someone You've Already Gone on 1,000 Dates With." The ultimate goal of all of this is to create a sense of "*hygger sig*," feeling "cozy around together." That was the aim for our night on the town in Copenhagen.

....

"Do you both eat all the things in the world?" our waiter at the gourmet pizza restaurant Bæst asked when we solicited a menu recommendation from him.

"We do," I replied.

"That makes me happy," he said. The connection between food and happiness is something that can't be ignored in Denmark. It's a country that thrives on preparing excellent food and delighting diners with dishes that taste as good as they look on Instagram. Without having to ask, our waiter brought us a bowl of the meltiest, gooiest, most intricately flavored burrata I'd ever placed in my mouth.

"This is incredible," I said through a mouthful of cheese. "Where's it from?"

"Upstairs," the server said. "We have a dairy up there. We make the cheese fresh every day."

"Do you teach cheese-making classes?" I asked, using my finger to sweep up the remaining olive oil and cheese on my plate. Nick raised an eyebrow. We didn't have that much longer in Copenhagen, certainly not long enough for me to learn to make cheese.

Our server scratched his dappled blond head and blinked at us slowly. "No. But you can probably just come up and we can show you how we make the cheese. Do you want to do that?"

Did I want to do that? Did I want to know how to make the happiest cheese on earth? *Hygge*, in that moment, was learning how to prepare this particular burrata.

"Let's go," I said, grabbing Nick's hand. "I'm going to make us buckets of burrata when we get home. *Hygge!*"

We made our way to the sweet-smelling second-floor kitchens. Bæst didn't just make delicious cheese upstairs. They also prepared handmade charcuterie from some of the happiest pigs in Denmark. "The pigs stay with their mother as long as they like and they wander around in the fields their whole lives," Bæst head chef Kris Schram told me after I barged into his dairy. "He kills them in the fields so they never need to leave the property. The pig is never scared. They live in a beautiful field on a beach. I want to live there. The same for the milk we get for the cheese. Our ingredients come from happy animals." Of course, even the animals are happier in Denmark.

"Do you think it makes a difference in the taste?" I asked, feeling like I was in an episode of *Portlandia*. "The happy animals?"

He nodded. "It does. It matters. Being conscious about where your food comes from makes the experience of eating it even better." His delivery was so sincere that I couldn't help but believe him.

It's not just meat that Danes cultivate with care. Their food-positive mind-set stretches to vegetables as well. Many restaurants in Copenhagen strive to serve veggies that are organic, biodynamically raised, and local. The vegetables aren't just seasonal; they're microseasonal, meaning that chefs shift their menus to serve whatever is coming out of the ground in a given week.

Kris is another American transplant to the happiest place on earth. He's from the Hudson Valley of New York and worked as a chef in the Sonoma wine country, about an hour's drive from our place in the Bay Area. Then he met a girl, a Danish girl. They moved to Copenhagen and got married.

"I wouldn't be married, with her and this happy if I were trying to do this in the States," Kris told me as we drooled over acres of fresh mozzarella being stretched and rolled into succulent balls.

"What?" I said, not sure that I'd heard him correctly. "Why wouldn't you have a wife if you lived in the States?"

"In the States being a chef is a young man's game unless you own your own place. Here we work hard, but you work less days, get more days for your family. We have five weeks' vacation. I just had a chef go out on paternity leave. In Denmark you can be a chef and still have a life and a family."

What comes first, the happy-making food or the happy family that makes the food? The concepts are so intertwined in Denmark that it's like separating the farm-raised chicken from the joyously laid egg. What I began to realize, as I learned to make fresh mozzarella from scratch at a very fancy pizza restaurant in Copenhagen's hipster neighborhood, was that creating happy-making meals for Nick and me was about more than just finding recipes on Pinterest that would look beautiful on Instagram. It was about being mindful about all of our food, where it came from, and how it was prepared, something Nick considered more than I did. For most of my adult life I shopped at the closest and cheapest grocery store. When I arrived in San Francisco, I bemoaned the high prices at Bi-Rite, the all-organic grocery store around the corner. But now seeking out better, healthier, and "happier" food sources seemed like a good use of our time. Don't get me wrong. I wasn't about to spend $10 for a basket of designer strawberries—I'm not a crazy person or a celebrity—but I did want to slow down, to take a breath and take care with what we purchased and ultimately cooked.

Back at our dinner table, nibbling on more mozzarella and crispy pancetta and asparagus pizza, Nick was getting irritated with me.

"What are you writing down?" he asked as I furiously scribbled in my notebook, listening hard to the music coming from speakers perfectly hidden in postmodern light fixtures.

"This playlist," I said. "It's the best playlist I've ever heard. So well curated. It rises. It falls. It's not pretentious. Listen. They're playing 'Hungry Eyes' from *Dirty Dancing*. And before that Stevie Wonder and the Temptations and Elton John's 'Tiny Dancer.' We need to create dinner playlists. This is happy-making music. This is *hygge*. We're getting *hygge* right now from this playlist!"

"Now that we have it, let's enjoy the rest of dinner." Nick allowed a smile to turn up the corners of his lips.

I'm accustomed to multitasking while I eat, glancing at my phone, responding to e-mails, clicking on news alerts. I looked around the restaurant. No one, except for me, had their phone on the table. Surely that couldn't be normal? Everyone brings their phones to dinner, right?

Wrong. Wasn't that the first tenet of Sandahl's *hygge* oath? Put away your damn phone.

Treating our phone like a fifth appendage is not a uniquely American phenomenon. The French and British are just as bad. And the Russians? Forget about it. You can't get them off Facebook at the finest of fine-dining restaurants, but no one can dispute that the constant preoccupation with our electronic devices during what should be quality time is causing an erosion of civilized conversation and satisfied relationships.

"Is part of *hygge* keeping your phone off the table at dinner?" I asked one of my Danish friends. "When you're eating with your husband or your friends?"

She gave me a strange look. "It could be. I guess. But really, isn't it just a better way to live? Why do you need to check your phone during dinner?"

"Don't you want to Instagram your food?" Even though I was a novice in the kitchen, I still derived great joy from Instagramming everything I ordered in a restaurant.

"No." My Danish friend shook her head and looked at me as

though I had recently arrived from a faraway, less civilized planet. "We just want to enjoy the food with the person we're eating it with."

Plenty of research shows that real-life interactions suffer when one partner is constantly on their phone rather than interacting with the other. "Studies of conversation both in the laboratory and in natural settings show that when two people are talking, the mere presence of a phone on a table between them or in the periphery of their vision changes both what they talk about and the degree of connection they feel. People keep the conversation on topics where they won't mind being interrupted. They don't feel as invested in each other. Even a silent phone disconnects us," the author and academic Sherry Turkle wrote in the *New York Times* Sunday Review. In a 2015 poll by the Pew Research Center, 89 percent of cell phone owners admitted to using their phones the last time they gathered with family and friends. Of those, 82 percent said they weren't happy about doing it.

Baylor University's business school even gave a name to the phenomenon: "phubbing," which means snubbing someone for your phone. "What we discovered was that when someone perceived that their partner phubbed them, this created conflict and led to lower levels of reported relationship satisfaction. These lower levels of relationship satisfaction, in turn, led to lower levels of life satisfaction and, ultimately, higher levels of depression," James A. Roberts, a member of the research team, explained.

Both Nick and I are guilty of spending too much time on our phones, but he's much more self-aware about it. While I dive into a rabbit hole of Instagram or panda videos, he's much better at quickly checking his e-mail and then putting the phone away at the dinner table.

I stashed my phone and notebook in my purse and enjoyed the rest of our pizza dinner.

....

Danes value good design more than almost any culture in the world. Since they tend to get married later, couples often come to a marriage with their own nice chairs, dishes, potted plants, and picture frames made of blond wood. Nick and I were plenty old when we got married, comparatively at least, but since I'd moved all the way across the country and Nick lived in a small studio prior to our cohabitation, neither of us came to our union with grown-up furniture or home accessories. Our home wasn't just un-cozy, it was empty. We couldn't afford anything new yet.

Creating a cozy home is one of the central tenants of *hygge,* and it was time we embraced it.

"In Denmark, we are very much indoors—I guess mostly because of our changeable weather. Therefore creating a cozy home, which is personal and relaxing, means a lot to us in relation to feeling good," Iben Sandahl informed me. "I would argue that many of us are trying to create the 'invisible' cozy spirit that characterizes *hygge* in our homes, because we need that place to relax. If you enter into a cozy home, you enter at the same time into a good and lovely energy that makes you happy. If you are happy when you come home from work, it rubs off positively on your spouse."

That's why our next *hygge*-gathering mission took place in Copenhagen's Østerbro neighborhood, on a search for beautiful things for our home that would fit in my one suitcase—yummy candles, throw pillows, and soft blankets. I discovered a beautiful blond-wood birdcage meant to house the toilet paper in one's bathroom and a garlic press chicer than all of my shoes.

My first purchase was a set of geometrically interesting blond-wood napkin rings. When Nick was growing up, his mother, Patsy, was insistent that family dinnertime include cloth napkins folded neatly into napkin rings, and Nick seems to still agree with her. I wanted to make a practice of sitting down together for dinner a regular thing even before we had kids. We didn't do that in my house when I was growing up. My dad was rarely home in time for dinner, and I often balanced my plate on my lap in front of the television with my mom. Nick recalls plenty of family dinners; I remember episodes of *Married . . . with Children* and *The Simpsons*.

Like the Asters, the Danes are also focused on sitting down to dinner together, and it's one of the reasons that most offices let their employees out of work by four, or at the latest five, so they can make it home in time for dinner with their families. "The desks are empty way before six," one tech executive in Copenhagen told me.

Nick began fingering a pair of glass candlesticks.

"We always had candles at dinner when I was growing up . . . big tall ones. I got to light them!" he said. I pictured a little blond boy delicately leaning over a dark wood table with a match. And then I thought about me, the messy little girl balancing a Lean Cuisine on her lap on our secondhand couch.

"Do you want us to have candles on the dinner table?" I asked. Did I really marry someone who wanted to have candlelight dinners every night? I didn't know what to make of that.

"Oh, I don't know. We don't need them. I guess." But his eyes said he wanted the candlesticks. I checked the price and decided to order something equally adorable but more affordable on Amazon or Etsy.

We found pillows made from upcycled denim and rags, pillows made from Tibetan yak wool, pillows hand sewn in intricate Scandinavian designs. I even found a pillow with a crocheted cat wearing a fancy dress. Mindful of the high prices, I was careful to peruse only the bargain-bin throw pillows, which were still of a much higher quality and aesthetic than the ones from Target.

The owner of one Danish boutique laughed at me as I tripped in her shop, arms piled high with cut-price Scandinavian throw pillows and an alpaca-wool blanket that would perfectly hide that red wine stain on the couch.

"Are these for gifts?"

"No," I said. "For our house. I'm buying *hygge*."

I would call the noise she made a snort if Danish women weren't too proper to ever snort in public.

"You can't buy *hygge*," she said. "Getting *hygge* is a feeling. You have to make your own *hygge*. You can do it just by spending time in your home with the people you love."

"With beautiful chairs?" I said.

She sighed. "You should have beautiful chairs."

Since we'd bought our place, Nick and I had spent less than 50 percent of nights there. Even when we weren't traveling for work, we were frenetically, almost pathologically, busy with weekend trips to visit friends or family, weddings to attend, or camping trips into the wilderness with Lady Piazza. Even through my homemaking experiments, our refrigerator would often stay empty for weeks at a time. Why buy groceries when you're both leaving in a couple of days? I was often in the office for ten hours a day. Add on another hour for commuting, an hour for the gym, and then another two hours of preparing at home for the next day's work. Factor in eight hours of sleep and that left two hours of time for family dinners, conversation, and general relaxation in our space. And rarely, if ever, would those two hours line up for Nick and me. Sometimes we'd never see the other one awake. We'd grown adept at communicating affection through sleepy tangled limbs.

It couldn't be healthy for a marriage to feel like we were living in a hotel, like two business travelers just passing through a shared space for a little while.

On our last day in Copenhagen Nick and I rented our very own solar boat to cruise the canals alone. I picked up some biodynamically farmed red wine, *snegles*, and *smørrebrød* smothered in cheese and humanely raised meat. We cruised out to catch a glimpse of the famous *Little Mermaid* statue, surprised at how little and uninspiring she was compared to the hordes of tourists desperate to take a selfie with her. I left my phone back in our Airbnb for the entire day, Instagram be damned.

"This is delightfully hoo-gahhh," Nick shouted into the air, his words catching on the warm breeze.

"The most hoo-gah-y hoo-gah of all," I grinned. "We've got this."

But did we have it? In order to feel cozy in our home something else would eventually have to change. I knew we needed to carve out more time to actually be in our home together.

6

France

Be Your Husband's Mistress

She was as sated with him as he was tired of her. Emma had rediscovered in adultery all the banality of marriage.

—GUSTAVE FLAUBERT, *MADAME BOVARY*

"American men are afraid of American women. Can you blame them?"

Poupie Cadolle, the CEO of one of the oldest and fanciest lingerie shops in France, told me this plainly and simply when I met her in Paris. "American women just don't care enough about making their husbands happy."

"You don't really believe that, do you?" She nodded. Poupie believed it.

How do you respond to that? I cared about making Nick happy. Didn't I? I'd just ordered nice candlesticks for the dining room table.

Poupie, a bold blonde with a companionable manner, has been happily married for more than forty years while running a lingerie company that has made her an anthropologist of human intimacy.

She continued to deliver rapid-fire tidbits on why French women are better suited to being wives than American ones.

"For a French woman, a beautiful set of underwear is part of her personality. She does not save it for a special occasion. She wears it because she wants to feel beautiful every day. American women wear underwear like a uniform." (Mental note not to tell Poupie I'd been wearing the same threadbare white sports bra for three days.)

"The French woman, she always aims to please her husband. She's not mad that he would insist on her wearing a particular kind of underwear. She likes it. She wants him to tell her what to wear."

"French women love men. We love being married. We do everything we can to keep being married."

"I love men," I insisted. That was a lie. I loved Nick, but I generally thought most men could be real jerks.

"Men and women are not the same." Poupie raised an eyebrow. "If you want to make a marriage work, you need to forget about your feminism."

Shit. She was making me nervous.

"French women want their husbands to be happy, and it's not because they are weak or stupid. I am not weak or stupid."

No one would ever mistake Poupie Cadolle for being weak or stupid.

....

Weeks earlier in San Francisco, Nick and I went out for dinner with another couple. Our dining companions were around our age and had been married for five years. They'd dated for another five before that. Ten years total. Nick and I had ten months under our belts at that point. We were in no place to judge a decade-long relationship.

She was early for dinner, and he was late. The look of derision in her eyes when he finally walked into the room made me want to get up and hug him and kiss him hello myself. Throughout dinner she consistently rolled her eyes at his jokes and spoke to him in a voice that should be reserved for very small children or bichons frises. In return he stared hungrily at the waitress's ass as we debated whether to order a molten chocolate cake. This is sadly a common pattern among many of my married friends. After a year or two of marriage they become exhausted by their spouse and are quickly irritated, mentally downgrading them from lover to friend to an annoying roommate who never unloads the dishwasher. There are little things that bug me about Nick. Same for him. Nick wants to cry when I order an Uber instead of taking public transit. He doesn't understand why I mix up the composting and recycling. He becomes a socialist philosopher after three beers, he corrects my grammar, forces us to take flights based on frequent-flier miles, and gets a horrified look on his face when I drink bottled water instead of tap. I despise his fancy Chemex coffeemaker because I don't have the patience to wait for snobby slow-drip caffeine. He thinks I'm a jerk because I don't tuck the sheets into the mattress.

I look at my long-married friends and wonder if perhaps the quotidian nature of daily married life—the repetition, routine, and perpetual proximity of another human—makes it dangerously easy to become numb to whatever made you fall in love in the first place and to search for imperfections where you once only found delight.

I'd recently noticed a degradation in our own conversations. We'd gone from thoughtful discussions of philosophy, global politics, and elaborate plans for the future to a running commentary on the dog's digestive habits. "Did Lady Piazza poop today?" I'd find myself asking while I stood in the kitchen without pants applying deodorant.

"Huge poop," Nick would reply and pick a piece of lint out of his belly button. "Biggest this week."

I kept pondering whether it *had* to be that way. Did familiarity necessarily breed contempt and complacency? French women don't think it *has* to be that way.

....

Next time you find yourself in Paris, notice the way French women's husbands look at them. Even after years of marriage, having babies, losing jobs, losing elasticity in all the body parts that matter, flirtations with other people, failures and successes, husbands still gaze at their wives with an intense mixture of passion and curiosity.

Nick was going to Paris to cover one of the biggest stories of his career—the COP21 conference on climate change. Presidents, prime ministers, CEOs, celebrities, and journalists would convene on the City of Light. I took a week off from work so that I could tag along and eat all of the cheese while I learned French women's secrets for keeping the spark alive in their long-term relationships.

Long before everyone was crowing over the wisdom in *French Women Don't Get Fat*, I was already keenly aware of French women's talents at imparting advice to non-French women. One of the most invaluable things I learned in my twenties came from an incredibly chic editor for French *Vogue* whom I once sat next to during a fashion show in New York. She looked at me, disheveled, barefaced, and smelling of last night's cheap martinis early in the morning, and said, "Always wear red lipstick. No one will know you are hungover." For the past ten years I've carried a tube of Chanel Rouge with me at all times—and it has served me well.

"I'm going to pack like a French woman," I announced the night before we left as I folded clothes into my suitcase.

"I don't know what that means, Squeak," Nick said as he went about carefully packing the nine practical items he packs for every trip (a pair of jeans, two button-down shirts, a sweater, two T-shirts, a sport coat, dress shoes, and hiking sandals).

I twirled like a ballerina and banged my shin against the bedpost. "*Fuck! Ow!* It means I'm going to be light and carefree." My French friends have a universe of acceptable clothes that is quite narrow—leather jacket, skinny jeans, ballerina flats, and a trench coat. I told Nick that's what I was planning to pack, along with a sweater that would fall effortlessly off my shoulder.

"Is it effortless if you're planning for it to fall effortlessly off your shoulder right now?" Nick said, a wry smile bending his lips.

I just rolled my eyes. My intensely American need to be prepared for every possible situation defeated my desire to be French, and before I knew it my two suitcases were filled with four dresses, five pairs of pants, three pairs of shoes, five sweaters, two skirts, a cape, and three pairs of yoga pants . . . for a six-day trip.

I landed in Paris an hour before Nick (separate flights maximize frequent-flier miles, or so I had been told). As I lined up for coffee and a buttery warm *pain au chocolat* in Charles de Gaulle Airport, I couldn't help but stare at one particular couple in the café. He had a very French nose, bony and crooked, but not unattractive. It reminded me of Serge Gainsbourg's nose, even though I couldn't recall the rest of the French singer's face. His hair was short but thick, and he wore a turtleneck in an unapologetically Parisian way. She was beautiful. But then, I've never seen an *ugly* French woman. They embrace their imperfections in such a confident manner that all French women appear beautiful, no matter the configuration of their features. "Let's leave the obviously pretty women to men with no imagination," the French novelist Marcel Proust once wrote. The French even have a phrase for beauty coupled with imperfection, *jolie laide*, which translates very loosely to "ugly pretty." She was tall and reedy with thin lips and sharp cheekbones, elegant with a sophisticated insouciance. Her husband stared at her as though she were the only reason he had to live.

....

We had a lazy day before Nick had to start covering the conference and spent it walking and talking and eating and drinking. The sweet smell of roasting chestnuts filled the air as we bought *vin chaud* on the street outside of the Louvre for just two euros. Some of my American friends claim that the French are snobs, to which I reply, "Would snobs heat up red wine in a pot and serve it in a Styrofoam cup on the street?" We lit a candle to Joan of Arc in the Cathedral of Notre Dame and ate *frites* at a bar, seated next to a dog eating a pork chop and wearing a tricolor French flag scarf around his neck. We walked and walked, avenues and streets and alleys all mingling together: rue du Temple, rue de l'Abreuvoir, cour du Commerce, rue Cremieux, avenue Winston Churchill, quai de Jemmapes. I stopped to admire the chunky love locks on the Pont des Arts—padlocks that couples write their names or initials on and lock to a public place to symbolize their love, tossing away the key together.

"If I were going to declare my love and fidelity for you with a lock, I wouldn't put it here with all the others. I'd find a nice empty bridge somewhere in Omaha," Nick said.

I wound my arm through his and admired the motley collection of padlocks, as the words love and fidelity lingered in the air.

"What do *you* think of the French take on infidelity? What do you think about cheating . . . generally?" I suddenly asked, my brain leaping from love that inspires locks and chains to the kind of love that can induce you to break them.

"Well, you should probably interview all eight of my mistresses," Nick joked, pausing to take a picture of the Seine. I paused too. I have a serious problem with cheating. Namely, I have a problem with being cheated on. In the fifteen years before I married Nick I'd had a total of seven serious boyfriends, five of whom had cheated on me. One of them cheated on me with thirty-seven women in a single year, which I think is some kind of world record, even though Guinness has yet to get back to me. My father adored the attention of other women besides my mother, often to an egregious extent. One of my earliest memories is of my mother confronting my father's secretary turned mistress in the parking lot of the grocery store. My chubby toddler legs kicked out from the cart's basket as my mother screamed, "Stop destroying my family." Yeah, infidelity was a serious issue for me, one Nick greeted with an annoying nonchalance. He'd never cheated on a significant other. "It would never even enter his thoughts," his ex-girlfriend Jen told me. "Cheating is something that would make no sense for him. He would be so confused if another woman hit on him." Or as Glynnis put it: "Congratulations. You won the marriage Olympics. Not only did you marry someone good-looking, kind, and caring. You didn't marry your father!" Yet no matter how much I trust Nick, it had been impossible for me to rid myself of the knee-jerk reaction that all men, under the right circumstances, could be cheaters.

Approximately 20 to 40 percent of American married heterosexual men will have an extramarital affair during their lifetime. The number drops to between 20 and 25 percent for American women. And yet a large majority of Americans say affairs are wrong, unacceptable, unforgivable! The French see things a little bit differently.

According to research from the Pew Institute, only 47 percent of the French say it's not okay for married people to have an affair. France was the only country of the thirty-nine surveyed where fewer than 50 percent of respondents described infidelity as unacceptable. This is compared with 84 percent of Americans who say affairs are wrong. Let's be honest here. Both of our countries have a history of high-profile affairs, but the difference is that the French are less likely than American public figures to be castigated for them.

The Emperor Napoléon was famously unfaithful to his wife, Josephine, despite declaring she was the absolute love of his life. In 1899 French president Félix Faure died in the arms of his mistress. When François Mitterand, the country's longest-serving president, passed away in 1996, his wife and his mistress stood side by side next to his grave at his funeral, accompanied by both of their children. The famous French intellectuals Simone de Beauvoir and Jean-Paul Sartre made a pact to follow their hearts into the beds of other people. And while they had their ups and downs, their open-minded philosophy did lead to a long and successful partnership, although they never married.

But not all French women tolerate infidelity with such laissez-faire.

More recently, when it was revealed that François Hollande, the president of France, was having an affair with a journalist, his long-time partner, Ségolène Royal, chucked him out of their home. That's not the end of the story; this is France, after all. Royal wouldn't tolerate the man she loved sleeping with another woman. But she would work with him as a political ally. Several years later Royal became the president's minister of ecology, de facto vice president, and closest adviser. The two maintain a platonic and healthy working relationship, but not a romantic one. I ran into Royal at a party at the Ecology Ministry during the COP21 conference and marveled at her poise, beauty, sophistication, and pink cashmere coat. All night I worked up the courage to ask her about her thoughts on love, infidelity, and long-term relationships, but after I was champagne-pickled enough to do so, I attempted to pet the back of that glorious coat and her security detail gently ushered me away.

Unable to talk to the most powerful woman in France about infidelity, I asked my friend Hélène, a Parisian model who has two kids with her long-time partner, about her take on whether infidelity was something viewed more favorably in French relationships than in American ones. I thought she might hit me.

"Do I wish for my man to fuck someone else?" she spat back. "No. This is not what I want, and it is a silly cliché that you Americans believe this is what French women want."

She softened once I apologized and mentioned my own history with infidelity. "It's okay, my darling. You American women have a lot of stupid ideas. Here's what it is like. Okay? I don't mind if my president has sex with other women," Hélène said. "That's not my problem. But a man who disrespects his woman and hides it is not treating her right," she said. "Of course I hope my man does not do it to me."

"But what if he did?" I pressed.

She pondered that for a bit. "I love my man dearly. I do hope he's going to be sitting next to me tomorrow," she said. That was true. The two of them were obsessed with each other. "But it's work. He still needs to conquer me every day and I need to make him want me every day. I need to put in the effort," she said in her low and guttural voice, a voice so sexy it made me want to take up smoking again. "And here's what's important: I want to do the work."

I nodded. I didn't want to seem like I didn't want to do the work.

But that sounded stressful, making sure your husband wanted you every day! One of the things I loved about being married was that the constant conquest was over. I no longer dressed to please men. I dressed to please me, not worrying about how my ass looked in a pair of jeans or whether the plunge of a top would preclude me from being invited home to meet a boyfriend's mother. I'd thrown away all of my thongs. It was one of the best things about getting married—tossing those recalcitrant strings in the trash.

Eliminating these worries gave me more energy to do other things. I could read entire novels, go to yoga class, binge-watch *Broad City*, and build a drought-resistant herb garden. But Hélène would not be deterred, and maybe she was right. Maybe some marriages fall into a rut because we allow that sense of relaxation to turn into laziness. Maybe we all need to be more honest about what it takes to maintain passion and love in the long term.

Hélène continued. "I don't want him to come home at night and kiss me on the lips without even looking at me. I'm not interested in having the average relationship. I won't accept it."

"I won't accept it either," I agreed with sudden fervor. *Vive la France!*

....

The symbol of the French Republic is a woman, Marianne, a warrior goddess with a bayonet in one hand and the French flag in the other. Not only is she armed and vaguely dangerous, but her gravity-defying breasts are bare to the world. She's fierce and brilliant and sensual and nurturing—all at once. I learned this fact from my own friend Marianne, another Parisian woman. We'd met when she lived in the United States for a decade after attending school in New York. She'd recently moved back to France with her husband, Jean Paul. A couple of days after Nick and I landed in Paris, Marianne invited a coterie of her very French friends, of all different ages, all of them married or in a long-term relationship, to have coffee with me at a cozy little café in the Marais. It was one of those places with red wicker chairs where you can still smoke cigarettes without someone glaring at you. French women are incredibly social creatures but skeptical about outsiders, and I was pleased to be invited to one of their gatherings.

I'd carefully selected my outfit of skinny jeans, a red and white striped shirt, and conservative yellow loafers to emulate Parisian chic. "Stripes look good on you, Coco," Nick said before I left. "You look like a French girl." But when I arrived at the café the other women were decidedly more elegant in linen pants, crisp button-down shirts, and sweaters that really did fall effortlessly from their shoulders. Each of them painted a sophisticated silhouette, their look a part of their public performance. It made me feel like a child who'd just learned to dress herself.

As everyone settled in, the small talk ranged from French politics and the current climate talks to the disturbing rise of Donald Trump in American politics.

"He looks like a large leprechaun, yes? He's practically orange," one woman noted. French women have strong opinions about everything from fashion to politics to recipes for coq au vin. They're always game for a debate, and I suspect their curious minds and readiness to verbally spar keeps their husbands on their toes, another facet of what keeps their partners so interested in them in the long term.

"I feel sorry for his wife," another woman chimed in about Donald Trump. "What's in it for her except for the money? How can she stand it? What does she tell herself when she goes to bed with him?"

From here our conversation shifted to marriage, first Donald Trump's, then more generally. The very first thing I learned from this Parisian cast of characters is that marriage is not the institution in France that it is in America. Men and women in France, particularly in the urban areas, engage in long-term relationships for years, live together, have children together, but may never officially marry.

"We don't need a piece of paper to prove we are in love," said Elena, a woman in her twenties with alarmingly short bangs that she was really pulling off. "French women don't believe in your silly fairy tales." In Paris, although not necessarily in the rest of France, women are often the ones to propose to men (or they simply say, "It's time to get married") if they do choose to get married, and they don't wear a large diamond engagement ring, opting instead for a simple gold band. They prefer a small wedding at City Hall in a sexy dress they'll wear over and over again, and afterward they'll have a champagne toast in their favorite neighborhood bistro.

From talk of weddings we moved on to the advice-gathering portion of the afternoon, or rather, the instructing of the American girl in the art and science of French partnership.

"Sleep apart at least once a week to make him miss you," said another of Marianne's friends, whose name sounded like a breathy whisper I desperately couldn't pronounce.

"Flirt with your husband. Really flirt with him," chimed in Alix, a fortysomething doctor who'd been married for fifteen years.

"In fact, flirt with everyone. You Americans are such prudes about flirting." I had noticed that both members of French couples tend to be flirtatious with members of the opposite sex, particularly when their spouse is around. A French host would never seat a couple next to each other at a dinner party. Mingling of the sexes is encouraged, as is healthy flirtation.

"It releases some of the tension, and men think it is sexy to see that another man wants their wife," Breathy Whisper said.

"The more you love yourself, the more your husband will love you," Marianne added, as though she were explaining something absurdly simple to a very small and not terribly bright child. "American women think that they need a man to fulfill them. We fulfill ourselves, and then we find a man to come along and be a part of our journey. It's very simple. Your husband needs to know that you are comfortable in your own skin. Then he will be comfortable. None of the whining, 'Ooohhhh, I look fat in this dress. My face has spots. I look old!' He will believe what you tell him to believe about you. You tell him you feel beautiful and thin and young and sexy and that is what he will think of you. This is what will make him feel content and happy."

How many times had I bemoaned my love handles to Nick or talked about a giant blotchy zit on my face or said that the wrinkles on my forehead were beginning to make me resemble Ruth Gordon in *Harold and Maude*?

"Your husband wants you to tell him what to do and how to think. It's like how you program a computer," Alix said. "Or train a dog."

"Look at him like you want to fuck him," laughed Marianne. "Sex heals all wounds."

"Stop peeing with the door open. Why do you American women pee with the door open? Keep some things private!"

"Our bathroom is really small," I muttered in my defense.

"Play the role of the perfect woman even when you are a disaster on the inside." This was the opposite of what Nick and I had learned in Mexico from Bobby Klein, who had instructed us to talk about everything that was on our minds all of the time. But maybe there was a fine line. Maybe you could take it too far. I thought back to a conversation I'd had with Nick that morning that maybe I should have kept to myself.

ME: I think I forgot to put on deodorant this morning. Do I smell weird?
NICK: No.
ME: Can you smell me?
NICK: No.
ME: Come on.
NICK: You always smell good to me.
ME: I still think I might smell gross.

I liked talking to these French women. They forced me to flip over some of my long-held notions on womanhood, wifeliness, and marriage in a way that was uncomfortable and exhilarating. But I couldn't keep up with their rapid answers in a hybrid of English and French and I was having a hard time balancing my notebook and glass of wine on my lap, so I finished the wine and focused on writing down what they said.

One woman quoted the famous French novelist Camille Laurens: "When you have desire, words are excess baggage. Speaking, in fact, eliminates desire."

This seemed a paradox, since French women are so outspoken, and I said as much.

"You don't get it. What we mean is that you choose your words. Speak about things that are interesting, but leave the nagging to his coworkers. Don't pick small fights; don't speak of small things. And above all else, never be boring." It reminded me of the *hygge* oath—Do not complain unnecessarily, share fun and uplifting stories, leave your drama at the door.

"When you go out to dinner, put down your goddamn phone and don't talk about the home things. Don't talk about work or the laundry or the broken toilet. Would a man talk about a broken toilet with his mistress?"

"So does everyone in France have a mistress?" I said in the same unprejudiced tone I'd used to ask all of my other questions.

I might as well have made the mass generalization that all women in France kill puppies. The room went silent and I stared at the floor, first slightly ashamed and then distracted by all of their sharp-toed shoes. Marianne was the first to break the silence, and her response echoed Hélène's.

"No one wants to be cheated on. No one wants their man with another woman. Does it happen? Sometimes. We don't want it to. You behave like his mistress and it is less likely to happen."

The other women unanimously agreed. No one wanted their husbands to cheat. They claimed none of them had ever cheated. Would they admit it if they had? I don't know. But I do know they took honest and aggressive puffs of their very thin cigarettes as they swore they'd been faithful.

"Would I like to fuck another man?" one of them said. "Of course I would. Who wouldn't at some point? But it is much more interesting to keep myself from fucking someone else."

Their thoughts on the subject were clear and final and, not wanting to alienate my new friends, I quickly steered the subject back to how I could keep my husband enthralled with me.

"What does it mean to behave like his mistress?" The closest I'd ever come to being someone's mistress was a bumbling flirtation with a middle-aged grad school professor that never went beyond a few embarrassing text messages.

"Walk around naked or in beautiful underwear, but do not let him see you in sweatpants," Marianne said. She said "sweatpants" the way some people say "toenail clippings." I don't think these women understood how much money I'd invested in cute yoga clothes.

"Spend a fortune on lingerie," asserted the unassuming steel-haired matriarch of the bunch, so chic in her skinny jeans and a wispy scarf.

I recognize that some women may be offended by this call to look pretty and feminine all the time. It made me think about the many drawers I had at home filled with sweatpants and how I'd spend entire weekends wearing nothing but sweatpants. The truth was it didn't matter what I wore. Nick makes me feel sexy as hell all the time. Even with the twenty-five pounds I gained after the wedding and a zitty face and a sometimes-bloated cheese belly, even with a new haircut that made me look more like the little boy from *The NeverEnding Story* than I would have liked and even when I'm wearing shitty sweatpants.

For some women feeling sexy and confident might mean lingerie. For some it might mean something totally different. And that was my takeaway from these sophisticated French chicks. Dress in a way that makes you feel sexy and alive and wonderful.

The older woman, the one who mentioned the lingerie, looked at me with a slight frown. "You think it's silly. I can tell. It's not silly. I've been happily married forty years."

They wanted me to know when to be silent and yet interesting. I needed to be in control of my husband while maintaining a calm confidence. They despised adultery in their own lives but accepted it in others' and even recommended behaving like a mistress and flirting with other men. The paradoxical mystery of French women was enough to keep *me* intrigued. No wonder it worked so well on their husbands.

....

I needed to understand more about the French woman's obsession with sexy (and wildly expensive) lingerie. What I'd learned so far was that lingerie is not simply underwear for Parisians. It's an art, a necessity, and it could be one of the many reasons French husbands gaze upon their French wives as though they are the most perfect creatures on earth. They're intrigued by the things they cannot see.

That's how I found Poupie Cadolle—the expert on French lingerie.

According to Poupie, her great-great-grandmother Herminie invented one of the very first bras.

Herminie was a revolutionary, an anarchist, a badass chick who, Poupie told me, was expelled from the country in the nineteenth century for her radical views on feminism and fled to Argentina. Before leaving, she was quoted in the Parisian newspaper *Le Figaro* saying that she didn't expect to be an equal to a man, but she did expect to make as much money as him. In Argentina Herminie broke into the corset business, but she soon grew to see the corset as yet another constraint placed on women by the patriarchy. The stomach should be free, she thought. Women deserved to be able to breathe. And so, at the Universal Exposition in 1889, Herminie unveiled an ingenious creation. She'd cut a traditional corset in half, thus inventing one of the world's very first modern bras, built from lace, elastic straps, and underwires made of whalebone that Herminie had heated and shaped all on her own.

It was a spectacular failure.

But Herminie wouldn't be deterred. She traveled all over the world to extol the virtues of freeing a woman's belly from the bind of the corset, but no one would listen. Soon the First World War broke out and women all over the world began working. Hard labor was nearly impossible when you couldn't breathe. This is one of the tales of how the bra, as we know it today, went from bust to your bust.

Herminie's great-granddaughter Alice grew the bra business and became a legend for outfitting both Coco Chanel and the Duchess of Windsor with the Cadolle brand of fine undergarments, bras, underwear, and slips bedecked in the most delicate French lace and bows in every color of the rainbow.

Today Poupie runs the business. An exclusive clique of very wealthy and very fashionable women regularly travel to Paris just to see Poupie at her couture atelier across from the Chanel shop on rue Cambon. Over a six-week period they attend three different fittings for their custom-made underwear—more fittings than most women have for their wedding dress. Poupie studied as a lawyer, which is clear when she fixes you with her intense prosecutor's stare to determine exactly the right fit and fabric to complement your particular bosom and shape. Poupie had recently turned sixty-nine when we met. I complimented her on how good she looked for her age, and she wrinkled her nose and made a sine curve with her elegant hand to inform me this was not an achievement of any merit. Women should continue to look good well into their seventh decade. Poupie didn't believe in letting yourself go.

One of the first things I tried to explain to Poupie was that Nick has no interest in sexy underthings.

"I'm just going to take it off of you," he always says with his trademark practicality, and adds, "I think you're cute when you wear my boxer shorts."

I'll sleep in anything, but more often than not I fall asleep in some version of Nick's boxers, tattered lacrosse shorts from high school, a T-shirt worn thin from hundreds of washings, or, in the winter, plaid flannel pajamas that I stole from my father. Nick sleeps naked as a baby. I'm terrified of sleeping naked, in case there's a fire or natural disaster in the middle of the night. My fear has only intensified now that we live in Northern California, where an earthquake could strike at any moment. When that happens, I will be fully dressed and ready to help drag survivors from the rubble. Of course, Nick will also spring into action, save all of the neighbor children and dogs, and will probably end up on the front page of the *San Francisco Chronicle* as the hero without pants.

For my bachelorette party my well-meaning girlfriends played that game where they bought me racy lingerie, hung it along the wall with clothespins, and made me guess who bought me what. Everyone bought underwear that perfectly matched *their own* personalities. My girly friend Danielle bought something pink and frilly and complicated where the underwear was just three pieces of string. My sexy friend Jaclyn gifted something black and slinky. The sophisticated one, Jackie, purchased a simple cream and lace slip that felt expensive. The Megs, my very practical lesbian friends, bought me Patagonia hiking underwear and sports bras. I wear those all the time.

I had a drawer filled with pretty things that I rarely put on because they often made me feel more embarrassed than sexy.

When I explained this to Poupie she informed me I was committing a cardinal sin for my marriage.

"Lingerie, beautiful things worn under a woman's clothing, should be something shared between a man and his wife," she went on. "I think that is love." Poupie wouldn't dare wear a piece of underwear that her husband didn't like if she knew he would see it.

"Why would I do that?" she scoffed. "A man shouldn't be disappointed. If a man doesn't want his wife to wear a T-shirt for sleeping, she shouldn't do it. Poor American men. They are not spoiled."

Poupie loves spoiling men. She welcomes them warmly into her shop, inviting them to inspect the fine silks and laces as she coquettishly but assertively asks them what they like.

Poupie has great pity for the women who come lingerie shopping alone.

"If a woman leaves and says, 'Let me ask my husband what he would like me to buy,' then I know they will last forever," Poupie said. "If she buys something on her own, who knows!"

When a husband comes shopping with his wife, Poupie encourages the woman to show her man the bras as she tries them on. "The men should be involved. American women do not understand this. They would never bring their husbands with them into the shop and ask them what they like," Poupie said. "I compare it to a woman who cooks only potatoes. Potatoes every single week, even though her husband hates potatoes. In France we care what our husband likes. We have a confident relationship with what our husband likes. We let him come and see and choose. And then . . . we let him pay. French husbands always pay."

She leaned in conspiratorially, her red-rimmed designer glasses bouncing cheerfully on her perfect Roman nose.

"I am going to tell you a story now. I had a client. Very wealthy. Very elegant. Complete bitch. She came to see me four times a year with her husband. *She* picked out what *she* wanted and then *she* was the one signing the checks. Well, later in the afternoon the same husband always came back to my shop with his mistress. It was the same woman, just thirty years younger. Same bitch. Except the difference was that *he* picked things out. *He* wrote the checks."

Treat your husband like your lover and your wife like your mistress.

The prolific author, essayist, and quintessential Frenchman Honoré de Balzac once wrote that passion is an essential part of the happiness of marriage. "But to be passionate is always to desire," he wrote. "Can one always desire one's wife? Yes. It is absurd to pretend that it is impossible always to love the same woman as to say that a famous artist needs several violins to play a piece of music and create an enchanting melody." But, as I was learning over and over again, maintaining that passion requires effort and work.

I thanked Poupie. When she asked me if I wanted to come with her to pick out a bra, I smiled coyly and said, "I think I'll need to bring my husband to see what he would like." She clapped her hands and nodded approvingly.

"You know what you're doing," she winked.

I still had no idea.

....

I made a reservation that Friday night at Lapérouse, a historically famous haunt for adultery in Paris with intimate private dining rooms where men have been meeting their mistresses for more than 150 years. A French law passed in 1870 made adultery legal if it happened in a public place. The owners of Lapérouse took full advantage of the loophole and welcomed men and the women who were not their wives into *les petits salons* on the second floor for their amorous trysts. Secret back entrances into the restaurant led to tunnels connected to the French Senate building so politicians could meet their mistresses without the shame of walking through the front door.

A scratched mirror adorns the restaurant's wall: the marks are from over a century of courtesans testing the authenticity of diamonds given to them by their lovers on the glass. Some bold women would even use their rings to carve their names into the crystal.

While I was hoping for a carefree night of lust and love, things were tense between me and Nick as we got ready to hit the town. Earlier in the day I had grabbed a T-shirt off the rack at my favorite French shop, Merci, without paying attention to the price tag. After we checked out and left the store, Nick glanced at the receipt.

"You spent two hundred euros on a T-shirt."

"Nooooo," I said. Now, I've spent ridiculous amounts of money on clothes, particularly yoga pants, in the past, but on this particular occasion I hadn't planned to spend that much, particularly not on one T-shirt.

"Yes, Squeak. Two hundred euros on a T-shirt. What's it made of? Baby seal?"

"I don't know. I think I read the price tag wrong. Don't yell at me."

Nick has never blinked at any of my shopping habits or chastised me for spending money on nice things for myself, but even I had to admit that $250 for a T-shirt was excessive, especially at a time when we were so house poor we couldn't afford a dining room table.

"Whatever. I'll just return it. I just got it."

The store refused to let me return it.

I e-mailed Marianne.

"What would you do if you accidentally bought a $250 shirt on your husband's credit card?"

The reply was nearly instant. "Give him a blow job. Ha ha ha."

And then she sent a follow-up. "Tell him you deserve it."

I got very dressed up for our date night at Lapérouse, carefully applying eyeliner, which I hadn't worn since our wedding, to create the perfect smoky eye. I put on a teensy black dress that hugged my ass, and I curled my hair with care. I even shaved my legs, despite the fact that the shower in our Airbnb was the size of a shoebox and shaving required an elaborate mixture of yoga and courage.

"Don't I look sexy?" I said to Nick, coming out of the bedroom.

Nick looked up from his computer.

"I'm just checking out this menu. It's expensive, Squeak."

"Like how expensive?"

"Like between sixty and a hundred dollars an entrée."

"Shit." That's the last thing you want to hear after you spent $250 on a T-shirt.

He could see I was nervous. Nick hates making me nervous. "We can splurge for one night."

Everything inside of Lapérouse looks breakable. It's what I imagine the inside of Jackie Collins's living room must have looked like, all gilded mirrors and red velvet everything. I glanced at the menu. Was that $100 for a filet of pigeon? A birdlike woman with a clipboard approached us. She was wearing a tight black lace bustier with perfect half-moon B-cups peeking out.

"You have a reservation?"

"Of course we do," I replied.

"Aster," Nick said.

"Um, Piazza . . . Sorry." I was still getting used to using my new last name for things like reservations and bill signing and introducing myself to small women with clipboards.

"No," Clipboard replied.

"No?"

"No reservation."

"I have one. I swear. Is it under Aster?"

She ran a red-manicured finger down the page.

"No."

I grabbed my phone to look for an e-mailed confirmation and breathed a sigh of relief.

"Here it is. Piazza. Reservation for eight p.m."

She looked it over. "Wrong night."

"What?"

"Your reservation is for tomorrow."

I snatched the phone away from her. She wasn't wrong. Our reservation was for the next day. I couldn't imagine it would be that big of a problem to fit us in that evening. "Well. We are here now and we are all dressed up and we took a taxi and it is a special date night." I wanted to add, *And I shaved my legs!*

"I am sorry. It is impossible." With that she disappeared into the folds of a red velvet curtain.

"I'm sorry, baby." Nick smiled and shrugged. "It's fine. We'll come here tomorrow night."

"You have a work dinner tomorrow night," I whined. A mistress would not be whining right now.

"I'll change my work dinner and we'll have a special night tomorrow."

I pouted for no reason other than I didn't feel like shaving my legs again, and I knew I'd never replicate this smokey eye.

....

I broached the idea of lingerie shopping as we strolled the medieval alleys of the Marais the next afternoon. The sidewalks were packed with Parisians holiday shopping and dragging Christmas trees wrapped up like sausages down the street.

Nick was more excited by the prospect of shopping for bras and underwear than I expected him to be, and he agreed to accompany me.

The two of us were welcomed into a warm shop (a slightly less expensive one than Cadolle and handily located in the neighborhood where we were staying) by a kindly woman in her sixties with a bowl cut of steel hair and fragile-looking wire-rimmed glasses. When men walk into a Victoria's Secret in America, they are generally treated like perverts and sex offenders, but here the clerk smiled warmly at Nick as she pulled beautiful lacy things out of gilded drawers. No pattern of lace was exactly the same, and the silk was fine yet raw, with a slightly rough feel like the tongue of a kitten. I wanted a beautiful bra. Just a beautiful bra. There was no point in buying something with confusing ties and straps and openings in the fabric where there should not be openings. I wouldn't wear those. I *would* wear a nice bra.

"Do you like these?" I asked Nick, holding up three brassieres at once.

He liked a sincere navy blue with a tiny border of lace.

"Not too much lace. Lace looks itchy, baby," he said. "I want you to be comfortable."

My arms piled high with French lingerie, I made my way through the imposing curtains in the back of the shop to the dressing room. Nick lingered in the middle of the store, uncertain whether to follow or to walk out the door and into the nearest pub for a pint.

"Come along, dear." The clerk grabbed Nick by the hand in a motherly kind of way and led him behind the curtain. "I'll get you a chair." When is the last time that happened in Victoria's Secret? The answer is: never.

From then on we were a threesome, a strange ménage à trois. I would struggle into a brassiere and then shyly pull back the curtain to show Nick. At first he laughed as I shimmied my boobs. The clerk would bustle past Nick and frown, always frown. I was doing it all wrong. She loosened the straps and, without asking, reached her hand into the cup of the bra to scoop my boob up and toward the center of my body in a mammary tsunami, her index finger expertly flicking my nipple into place. Her hand swooped through a second time to usher my armpit fat firmly into the bra. She'd cluck and then beckon Nick forward to look again.

"Better, yes?"

Nick nodded.

"*Bon!*"

And so it went for over an hour until we'd narrowed down the choices to that same beautiful navy blue demi-bra with delicate light blue lace along the bottom that Nick had chosen in the first place. Adrenaline pulsed through my veins. I was excited, not turned on, but amped up the way I would be before a race or a particularly competitive episode of *The Voice*. I felt a sense of accomplishment out of proportion to the fact that I'd just spent the past sixty minutes in a two-foot-by-two-foot closet.

Old habits do die hard. I *am* a woman who is used to paying for things. I'd been doing it for more than fifteen years by the time I met Nick Aster. "Honey, can you get my wallet?" I asked Nick from inside the dressing room.

"No," he said. "I've got it."

"You?" I was surprised to see him taking to this Parisian sensibility so easily.

"Me. It's the nature of things. It's my duty to buy you lingerie. Yeah. I've got this." He winked. He was joking, maybe, but it did remind me of the time he told me that he wanted to take care of me. I heard a little voice inside my head, a voice with a distinctly French accent. *Let him buy you lingerie. You will not set the women's movement back fifty years just by letting your husband buy you a blue bra.*

"So be it." I smiled. "You really like it?"

"Of course I do. It looks comfortable and practical."

"And sexy?"

"Yes, darling, and sexy."

For the rest of the day, while we wandered around adorable neighborhoods and finished our Christmas shopping, I kept wondering: Was I putting in enough effort? Was I doing enough to make my husband happy? Just asking the question made me feel a little icky. I felt like I'd been trained to be concerned with my happiness first. But Nick definitely considers my happiness in just about every decision he makes. He was willing to shell out nearly $100 for a baked pigeon at Lapérouse if it made me smile, and he would change a very important work dinner to go to that same restaurant two nights in a row. He spent half the day shopping for wildly expensive underwear the day after I accidentally spent $250 on a T-shirt. And he paid for it.

I kept thinking: Did my husband really want to go to this fancy-schmancy restaurant and blow our mortgage money on odd, fatty French food? Would that make him happy?

"Hey, Monkey," I said when we returned to our cozy little Airbnb. "How about we skip Lapérouse tonight? Let's go down the street and have a pizza and some cheap red wine in the Marais."

"Really?" he said. "No hundred-dollar pigeon?"

I kissed my husband.

"If we're going to get a hundred-dollar pigeon, I would like it to do much more than just sit on my plate. Perhaps we can find a dancing pigeon or one who sings reggae or does my taxes! We can do much better things with a hundred dollars than purchase a buttered street rat. Maybe we can buy our first dining room chair."

So we ate pizza and we drank cheap wine. And we went home and I wore the sexy lingerie my way—paired with my husband's boxer shorts.

7

San Francisco

For Better or Worse

The strongest love is the love that can demonstrate its fragility.

—Paulo Coelho

The genetic mutation that caused my dad's muscular dystrophy lives on an obsure region of his fourth chromosome called q35. Growing up, our family doctors told me different things about whether or not my own q35 was faulty. First they said a blood test I'd been given as a teenager didn't show any signs of the disease. Besides, they told me, women rarely developed symptoms of this kind of muscular dystrophy. They claimed the chances were so low I didn't have to worry about it.

They were all wrong.

I don't remember much about the morning I got on the phone with Violet, the strangely chirpy genetics counselor, who told me I had reason to worry.

It was a Thursday. Nick had to take a conference call, so he went into the office early and I worked from home. It was raining and the dog didn't want to pee, so I was soaked and freezing when I got on the phone.

That's when Violet told me I had a fifty percent chance of having muscular dystrophy. I'd read once that some people swoon, actually pass out, when they hear bad news. My joints turned to butter and I sat on the floor.

If I had the mutation on my chromosome, it meant I'd develop the same symptoms as my father, a gradual degradation of my muscles that would make my body weak and frail and eventually put me in a wheelchair for the rest of my life. The really shitty thing about muscular dystrophy is that you can't do anything to prevent it. If you have it, the muscles just start deteriorating one day. But the condition rarely affects your brain, just your body, trapping a fully functional mind in a body that slowly stops working.

Modern genetic testing raises a host of questions, the majority of them centering on what you can live with knowing. If you knew you were going to get a disease that would kill you, would you rather know and plan, or would you rather wait and see? Personally, I would rather wait and see. But now that I was married to Nick, and we would eventually want to start a family, the decision wasn't only mine to make.

Two voices fought for supremacy in my head.

The first: *You should just give up. Stop working. Fuck it! Let your roots grow out, dye your hair green, and sit with the gutter punks down on Haight-Ashbury smoking crack . . . because why not?*

And the second: *It doesn't matter what the tests say. You'll fight. You're strong. You're stronger than you know.*

The first voice was so clearly mine. The second was Nick's.

I want to be one of those people who allows adversity to make them better. But I fear I'm the other type of person, the kind who surrenders in the face of misfortune, closes the shutters, and wanders her dark and dusty house wearing her wedding dress for eternity like Miss Havisham.

This new information from Violet was what led to my hysterical and admittedly dramatic plea to Nick that he should divorce me and marry a healthy wife.

"Maybe the good of being married to me doesn't outweigh the bad anymore," I said to him the night after I talked to Violet. "You should find a hot and healthy new wife." I paused. "Maybe not hot. But find someone nice, maybe a little plump."

He looked at me like I was nuts and scratched his head. "You know, I measured it. I had these tools to measure the good and the bad of being married to you, and I set up the machine and I did all of these calculations and you know what happened? The damn machine broke, the good outweighed the bad so freakin' much." Nick insisted he would never divorce me and said things like "Aren't these interesting and uncertain times we are living in." I had to trust him and accept the fact that he wasn't going anywhere.

But I began having nightmares where I was confined to a wheelchair, my legs useless, where I couldn't breathe on my own and had a tube shoved down my throat to do it for me.

We went back and forth about how much we wanted to know about my chances of having muscular dystrophy, but in the end we needed to find out. So I went to the hospital and handed over my arm, allowing them to take many, many vials of blood, during which time I distracted myself by watching YouTube videos of baby bulldogs trying to climb into a Cheerios box. Those vials were shipped off to a lab in the middle of Iowa.

That's when Nick and I first started talking about doing something big and scary and hard and physically taxing on my still fully intact body.

"We could climb a mountain," Nick suggested.

"Which one?" I asked, searching his face for signs he was kidding.

He shrugged. "There are plenty of mountains we could climb in California. Or in Colorado. Or we could do something serious. We could climb Mt. Kilimanjaro." At the time my entire knowledge of

Mt. Kilimanjaro, in Tanzania, came from the lyrics of the 1982 classic rock song "Africa" by Toto: *I know that I must do what's right, sure as Kilimanjaro rises like Olympus above the Serengeti.*

"Sure, honey." I smiled, convinced he was kidding. "We'll climb Mt. Kilimanjaro."

More than a month later Violet called me again. Her voice mail went something like this: *Hi, Jo! This is Violet, your genetics counselor. I'm calling to go over your test results, so if you can call me back at 415-833-****. Again, my number is 415-833-****. Hope to talk to you soon!*

I went to yoga before I called Violet back. My yoga instructor, Roy, a handsome gay Asian man who plays movie soundtracks instead of yoga chants during his vinyasa classes, put on the score to *Forrest Gump*. Tears slid down my cheeks.

"I need you all to focus on your hips and on your pelvic floor. Focus on it now and you'll be able to do this well into your nineties."

Maybe not, I thought.

I bought an overpriced, sustainably sourced mint-chocolate-chip ice cream cone from stupidly expensive Bi-Rite, on my way home. Coming out of the store, I walked right into a guy in his twenties carrying flowers, and wondered if they were happy flowers or sad flowers, *I'm sorry* flowers or *I love you* flowers.

"Hi, Violet," I said into the phone when I called her back. I licked one side of the ice cream to keep it from dripping onto my hand and felt a distinct chill, even though March in San Francisco is warmer than July.

"Hi, Jo," she chirped back. "Do you want to get Nick on the phone?" The news was bad. If it were good, Nick wouldn't have to get on the phone. "Not right now. He's stuck in meetings all day. We can keep going. Just us."

"Okay! Well, I was surprised by your results. You have the genetic mutation."

I wasn't surprised. Ever since she said the chance was 50/50 I'd expected it. Hadn't I known it deep in my bones?

My mother and I have very little in common, physically at least.

From the start I was a carbon copy of my father, with my dark hair and dark eyes. My mother would laugh about it, but I actually think it bothered her a little bit.

"This child couldn't possibly belong to me," she joked when I was little.

My dad and I have the same mannerisms. We scratch at our faces and pull on our earlobes when we get nervous. We each take four packets of Sweet'N Low in our coffee, a fact most people find disgusting. We read books the same way, furiously, often in a single sitting, as though we were in a race against time. In a way, I suppose he was. We have the same jowly cheeks.

Both our lips are a little off center and our left eyes slightly more round than our right.

"You're a strange case. Most people show symptoms by the time they're twenty," Violet said.

"My dad didn't." I thought about how badly my dad still wanted to live, despite being trapped inside a body that constantly fought him. Every time I talked to him he had a new scheme, a plan to find a transplant for whatever organ had newly begun to fail him due to complications from his muscular dystrophy, complications that no one could predict. Sick people, dying people, don't want to talk about being sick or dying. They want to talk about being strong and alive, and you have to talk to them about those things even if it breaks your heart every time you have to lie.

"I know. So we don't know what to expect. There's no telling how it will present."

How it will present. How it will present. The words skidded around in my head, making less sense each time I repeated them to myself. I knew they were a kind way of saying, *We don't know how much longer you will be able to use your legs.* I thanked her and scheduled an appointment to come in and meet with the doctor at a later date to figure out how the disease would progress.

There's a kitten café in downtown San Francisco at the corner of Gough and Rose Streets. At any given time they have ten adoptable cats roaming around while they serve strong Japanese tea. I walked there, paid my $15 entry fee, and let a chubby tabby climb all over me while I cried quietly to myself.

A man wearing a T-shirt that said "It's Meow or Never" looked at me quizzically but thankfully never said anything.

I waited to call Nick until I got home.

"I have it."

"Oh, sweetheart. I love you very much. And I don't think it changes our lives, at least not for a long time."

I stared down at the dog. Lady Piazza looked back at me with no comprehension of what was being talked about on the phone. She wagged her tail and looked over her shoulder to suggest we go to the backyard to play ball.

"It's frustrating. They know nothing. They know less than nothing," I moaned. The uncertainty was the worst part of it. I could live more easily with a clear-cut diagnosis, one that said, *You have X years before Y terrible thing will happen. After Y terrible thing happens, this is what your life will look like.* That I could handle. The unknown would destroy me.

"I think we have reason to feel optimistic about when it will happen and how it will happen. You're healthy and strong and there's new science every day. It doesn't fundamentally change anything. It only puts a certain perspective on life. Let me finish up here and I'll be home really soon."

"I love you."

"I love you too."

For some reason this made me think of the first time Nick told me he loved me.

We'd been dating only two months, and I was the maid of honor in a friend's wedding. Nick, being the new guy, brought the entire bridal party coffee and doughnuts as we got dolled up the morning of the wedding. "Love you," he said as he headed out the door, leaving us to be spray-tanned and spackled. I sipped my coffee while my friends erupted like a band of harpies.

"Did he just say, 'I love you'?"

"You hardly know him!"

"No," I said, slightly embarrassed. "He must have said something else."

But that is what he said, the first of many.

I hung up the phone and paced the house from the living room down the long hallway into our bedroom and into the second bedroom, filled with summer clothes, an untuned guitar, and a broken Nintendo, the room we kept trying not to call a baby's room.

I poured a generous glass of wine and began cooking Cajun catfish and brussels sprouts for dinner.

I Skyped one more time with Nick before he left the office.

[3:09:44 PM] Johanna Piazza: **Hi**

[3:09:54 PM] Nick Aster: **Hi love**

[3:12:30 PM] Johanna Piazza: **Are you really ok with all this? Are things OK?**

[3:17:05 PM] Nick Aster: **It's just one moment of our long lives together.**

[3:33:04 PM] Johanna Piazza: **I think my biggest fear is still that you will look at me like I am broken**

[3:33:59 PM] Nick Aster: **That's enough of that :-) I love you sweet girl. You're my darling, that's just how it is**

[3:40:13 PM] Johanna Piazza: **What do we do now?**

[3:41:36 PM] Nick Aster: **We live our lives.**

The next day Nick went out and bought me my first tennis racket and a pair of very serious hiking boots, the kind of hiking boots Cheryl Strayed wears in *Wild* when she takes on the Pacific Crest Trail, the kind you'd wear if you really did want to climb Mt. Kilimanjaro, the kind that give you confidence-building blisters.

We were going to live our lives.

8

Israel

Secure Your Own Oxygen Mask First

> Love yourself first, and everything else falls in line. You really have to love yourself to get anything done in this world.
>
> —Lucille Ball

A seventy-year-old Israeli woman was feeling me up. I'd been applying the Dead Sea's curative mud gingerly to my arms and feet with delicate pats and circular motions.

But I was doing it all wrong. Clearly I was doing it all wrong, because two elderly women approached me and, without asking, scooped up a pile of the mud and patted it directly onto my breasts above my bikini top. I looked up at the "beach" above us. It was more of a swamp filled with loud families with coolers and faded umbrellas. Dads and grandpas all wore Speedos, with their hefty guts protruding toward Jordan across the sea. Empty potato chip bags and plastic Coke bottles clung to the shoreline.

According to the many companies that sell products made of

Dead Sea mud, the murky, salty mixture is a kind of panacea, curing everything from respiratory diseases to acne to arthritis. I only wanted to coat myself in enough of it to take that obligatory picture of myself floating in the Dead Sea with mud on my face so that I could send it to Nick. It would be a picture that clearly conveyed a sense of relaxation. *I'm floating. I'm muddy. Look how untroubled and peaceful I am.*

"Good for your skin," the bigger of the two women, who had the sturdy authority of Bea Arthur as Dorothy in *The Golden Girls*, said in Hebrew, allowing the sludge to drip through her pruney fingers. A nearby English speaker translated for me. "You'll glow. You're young. You should have nice skin."

I'd taken a bus across the ancient Judaean Desert, below the Ha-He'etekim cliff and past the Qumran caves, where the famous Dead Sea Scrolls were discovered, to end up here, the lowest point on earth, the Dead Sea. I'd been expecting to recline and float in the dense, salty water, surrendering the stress of the past few months to one of the holiest places on the planet or, at the very least, to take a picture that conveyed this. I hadn't been primed for a chat, and so at first this intrusion into my space was irritating.

I want to not feel my body! I screamed in my head. *I want to pretend it doesn't exist for just an hour. I want to not worry about it.* I wanted my sadness and fear and pain and worry to sink into the biblical lake. But these women would not be deterred. Plus, they were kind and gentle and reminded me enough of my big Irish grandma that I let them pat mud into my armpits and the ticklish creases between my thighs and hips. Both of them were covered from head to toe in the brown gunk, which was now drying, cracking, and turning lighter in some places, giving them the appearance of creatures who had emerged from the depths of a swamp. Their teeth took on an anomalous whiteness within their wide smiles. Each of them wore a shiny gold wedding ring that managed to catch the sun despite the layers of mud.

Since we'd become so intimately acquainted in such an expedient manner, I thought it was only polite for me to make small talk, and so I asked if they had any advice for a long and happy marriage.

The bigger one of the two laughed. Her whole body shook and flecks of mud flew off her shoulders as they rocked back and forth. She looked at me and grabbed her substantial belly, one hand on each side of it, shaking it up and down. When she said something in Hebrew, my new translator friend chuckled.

"She says to make sure you feed him." This was a common refrain from the older generation in most cultures, a demographic of women clearly worried that no one was properly cooking for men anymore, fearful that all of the men were about to waste away due to women who used their ovens for shoe storage. I reassured her.

"I recently learned how to cook beer-can chicken, and I took a cheese-making class in Denmark."

The stout woman screwed up her face and made a rocking motion with her pelvis. My friend sniggered and translated again. "She says her advice is better: Don't stop having sex with your husband, even when you get really old."

The first woman lifted up my ponytail to make sure I had enough coverage on the nape of my neck. "Take care of yourself, *neshama*." *Neshama*, I'd learn during this trip, translates loosely to "my sweet one" or "my darling." "Take care of yourself."

"I'll try," I said and walked off into the sea to float alone. On my flight over to Israel I'd been caught off guard by the flight attendant's safety announcement. Safety announcements are usually just the soundtrack to the turf war with your seatmate over the shared armrest. But, for some reason, this time I was listening. "In the event of a decompression, an oxygen mask will automatically appear in front of you. Place the mask firmly over your nose and mouth and breathe normally. If you are traveling with a child or someone who needs assistance, secure your own mask first before assisting someone else."

Why did I feel like this flight attendant was speaking directly to me?

Secure your own mask first before assisting someone else. Take care of yourself. If you don't take care of yourself, then what use are you to anyone else?

With the past year's focus on learning to be married, building a home, building a future, thinking about planning a family, and taking care of an ill parent from afar, it had been easy to slip into crisis-management mode all the time, automatic pilot where I fell asleep due to exhaustion and woke with a pit of angst in my stomach over what needed to be accomplished next. It made me feel a certain kinship with my mom. Over the past decade, as my dad had gotten sicker and been increasingly confined to the house, I'd watched my mother place everyone else's needs ahead of her own. I was certain this was one of the things that had contributed to her having a nervous breakdown in the months before our wedding.

The last time I'd been home to see my parents had been a particularly painful visit. It was right before I'd been diagnosed with the muscular dystrophy, and my dad's doctors warned that his health was deteriorating more quickly than usual. His liver had failed. Nick and I both flew out to Philadelphia to see my parents and try to help my mom figure out how to manage their dwindling finances. A few years earlier, my father had taken a second mortgage on their house without telling my mother. The money was gone and he couldn't remember how he'd spent it. My mother's mental health was so bad she could no longer work. They had no income coming in and mom knew nothing about their savings or investments. My dad was only awake to talk about it for a couple hours a day. At my parents' house I sat in an armchair next to my dad's hospital bed. He couldn't lift his hands to feed himself, so my mom sat on the other side of the bed, spooning soft cheese into his mouth. He stuck his tongue out to receive it like a small child. Most of his teeth had fallen out because his gums could no longer hold them. His entire body was so swollen, he looked like he was covered in a blanket of himself.

My mother's hands shook from nerves and anxiety as she lifted the spoon to my father's mouth. It was as though I were watching a performance that took place several times a day, one in which the actors had long ago ceased to put in the effort to pretend. For my mom, caring for my father had become like caring for an infant—frantic, uncertain, exhausting, and often gross—but with none of the unconditional love a mother has for her child.

I always loved the story of how John and Tracey Piazza met. It's the one story of my parents as a couple where it sounds like they were truly happy. My mother was a striking debutante from Denver with corn silk–blond hair cascading down to her butt. She grew up riding horses imported from South America and hiking in the Rocky Mountains. She went to Drake University in Des Moines, Iowa, with no ambitions beyond finding a husband, preferably a doctor or a lawyer. My dad was the scrappy and brilliant son of a truck driver and a nurse from Scranton, Pennsylvania. One of five kids, he hitchhiked his way to college, also at Drake, and paid his own tuition as a bartender at the campus bar, the Doghouse.

He met my eighteen-year-old mom in the bar on her very first day of college, fresh out of a Delta Gamma sorority meeting. Dad was very handsome, like Al Pacino in *The Godfather*, with a hippie vibe, black hair, mysterious eyes, and a serious jaw—nothing like the boys back home in the Rockies. He said she was the prettiest girl he'd ever seen. My mom later joked that was because his hometown, Scranton, wasn't known for pretty girls. As family legend goes, he charmed her with dirty jokes and plied her with strong margaritas before convincing her to come back to his apartment to go swimming in his pool. With a flick of her silky blond hair and a giggle, she agreed.

Only once she was in the water did she realize my dad had brought her to trespass in someone else's pool. When I first heard the story, I loved the fun and frivolity, but looking back, I saw it as a metaphor for a forty-year marriage based on half-truths, paper cuts that became gashes, and broken promises.

At home with me four decades after that first date, my mother sat on their back porch with a faraway look in her eyes. This bout of depression had transported her to a place that felt very far away from me.

I tried to hold her hand, but she winced. This wasn't the mom I was used to.

Before she got sick and before I met Nick, Mom would take the train from Philadelphia to New York to visit me for a few hours almost every Sunday. We'd have lunch at a grungy diner across the street from my apartment. She was my biggest cheerleader back then, particularly on the mornings where I was slightly hungover and nursing a bad breakup. "I'm not worried about you," she'd say, shoveling eggs and home fries into her mouth, her diet of the month always put on hiatus when she visited me. "You're going to find the perfect person for you one day, Jo. I know it in my bones."

Now I had found the perfect person, but my cheerleader had misplaced her pom-poms. She was deflated. I wanted to tell her I was still disappointed that she hadn't been a bigger presence at our wedding. She was the one thing missing from that day. In the weeks leading up to the wedding she was bedridden with depression and wasn't sure she'd be well enough to make it to the ceremony. I didn't see her until I walked down the aisle. It was Nick's mom, Patsy, who came to see me in my bridal suite, hugged me, wished me luck, and gave me a pair of earrings she'd asked the jeweler to make me just for my wedding day.

It wasn't my mom's fault. She was sick, but I resented her for it all the same. I wanted her to snap out of it, to be the mom in the diner, my cheerleader, my friend, and then I felt selfish for not having more compassion.

"I'm sorry you're going through this," I said. I looked at her matted hair and the dried skin peeling off the backs of her hands. The truly unfair difference between my dad's disease and my mother's was that his was so apparent, so physically imposing. Because everyone could see he was sick, they treated him like a sick person. But mental illness takes cover inside a normal-looking body. No one tended to my mother or treated her with kid gloves, because it was easy to dismiss her depression as a choice, even for me.

"Are you happy for me?" I asked her, regretting the words the second they left my lips. What if she said no?

"I like Nick," she said in a remote voice. "Your father and I were children when we got married. We didn't want the same things. We fought all the time. We fought so much." I could see the tears welling up in her eyes and I reached out to put my hand on her arm as gently as I could.

"You made a better choice than I did. I lost myself in our marriage and I don't know how to get it back," she said. It was the first real thing we'd talked about in more than a year. *I don't want to end up like you*, I thought, feeling terrible that the words had even entered my brain.

....

I traveled to Israel to work on several assignments, some of them light and frothy ("The World's MOST IMPORTANT Hummus!") and some serious ("Is Israel Safe for Tourists?"). And when it came to marriage advice, I knew I was looking for something; I just wasn't sure what it was. I was fascinated by the Jewish laws that governed a husband's and wife's behavior in a marriage. I also wanted to understand how wives and mothers managed to stay strong and keep a family together in the midst of such a chaotic world, living in a country constantly rocked by violence and political tension.

I was having a hard time keeping my shit together in the midst of my incredibly safe and privileged life. Granted, our first year of marriage was more difficult than I'd expected it to be. I hadn't expected to find out I was sick or for my parents to fall so ill. But Nick was the best husband I could have asked for, better than anyone I could have dreamed up. I had no reason to complain, and yet I was worn down. On my flight to Israel, I looked at myself in the bathroom mirror. I hadn't gotten a haircut since our wedding, and my eyes were bloodshot, with deep navy circles indented beneath them. I looked exhausted. I looked like crap. Something had to change.

....

After a long day floating weightlessly in the Dead Sea, I arrived in Jerusalem, a welcome antidote to the previous night I'd spent in Tel Aviv, a city that reminded me too much of the worst parts of New York and Los Angeles—the crowds, the lines at nightclubs that seem like they never close, the muscle heads working out on the beach in as little clothing as possible, and the residents' obsession with telling me they were the best at everything.

Despite its being a city mired in a perpetual state of flux and often violence, the people in Jerusalem were much kinder, more soft-spoken, and more welcoming to foreign visitors than those in Tel Aviv, and I never once felt unsafe in the ancient city. I spent hours strolling the labyrinthine stalls of the Old City. I bought a rosary for my dad, who was raised Catholic, and had it blessed in the Church of the Holy Sepulchre, the site where some Christians believe that Jesus Christ was crucified. Most shops in the meandering alleys of Old Jerusalem don't have proper names. The stalls, no bigger than closets, are filled with precious stones from the Red Sea, frankincense, Stars of David, wooden rosaries, T-shirts with Hebrew words that say curses when viewed upside down, rip-off Hard Rock Café paraphernalia, bobble heads of every famous Jewish person ever, prayer shawls, and holy water. They trip over one another down the dim and dank alleys of the sweet-smelling old market.

That night I was going to meet Chana, an Orthodox Jewish woman who counsels secular women on the intricacies of Israeli marriage laws and teaches them how those laws can actually improve and strengthen any marriage, even one between two people who aren't religious. I was raised Catholic and Nick, Episcopalian, but neither of us had been to church in twenty years. We adhered to a shared moral code of being kind to your fellow man, doing the right thing, and resting on Sundays.

Israeli law doesn't allow marriages between Jews and non-Jews, or between Jews by birth and converts to Judaism, to take place within the state. In order to be legally married in Israel, the bride and groom must perform traditional Orthodox Jewish wedding rites and rituals and be married by an Orthodox rabbi (the vast majority of whom are men), even if they aren't particularly religious.

The Israeli system for marriage is wildly complicated and controversial, even for practicing but non-Orthodox Jews. I had friends from college who lived in Israel for years but left the country to get married in Europe (Cyprus was a pleasant sun-drenched option) or even on a boat out at sea, just to avoid the hassle of having a religious wedding.

Chana makes it more pleasant for secular Jewish women to have their weddings in Israel by meeting with them and talking them through the actual meaning of the ancient Jewish rituals. Her philosophy is that understanding the rituals makes things less scary and awkward.

"No one should dread their wedding," she explained when I met her. "That's just not fair." I'd expected Chana to be older, like the women I met at the Dead Sea, but she was my age, thirty-five, and already had six beautiful children. Chana was twenty-two when she got married, an old maid in Jerusalem's Orthodox community. Her husband had been twenty-eight.

With pale skin and a lace-embroidered beret, Chana's face conjured a Vermeer painting. She met me in her eighth-floor apartment and led me to her balcony to admire the view of the Old City before we settled easily onto her couch. Her oldest daughter brought us a plate of *macarons*, the French kind, not the Jewish kind. Her husband took the kids out for a few hours, which made it feel like we were old friends talking marriage.

Secular marriage comes with a lot of shoulds and shouldn'ts. You should love your husband or wife. You shouldn't have sex with other people. You should cherish your spouse and protect them. You shouldn't sneakily read their e-mails while they're in the shower. But

Orthodox Judaism comes with a very specific set of rules, and not just for the wedding but for the actual marriage.

Chana began by complimenting me on putting so much effort into my first year of marriage. "The first year is so important. That's when you see the most divorces," she added. "If you make the first year work, then you're in a good place."

"Thank you." I paused. "So, what are the rules?" I jumped right in, ready to take dictation.

Chana let out a twinkly laugh.

"Where do I start?" she breathed excitedly. "Getting married is a journey into the unknown. But I should tell you about the mikvah first. That's the thing that can be stressful for nonreligious women here when they get married. You have to have a mikvah here before you're allowed to get a marriage certificate, and I think it's a good thing. Most people don't understand it and they don't like it because they don't understand it. I worry that secular people hate religion because they've had a bad experience with it. I want to fix that. A mikvah should be wonderful."

A mikvah is a ritual bath undertaken by both men and women in which you immerse yourself in running water from a lake, a sea, or a natural stream. Israeli cities like Jerusalem and Tel Aviv have bathhouses specially designed for this purpose where at least some of the water is supplied by rain. You enter the water naked, with your arms and legs spread so that every inch of skin and hair is exposed to the water. As you duck under the water, you say a blessing. The most common one for brides and grooms is the *shehecheyanu,* which thanks God for preparing the bride and groom for their marriage: "Blessed are you, Lord our God, Ruler of the Universe, who kept us alive and preserved us and enabled us to reach this season." For women the mikvah is overseen by an attendant, often an older Orthodox woman. Chana admitted that they can be a little harsh as they physically inspect a woman's body before she is allowed to immerse herself in the water. No one really wants to be inspected when they're naked. I thought back to the women on the shores of the Dead Sea, carefully moving their hands along my body in places Nick hadn't even explored.

The mikvah is a cleansing ritual, plain and simple, and in some ways it reminded me of the *temazcal* in Mexico, a way of purifying your body before you enter a new stage of your life.

Most nonreligious women go to the mikvah once, get their marriage license, and never go again. Chana goes every single month seven days after her period. She loves it.

"It's a time just for me." Of course she needed a time just for her. She has six children!

For Chana the mikvah is her time of self-care. It gives her a sense of renewal, of finding herself again. She doesn't just go to the bath. This is like a monthly spiritual spa day. She immerses herself in the water, does her nails, moisturizes her entire body, and trims her hair.

"You spend one whole day focusing on your own body," she says. "Think of it like a reset button. I don't know for sure if that was God's intention, but I think it was. I think that's the reason we do it, to give women a time to take care of themselves. It's very easy to forget to do that in a marriage."

"I think I had a mikvah in the Dead Sea. It felt like a mikvah."

She peered at me with curiosity as I explained about surrendering to the water and the old women with the mud.

"Sure, maybe," she said with the right amount of skepticism.

Chana's insistence on self-care made sense, here of all places. I thought back to the safety briefing on the plane. *Secure your own oxygen mask first.* This part of the Middle East was roiled with uncertainty, and keeping a family safe required a wife and mother to remain strong, to take care of herself so she could ultimately take care of everyone else. Taking care of herself was something my own mother had never been good at, especially in times of crisis.

I finally felt comfortable enough to tell Chana I was curious about the Orthodox rule about when women could have sex with their husbands or, more specifically, when they couldn't. I'd heard that Orthodox couples were forbidden from having sex during specific times of the month.

Chana raised a very well-manicured eyebrow in amusement and lifted her hand to stop me from saying something embarrassing.

"You've got it all wrong," she said. "According to Jewish law, sexual relations between a man and a woman are sacred and holy. But sacred and holy in a very positive way. Sex is a really good thing to Jews. You can only have sex within marriage and only with your wife. And then, after you are married, you can only have sex at certain times. That's true," Chana explained.

She caught me making a face and gave me a look that said, *Stop being a judgmental twit.* "We aren't supposed to have sex during our period or for seven days after our period."

"Because that ensures you have sex when you're most fertile, right?" I responded. As a woman over the age of thirty-five, I was now well-versed in the science of fertility. "You want to maximize the opportunity to make babies." I regretted the words as soon as they'd left my mouth. I could feel how I was reducing her spiritual beliefs to biological imperatives.

She shook her head and leaned into me as if she were revealing a great secret.

"People think these rules are all about having children, and that's just not true." As she sighed, I remembered the basketball team she was raising in this apartment. "That's when sex is better for the woman. We believe that sex needs, *seriously needs*, to be good for the woman. During the times we have sex is when all of the hormones are right for sex to be very enjoyable for the woman. Your libido is great if you wait until seven days after your period."

I chewed on my *macaron* longer than necessary to consider this.

Chana continued. "Now also imagine not being able to touch your husband for that time. Imagine how great that is when you can finally touch him and release all of that pent-up energy." She told me that Orthodox Jewish marriage comes with a special bed. During the two weeks when a couple are not allowed to touch each other, it splits apart. Then it comes back together during the two weeks when they can touch.

"Wait." I stopped her. "I understand about the sex. But you can't touch for those two weeks? You can't hug or kiss or tickle or squeeze?"

She shook her head. "You can't touch. It makes it so much more exciting when you can. It's easy to lose yourself in a marriage, especially when you become a mom. The two weeks apart lets you connect with your body, return to your womanhood. You learn to love your body again. The two of us move apart in order to get to know ourselves better and then come back to each other more complete. It keeps the passion in your marriage. Everything is lining up during that time, your hormones, your libido. Everything is great," Chana said. I felt like I was reading *Cosmo*.

I thought about Chana's advice. When did Nick and I have the best sex? It was usually after I came back from a long trip, having built up all that desire and anticipation for days and sometimes weeks at a time. This trip was a prime example of that. I'd only been gone a week, but it was evident from his texts that Nick had started to miss me like crazy. "I was bouncing up and down in my chair at work thinking about picking you up from the airport," he'd written. "I was looking at our wedding pictures last night. I'm a lucky guy."

I'd come into our talk with plenty of misconceptions. One was that Orthodox Judaism was inherently antifeminist, turning women in baby-making machines. I hadn't expected to get enlightened and progressive advice on how to care for yourself, your satisfaction, and your relationship.

"Take some time apart," Chana said. "For me, it's like getting to have a whole new wedding night every single month. . . . You know, Jo, it's the relationship between the husband and wife itself that is seen as sacred and holy in the Bible. God dwells within each couple if you choose to let him in."

"But what does that mean?" I asked like an impatient child. Since

Nick and I are not particularly religious, saying that God was dwelling within our marriage made it sound like we'd invited a complete stranger to come over and watch us have sex.

She considered it thoughtfully. "When I think about letting God in, I think about the little things. I think about being nice to my husband at the end of a long day. I think about smiling at him when I don't want to smile. It is so easy in our world to think about me, me, me. But now you need to think about the two of you. It is about those little things."

I nodded.

"In Jewish law we talk about the marriage covenant. It's something so much bigger than a contract. It's about a desire to create good things in the world together. To have the same desires about goodness and changing the world together. When you're focused on these shared rules, then you truly focus on getting through the little things and the big things together."

Still trying to wrap my head around the meaning of the laws, I'd later talk about it with an Orthodox scholar back home in the States. Alissa Thomas-Newborn is the first Orthodox female clergy member in Los Angeles and one of only a handful in the entire country. She echoed Chana's ideas, telling me that the Orthodox rules truly did allow time for a woman to take care of herself, to feel renewed and refreshed each month, and for a couple to reset their relationship on multiple levels.

"Think of it as a time to work on your communication muscles, to talk without thinking about the physical aspects of the relationship," Thomas-Newborn told me. "Look at it as an opportunity, a wonderful one! It can be a time to explore the relationship in different ways."

Chana also told me her theory of bricks, which is not in the Bible but is wonderful advice all the same. Every married couple should think about the theory of the bricks.

"Every crisis, big or small, is a brick. It's up to you to decide what to do with that brick. You can use it to build a wall between you, or it can be a brick in building the foundation of your home together. You can choose to let that brick tear you apart or make the relationship stronger. Anytime I reach a low point in my marriage I try to think about how that crisis will eventually get us to a better place."

Her husband came home with the children soon after, and amid the glorious cacophony I could see why Chana equally cherished both her family and her time alone. She hugged me warmly as I left and whispered in my ear, "Take care of yourself."

....

I thought we'd have days of great sex when I returned from the Middle East. We'd moved apart, so we could come back to each other more complete. Right? Instead, Nick and I got into a fight, a really shitty fight.

It started small. We couldn't figure out how to set up a bank account that would automatically pay the mortgage. Then we finally set one up with Wells Fargo, but it locked us out because we entered the wrong password too many times.

The obvious way to mitigate this marital stress was to do something simple and relaxing together. And so we decided to assemble some Ikea furniture. As we searched for lost screws and Riktig Öglas we began wondering if we should put the mortgage on a credit card, which led the conversation to my desire to get rid of most of our credit cards. Nick, on the other hand, wanted as many credit cards as possible to maximize our frequent-flier points. This made my stomach tighten and my breath get short. The thought of looming plastic debt each month gave me an anxiety attack. But we somehow got back to the matter at hand and logged on to our credit card account to see if we could link it to the bank to link it to the other bank to link it to the mortgage. The Riktig Öglas were now nowhere to be found and tensions were running high.

I perused the last month of charges. "Why do we eat out so much?" I asked. "Do you hate my cooking? The beer-can chicken wasn't any good?"

Our talk grew more and more heated as we quarreled over how we spent our money. Did we even need this crap from Ikea?

Nick thought we could get rid of our car. We lived in San Francisco; why did we need a car? I loved the freedom of having a car to escape the city for the wine country or to buy toilet paper in bulk at Costco.

"We wouldn't need a car if we lived in New York, but we definitely need it here," I said. Before I knew it, I began listing all of the things I hated about San Francisco and reasons why living there was making me miserable—being yelled at in the grocery store for not bringing my own bags, getting disapproving stares because I'd never been to Burning Man, the fact that everyone looks down on you if you don't work at Google or Facebook, the chilly fog that seeps into your bones and never lets you truly get warm.

I wasn't completely miserable on the West Coast. Sure, I didn't have any friends and the hills made my glutes constantly sore and I felt like a pariah for not composting my own garbage, but San Francisco wasn't as terrible as I was making it out to be. I was looking for things to attack with. I was tense. I grew up believing that married couples fought every day. I'd watched my parents wear each other down with constant bickering. In the past I'd imitated them. I'd needle boyfriends with the same perverse pleasure I'd get from popping a particularly ripe zit, becoming calm only after a huge release of tension. But until now I hadn't done this with Nick. He was the first human things had felt normal with. The inertia of this argument catapulted us into a darker and darker place, bringing long-forgotten tensions to the surface. I'd shifted into a danger zone where sharp words came too easily.

"Why do you always have to be right?"

"Sometimes you're such a fucking snob."

"Why do all your female friends hate me?"

We'd recently had one of Nick's friends over for dinner. She sat next to me, pecking away at her phone for an hour and a half. When I looked over at her screen, wondering if she had a work emergency,

I saw she was playing Words with Friends. She was the least *hygge* dinner guest I've ever had.

"And speaking of your female friends, why'd you have coffee with your ex-girlfriend and not tell me?" I broke the rules Bobby Klein had taught us in Mexico, bringing up long-resolved issues, the kind that rot a marriage if you keep mentioning them after they've been put to rest.

"Oh my God, I don't have to tell you everything. I forgot! Why do you get weird and jealous when you're mad about other things? Also, did you stick your fingers in the Brie cheese and eat it again?"

"Yes, you do have to tell me! That's what marriage is about—telling me everything! Maybe I did. So what? It's Brie. That's how you're supposed to eat it. And yeah I have a bee in my bonnet about your ex-girlfriend. I'm sorry," I said. "Even though she's awful."

"When you apologize like that you sound like Donald Trump. Maybe it's your fault you have no friends here. Look at how you're acting."

Nick's words trampled me. Exhausted me. Enraged me. He couldn't unsay them.

"Fuck it. Leave me alone."

Nick called me a spoiled brat. I called him a word I'd prefer not to repeat.

We retreated to separate rooms, the silence heavy with defeat. Lady Piazza paced up and down the long hallway, refusing to take sides. "I rescued you from a trash bin," I reminded her. "He's brand-new and he doesn't even let you sleep in the bed!"

I seethed in the living room and distracted myself by eating a brownie and watching the scene from *Casablanca* where Rick puts Ilsa on the plane. I thought, for the hundredth time, about whether she was better off with Victor Laszlo. Victor Laszlo would never have coffee with his ex-girlfriend. *He* knew something about loyalty. I opened Skype. The little green dot blinked next to Nick's Skype photo, the one I keep trying to get him to change because he looks like a twenty-year-old German exchange student in it. So he was online. *Why is he on Skype?* I thought. *Who is he talking to? Is he talking about me? Should I Skype him?* No, I decided. I was not going to Skype my husband from the same house.

I grabbed my purse, left the house, and headed to the yoga studio down the street. An hour of stretching and breathing with strangers who neglected deodorant would do me good. As I bent over to touch the floor in the crowded vinyasa class, I noticed my toes looked gross, gnarly, and ragged with only the tiniest chips of red polish still clinging to the cuticles.

"Ewww," I said out loud.

"Are you okay?" The teacher rubbed my tailbone and moved her own perfectly pedicured turquoise toenails next to mine.

"Ahhhh," I said. "Just relaxing into this pose. Ahhh Namaste!" My answer satisfied her, and her perfect little blue toes moved on to help the woman next to me correct her downward dog.

I hadn't gotten a manicure or pedicure since we'd moved to San Francisco. I blamed this on not having any friends to go with me. Nail care back in New York had been a communal activity on Sundays with my girlfriends, a time to catch up and gossip and bitch about our significant others. Going alone to the nail salon felt stranger than eating out by myself. Yoga has taught me a lot about myself over the years, and in that moment it taught me I needed a pedicure.

I chose one of the many nail salons on Divisadero Street and indulged in shiny pink fingers and toes. The stress melted out of me and into the green tea–scented porcelain toe tub. Why had I stopped doing this? Taking the time to take care of myself had been such a priority when I was single and living in New York. Since I'd been married my time had been increasingly filled with "us" time or "having awkward dinners with other couples" time. In an attempt to feel less lonely I began texting with my friend Sarah, who was going through a nasty divorce. Before filing for divorce, Sarah and her ex were one of those couples who constantly posted goofy selfies of themselves in exotic locations with perfect hair with invented hashtags like #BestHusbandEver and #ArentWeCute. Sarah was one of those people who made me feel like every other married person had already been let in on the secret of having a perfect marriage. Those goofy selfies were hiding the truth. Now they only talked to each other through their lawyers.

Sarah began detailing the demise of her marriage through clipped sentences and descriptive emojis over text message while I waited for my nails to dry.

It turned out that there wasn't a single bombshell that ended their marriage. They began fighting over the little things. He wanted to get Yankee season tickets. She thought they were a waste of money. She put the toilet paper roll on wrong. He wouldn't stop eating cereal in bed. She thought *Silicon Valley* sucked and he thought it was a masterpiece. He wanted a Hamptons share house. She thought he just wanted to fuck teenagers.

"He can't stand my friends," she texted. "Including you. Sorry. We fought once a month, then once a week, twice a week, every day. The resentments got bigger and bigger. I had a dream I set him on fire. Then we stopped having sex . . . which was good because his balls smell. Seriously."

A divorce in your circle shakes your own foundation and makes you reconsider the things you can and can't live with. Maybe I didn't need a car so I could drive to Costco to get thirty toilet paper rolls to store in the closet.

I stared down at my rosy toes and felt a sense of happiness and accomplishment that was clearly not in proportion to either the expense or the amount of effort I'd put in.

I'm getting a blowout, I decided.

I texted Glynnis about the fight, my pedicure, and whether I should ask the hairstylist for beach waves.

"You know you're dealing with a lot," she texted back. "It's OK to take a breath and take care of yourself, you know. Your toes look perfect! Yes on beach waves."

I felt better. This was what it felt like to reset. All the marriage advice I'd gleaned so far had been about *us*. But keeping us strong was also about keeping myself strong and healthy and happy. I thought about an interview I'd seen recently between Oprah and Michelle Obama. Former FLOTUS + Oprah was like the "Be your best self" equivalent of crossing the streams in *Ghostbusters*. Michelle described moving into the White House and realizing that in order to be a good wife and mom she had to make sure she took care of herself. "If you do not take control over your time and your life, other people will gobble it up," the First Lady said. "If you don't prioritize yourself, you constantly start falling lower and lower on your list."

I'd stopped making myself a priority. For years I'd been disgusted with my mother for losing herself in her marriage and her role as constant caretaker, and yet here I was, married for less than a year, completely losing myself.

My calm was short-lived. The moment I walked back into the house, my anger returned, triggering a physical change in my body, like when a hyena smells a kill, a celebrity senses a paparazzo, or Lady Piazza gets a whiff of pizza. All the lights were out.

Did that fucker leave?

If anyone was going to leave, it was going to be me, but he up and did it first.

He'd left.

I'd made him leave.

Shit.

Every married friend I have (even the happily married ones) has their own unique marriage escape fantasy. When her marriage was still about taking goofy selfies, Sarah told me she'd go back to school to be a large animal vet if she ever broke up with her husband. Erin always told me that if she left her husband she'd go to Taos, New Mexico, with her two daughters and live in an adobe house and make jewelry out of feathers. Eliza would become a bartender in Bali. Annie would join me in San Francisco and become a lesbian. I didn't have an escape fantasy yet. Nick and I were still so shiny and new. I wondered, where would I go? The image formed almost instantly: I could go to Paris, sublet a flat in the Marais, get bangs, start smoking again, and buy a pink cashmere coat.

But the fantasy made me sad. Paris would be really lonely without Nick. Who would spout off obscure facts about the construction of the Eiffel Tower or tell me which side of the plane to sit on when we landed at Charles de Gaulle?

As I fumed in the living room, my shiny pink toes looking a little dimmer in the lamplight, I thought about what to do next. Talk to Nick? Or just go to sleep, because frankly I was exhausted. When you get married, everyone will give you the same advice: Never go to bed angry. That felt like bullshit to me. Sometimes you need to sleep to clear your damn head, right? One of the best pieces of marriage advice I'd gotten during my journey around the world actually came from Hollywood, from the actress and writer Jenny Mollen. I fell a little in love with Jenny when I was interviewing her for a *Forbes* story on how to succeed in life by failing miserably. The story was fine; talking to Jenny was wonderful. Jenny had been married to the actor Jason Biggs for five years, and her two *New York Times* best sellers talk a lot about surviving their marriage and having their baby, a little boy named Sid. Jenny's marriage advice was the refreshing opposite of "Don't go to bed angry."

"You know," she said, "I think it's normal to hate each other from time to time. You can't be afraid of not liking each other. Sometimes you're going to roll over in bed and wish he was someone else. Girls grow up with this idealized version of what their marriage should look like, and the reality is that it does ebb and flow. As much as I want to murder Jason sometimes, I know we're not getting divorced and it's not ending. There are times when you want to fuck them and times when you want to fuck anyone but them."

I walked toward our bedroom.

Lady Piazza jauntily trotted next to me down the dark hallway. If she had any awareness at all that Nick and I had had a fight, the only thing she cared about was whether that fight gave her license to sleep in the bed. I walked past the framed photo we'd blown up from our second date in Joshua Tree, right before the thunderstorm rolled in, the sky bruised purple but the desert calm and still.

Nick had turned on the reading light on my side of the bed. He hadn't left after all. I listened to his long, low snores.

I thought about what Chana said back in Jerusalem. Nick and I had had a fight. It was a brick. We could build a wall or we could keep building our house. We would fix it in the morning. For now, I was angry, and that was okay. My husband was still here, at home, in our bed. I combined the advice of the Hollywood actress and the Israeli Orthodox Jew.

I sucked in a deep breath, took an Ambien, and went to sleep next to Nick.

9

Kenya

It Takes a Village

Love is like the wild rose-briar,
Friendship like the holly-tree—
The holly is dark when the rose-briar blooms,
But which will bloom most constantly?

—Emily Brontë

"Do you want to have a cowife?" a stunning Maasai woman named Naropil asked me kindly as I sat down next to her in the dirt. "Would you let your husband have another wife? Would you like to have one?"

I wanted to shake my head. I looked over at Nick, who was sitting off to my left. My husband with other women? No thanks. I already had my hands full with his harem of platonic yet needy ex-girlfriends. But I knew that was the wrong answer, the rude-white-person answer, and I shrugged my shoulders instead.

"Maybe? Under the right circumstances. If she was cool. It's a hard thing to say, really. Does she cook?"

That *was* right . . . or closer to right. As soon as my translator communicated my answer to the clutch of women surrounding me, they cheered and thumped their bare feet on the dirt. As a traveler I'm often frustrated by my tendency to make assumptions before I fully understand a situation. Visiting Kenya was one of those times. Polygamy made me uncomfortable before I even came face to face with it. Marriage to multiple spouses is legal in Kenya. In 2014 the country's president, Uhuru Kenyatta, signed a controversial law legalizing the long-held practice, even though in East Africa's tribal regions polygamy has long been standard without being recognized by the state. Legal or not, the practice didn't sit well with me.

"It is hard to take care of all of this," Naropil said, sweeping her hand around the rural village of Naurori in the Maasai Mara of southern Kenya. Every inch of the family compound was blanketed in children, goats, and sheep. "When you work very hard, you need a cowife to help you take care of the children, the home, the cows, and the goats."

In many parts of tribal Kenya men tend to remain in a monogamous relationship with their first wife until they turn thirty-five. But as they acquire more wealth, they also acquire more wives. At age forty-one Nick would have at least two wives if he were a Maasai warrior. He was now making do with just me and not a single cow, goat, or sheep, unless you counted Lady Piazza.

The women in the village began inspecting Nick the way I look at avocados in Trader Joe's. They circled him and poked at him, squeezed his biceps.

"Why is your husband so old with just one wife?" one of them asked me. "Why don't you have any children?" Having one childless wife, in her eyes, meant we were a very poor couple. There were perhaps a dozen women sitting with us and more children than I could count running rowdy and free. One of them, a curious toddler shaped like a bowling ball, waddled over to pet Nick's blond head.

Yellow hair was funny and strange to them and clearly an invitation to stroke him.

"I have all the wives I need." Nick said with confidence, rubbing small circles along the small of my back. "But if we get more goats, I'll consider it."

....

The Maasai and Samburu tribes of Kenya live in very much the same way their ancestors did a thousand years ago. The major difference is that they now have cell phones and everyone is on Facebook. There are other differences too. Today there are agreements about sharing their land with the government for game reservations, the tribes are much more conciliatory to the wildlife (no more hunting lions), and they're more apt to send their children to government schools where they learn to read and speak Kiswahili.

Yet many of the remaining Maasai and Samburu still live in primitive villages without electricity or running water. A man's worth on the Mara is judged by sheer numbers—number of cows, number of wives, number of kids.

Even on Nick's worst days I don't feel like pawning him off on a cowife—yet.

But what the hell did I know? I could feel very differently a year from now.

Understanding polygamy in tribal Africa, really understanding it, requires a certain fluidity of Western moral thinking. There are three things worth mentioning right off the bat: The first is that Maasai and Samburu polygamy isn't about sex. It's about division of labor. More wives mean more hands to do the work. The second is that the first wives are usually the ones asking their husband to get another wife. And the third is that the women, for the most part, have made their peace with these arrangements. One researcher in Kenya, Dr. Crystal Courtney, has been living among the tribe for several years, working on conservation and development with them. To better understand the prospects of Maasai youth, she asked around one hundred of them to draw her a picture of what they hoped their lives would look like when they grew up. Nearly all of them drew her a picture of them with at least three other cowives and between five to ten children.

It wasn't until I sat down with the women of the Maasai village that I understood how having cowives is less about sharing a husband than about sharing burdens. To many Western women this may seem like the opposite of a feminist choice. When I explained it to a friend of mine in New York, a type-A tiger mom investment banker, she was so angry she nearly spat on the floor.

"Why don't they just tell the men to work more?" she erupted with irritation for a culture half a world away. The simple answer is that the men won't do it. And so the women work with what they have—other women.

Gaining cowives is also about the creation of a community. Maasai women view their cowives as a blessing because an extra wife means less work, an extra pair of hands when they are sick or recovering from childbirth. This is just good home economics—and a matter of life and death. When I saw how much labor the tribal women did, I felt like crying. The work of caring for the cattle, collecting water (from miles away), searching out firewood (also from miles away), cooking, building houses—it would be all too much for one woman on her own. The men won't do it. Other women will. The women take care of one another.

....

It had taken a day of travel to meet up with Naropil and her cowives. Nick and I stayed in the Maasai Mara's Rekero Camp, and we'd had a rough night, thanks to its position right next to what the locals call the "hippo highway." Gangs of the giant beasts surrounded us to graze all night long, grunting and moaning, their giant rumps rubbing against the canvas of our tent. "There's an animal the size of a Volkswagen out there," Nick mumbled, half asleep. "I don't think we should go outside." Next came the shrieks of the bush babies, a cross between a monkey, a rat, and a gremlin with giant eyes that glow in the dark. They flew through the air and landed on our tent, where they proceeded to tap-dance for hours.

"You're not supposed to feed them after midnight," I moaned, slightly delirious.

Around three in the morning the hyenas joined in with their cacophonous barking and laughing. Before sunrise a water buffalo had been devoured by a pride of lions in the river outside the tent. There's never a dull moment in the Mara.

We headed to the Naurori village by jeep first thing in the morning, fording muddy trenches filled with bored crocodiles. Giraffes peeked their heads over the orange-leafed croton bushes to inspect us. Topi, massive antelope with striking colored coats that make them look like they are wearing blue jeans and yellow socks, trotted along in a line behind us.

As we drove alongside the ridge, our guide Pius, a jolly fellow in a traditional red-checked Maasai wrap and a baseball cap, informed us he had big news. "I have just gotten a second wife," he announced proudly as he skirted a family of elephants.

"Congratulations!" I said.

Pius, who is a Maasai, was clearly used to American attitudes toward polygamy and began to defend himself. "You know we do not take a second wife only because of the fun." That's what many Americans think. "It *is* based on need. My wife wanted it. She needed it. She is happy now. She told me, 'Pius, I have too much work to do. Get me a cowife.' So I did. Two is not very many. My uncle has six wives and forty-five children. We can be like the impala." Because the Maasai have lived among the wildlife for so long, comparisons between their own lives and those of the animals pepper their speech. In this case Pius was equating himself to a male impala, which has a harem of many mates, sometimes more than twenty. He impregnates them all and guards them from other males. You often see groups of female impalas roaming the plains in a tight-knit troop with a single-horned male nudging them on from behind. That male impala always looks exhausted.

"What makes a good Maasai wife?" I asked Pius as we continued driving toward the village. He scratched his head and considered it for a second.

"Hardworking. Kind. Caring. She must be able to take care of the goats, the sheep, and the cows, find the firewood, cook the meals, build the house. They work hard, Jo. They work very, very hard. Life isn't always easy."

The harsh reality of Maasai life for both men and women could fill several books, and I only have one chapter here. The short and simple answer, the answer that isn't enough, is that it's complicated. Girls can be married off as young as eleven and circumcised even earlier. There are activists on both sides of the circumcision issue. One side criticizes it as a barbaric, cruel, and archaic practice while the other talks of preserving tribal culture and securing familial bonds. It is often the tribal women who both advocate for and perform female circumcision.

"Who the hell are you to judge these people?" I was asked by one white woman who had lived among the tribes her entire life as a rancher. "Who are you to say what they're doing is disgusting or wrong?"

We also heard stories of prepubescent girls fleeing their sixty-year-old fiancés to escape arranged marriages. On the other hand, we asked one young Maasai girl if she minded being married to a decrepit old man four times her age, and she told us it was perfectly fine because he was too old to have sex with her. He took good care of her and bought her extra sugar at the market. Many others assured us that when a girl was married off so young, she would be raised by her husband's mother and other wives until she was an appropriate age for sexual intercourse.

These are serious, complicated topics. Nick and I spent hours talking about the issues within the East African tribal societies, and we don't know the answers. My heart broke for young women forced to endure pain and trauma. It's eye-opening to see this wildly different way of life, and part of what makes the Maasai and Samburu so interesting is how they've managed to hold strong to their traditional culture in a rapidly changing world.

Most tribal men and women still don't choose their spouses. Rather, marriage is arranged by the elders of the tribe, who try to maximize the economic value of the marriage and find a happy and healthy fit between the two spouses. The husband's family pays a dowry to the bride's family composed mainly of cows, goats, and sheep, and fathers negotiate among their close friends to seek out an advantageous exchange of cattle. The Maasai consider genetics. They want a son-in-law who is healthy and strong to protect the women and children. They make sure he has no close blood ties to their clan. The joining of a bride and groom is also the joining of two families. The fathers of daughters look for a man from a good family with good morals. They care about the morals of the entire family. A boy with a nasty uncle who steals cows will have a more difficult time finding a good wife.

When I later explained the tribal arranged marriages to my mother-in-law, Patsy, back in Milwaukee, she shrugged.

"Oh, please," she said with a flick of her hand. "How is their arranged marriage that much different from what we do here? We send our kids to the right schools, we live in certain neighborhoods, we plan certain things, all so they'll meet a certain kind of people. Families behave the same way all over the world."

A week before a Maasai marriage is supposed to take place, a meeting is held between the fathers and other elders in the tribe called the *aadung inkishu*, which literally translates to "splitting of the cows." The number of cows doesn't depend on how beautiful the bride is; it's a figure determined by the prominence of the clan and the family that the girl is from. There's recently been a progressive evolution of the bride price, an increase based on the education of the girl. If the girl is highly educated and can make money for the family, her bride price is now often higher. The upshot of this is that there is more of an incentive to send girl children to school.

There are superstitions involved as well. The bride price is always paid with an even number of cows, because an odd number of cows in the dowry can curse the marriage. Pius paid eight cows for his first wife and ten for the second sixteen years later, due to inflation. Both girls and boys must respect their fathers' decisions about whom to marry. Very few dare to refuse.

"Why would I refuse?" one new Maasai bride told me, horrified at my question. "My father wants what is best for me. I respect my father. I love my father. Refusing to marry the man he chose for me would be disrespectful."

The thing that seems crazy to modern Americans is that the couple might never even meet in advance of the wedding celebration, when the groom travels to the bride's home with the required number of animals. He picks her up, gives her father the cows, and takes her back to his village. There's a huge wedding ceremony when the girl is brought to her new home. The women of her new village welcome her with singing, dancing, hugs, and kisses on the top of her head.

"It is a very, very special welcome that is given," Pius explained to us. "Such a warm welcome. Everyone gives them presents—bowls, utensils, goats. The woman is given advice for how to live in her new community. You are celebrating a very new and very special love. Love gets real after marriage."

"The more I know you, the more I love you, baby," Nick whispered.

"See?" Pius eavesdropped. "It *is* true."

The village then divides into smaller groups based on age and gender. Old men go with the old men and old women with the old women. A large bull and a large sheep will be slaughtered and roasted over a traditional fire made of cedar, olive wood, and elephant grass. The two types of wood symbolize the coming together of the two families. The bride and groom are decorated in traditional beads and covered in cowskins. The bride spends the next two nights with the women of the village, who help ease her into her new family and her new community. This whole ceremony is a process meant to marry the bride not just to her husband but to the entire community. I thought about that. In theory that was what most Western weddings are supposed to be about too. You invite your special people from different parts of your life to welcome your new spouse, to incorporate them even further into your world, bringing together your past, present, and future.

But community is one thing urban-dwelling couples from my generation have abandoned in too many ways. We isolate ourselves into smaller and smaller family units. We get married and move at the whims of our careers, often far from our own families and longtime friends. It's rare for extended families to live in the same place. Sometimes we forge friendships that are like family, but in our increasingly transient world they don't always last. Nick and I hardly even know our neighbors in our building in San Francisco even though we all live under the same roof.

After our long and bumpy journey, Pius finally delivered us to the village of Naurori and into a *boma,* a compound of sunbaked mud huts, home to one man, Dickson Naurori, and his many wives. Using only their bare hands, the women had built those huts and the foreboding wooden fence of sharpened spikes all around them that protected the family and their cattle from roaming lions.

"*Supa*," I said to the group, which Pius had taught me means "hello" in Maasai.

"*Ippa*," they called back, which means "Hello back to you."

The women introduced themselves to me, shyly at first. Long days spent toiling in the harsh African sun had carved premature lines on all of their faces. When I began asking them about love and marriage, they looked down at their hands, busy with sewing and making intricate beaded jewelry. I stood there stupidly. *This was a bad idea*, I thought. Who was I? A privileged white girl who had come here to ask these women personal questions about their family and their marriages. I felt like an intrusive alien standing there in my moisture-wicking safari pants from REI and my fake Fendi sunglasses.

"I just got married," I blurted out. "I don't know what I'm doing. I want to know how to be a wife." I paused and then added: "I need help." I glanced feebly at Pius.

He murmured a line of the Maasai tongue to them and received no response.

"No, I don't think you said it right. Please tell them exactly what I said," I urged him. "Use my words. Tell them I really want their help."

He began again.

Explaining to them the reason I was here, relating to them as a woman and a new bride instead of a nosy foreigner, shifted something in the atmosphere of the *boma*. They looked from Pius to me and back to Pius and then began answering my questions all at once, demanding Pius keep up with what they were telling me. One of the women pulled me down to the ground. If I wanted their advice, it was clear we should be on a level playing field. I relaxed into the soft earth, narrowly dodged a bit of goat dung, and stretched my legs in front of me. I looked at the Maasai women's smooth and hairless legs. My own had gone scraggly since I dropped my razor down a toilet that was more of a hole in the ground, and I hadn't been able to acquire a new one in the bush. For a moment I wondered what they used to shave but decided it wouldn't be appropriate to ask.

Another woman spread her blanket over my lap and poured a cup of brightly colored beads into its center. She handed me a piece of wire and encouraged me to work on making a bracelet as we talked. No moment for Maasai women is ever wasted.

Naropil was clearly the leader of this group. She was tall and slender and immaculately dressed in a yellow *shuka*. Her long black braids were pulled back from her face and a few lighter, caramel braids framed her exquisite cheekbones. Dozens of strings of beads hung from her neck and her waist. I asked her how long she had been married.

"I am the third wife," she responded.

Maasai women measure a marriage not in years but in the total number of wives their husband has married and where they fit into that hierarchy. It makes sense in a culture that doesn't keep track of time the way we do. Maasai live very much in the present, worrying little about what will happen following the day's sundown. They don't keep track of birthdays and many of them can't tell you how old they are. A new wife lives with one of the older wives in the same house until she builds her own house within the compound. Naropil pointed across the circle of women at a much older woman whose face was shriveled like a raisin left too long to dry, her mouth bare of teeth. "That's my first wife. I love her so much. I love all my cowives so much. We need each other. We are a team. We do the work together."

In our marriage, Nick and I were the team. Here, it was the women who worked together to accomplish their goals—to keep their lives sane.

The sun was going down and the *boma,* which had no electricity, was getting dark. Cows wandered in, single file, from their day out to pasture.

A woman named Nekiswa noticed me staring at her earlobe. It had a hole in it the size of a water chestnut, and rings of beads encircled the sagging flesh. She grabbed my hand and pulled it to her ear to let me know I could look at it and touch it. Then she pushed my own hair behind my ear and looked sad to discover only one empty hole. I wanted to make her smile again, so I raised my shirt up a little to show the women that I had my belly button pierced. All of the women gasped in unison and shook their heads. It was clear they thought my belly button ring was gross.

Nekiswa was the youngest of five wives, and she couldn't stop telling me how much she loved her cowives and how much she owes each of them for her livelihood. "I owe them my life. My life!" she insisted. "They taught me what makes my husband happy, what annoys him, what he needs, what food to make, how to make him proud, how to take care of the property. Everything I know about being a good wife I know from our first cowife. I respect her. I love her. I am like her daughter."

I'd long wished that Nick came with an instruction manual penned by all of his ex-girlfriends. Wouldn't it be nice to receive all the gifts on your wedding registry along with a finely annotated guide to your husband? *He'll eat garbanzo beans, but not pinto. He prefers the missionary position and hates it when you say the word "fuck." Sometimes he drinks directly out of the faucet and needs to be reminded not to do this in front of guests. He gives good shoulder rubs but snores if you let him sleep on his back.*

"The older women act like guides. Like helpers? I don't know how to say it in English," Pius said.

"Mentors?" I asked.

"Yes! Mentals!" Pius went on to explain that all of the older women and men in the tribe acted as relationship mentors for the younger ones.

The Western transition away from tribal culture has caused us a few great losses—one of them is the concept of true community. Without community we turn to the economy to replace what we've lost by hiring therapists, nannies, doulas, reiki healers, and housekeepers. But it's hard to hire a mentor, to find women and men who've been there before us and are willing to honestly counsel us about what marriage really has in store.

Naropil beckoned me inside one of the houses. We took a seat on the bed, the only place to sit, just a raised platform covered in a thin layer of cowhide. The children's bed was similar and about an arm's length away, separated only by the cooking fire. The small details inside the house struck me: how the pots were arranged by size, how the sheets were folded into fours.

"How often does your husband sleep here?" I asked her, hoping that it wasn't too personal a question.

"It depends. He splits his time between the different wives and houses," she said with a simple shrug of her shoulders, as if this were an issue of little consequence. The division of labor isn't just physical. They divide the emotional labor of a marriage too. More wives means more than one person to listen to the husband complain, brag, or repeat the same story over and over. "It's nice to have a break," Naropil said. Maybe that was how I should think about Nick's exes, as taking on some of my emotional labor.

But in the morning, Naropil told me, when everyone wakes up, it doesn't matter who slept in what house. All of a sudden, the chores are divided evenly among the women. One will start the fire while the other prepares breakfast and another watches the children. There's always someone to talk to, to bitch to, to help you braid your hair.

Pius motioned to me that it was time to go, and I waved my hand to put him off. I was finally being accepted into this complicated community of women, and it felt nice.

"Do you want to stay?" Naropil asked me. "You can be one of our cowives."

I thought about it.

Despite their many hardships, I began to envy what these women *did* have—their strong kinship with the other women.

Research shows that having strong friendships and strong community ties keeps a marriage together. A 1999 study by Chalandra M. Bryant and Rand D. Conger of Iowa State University found that having a strong social support network outside of the marriage predicted marital success.

Having strong friendships can also make you healthier. An Australian study conducted over ten years among an elderly population found that those with a large group of friends were 22 percent less likely to die during the study's duration. And a 2006 study of three thousand nurses with breast cancer found that women without a strong group of close friends were four times as likely to succumb to the disease than those with a formidable network of confidantes. In those cases having a strong community was literally the difference between life and death.

Nick has an incredible group of friends in San Francisco that he's been close with for twenty years. It's one of the things I love about him, the fact that he's managed to stay so connected to so many people for so long. We're similar in that way. I've also had a lot of the same friends for almost twenty years. But the truth was I felt like I'd left my own village behind when I left the East Coast. When you first leave a place, moving to a new city as I had, you kid yourself that you'll be back all the time. It had been almost nine months since I'd spent a night in New York City.

Once I settled into everyday life in my adopted city, I began to feel something I'd never felt before. I was lonely. When I left my mom and dad at eighteen to go to college, I was thrust into the robust community that freshman year instantly affords you via orientation, midnight breakfasts, communal coed bathrooms, and keg parties. It's easy to make friends when you all live on the same floor, drink too much cheap vodka, and have no responsibilities.

Postcollege all my friends migrated, lemminglike, to New York, and my circle, my community, the people cheering for my well-being, continued unbroken for the next twelve years. I left all of that behind when I moved to San Francisco.

A few weeks before we left for Africa we'd had a high school friend of mine and her husband over for brunch. They lived an hour outside of San Francisco and it was the first time I'd seen them since I moved to the West Coast.

"So, do you have friends here?" Karen asked me casually.

"Nope. None," I replied with a force and a touch of bitterness I hadn't expected.

"Yes, you do, Squeaky," Nick interjected. I looked at him and thought about the argument we had when I returned from Israel, the one where he told me maybe it was my fault I didn't have any friends.

"I have Nick's friends," I said. For good measure I added, "And they're great."

But it wasn't the same. When Nick went out of town for work, I was on my own with Lady Piazza, wishing I had someone to go to dinner with, someone who wasn't brand-new but comfortable and already broken in. As I looked around at the Maasai women, joking and laughing and fixing one another's beaded necklaces to place them in a pretty pattern around their long slender necks, picking up one another's babies with no mind for who belonged to whom, I mourned the friendships I'd left behind. I missed my girlfriends from New York and Philadelphia every day, and not having them around made me lean on my husband more than I wanted to. I felt needy and vulnerable. I hadn't realized how desperate I was for a strong community until right then.

This is the part where you tell me to cue the violins. I'm complaining about being lonely just months after meeting and marrying the man of my dreams. But despite the vow I'd made in Bobby Klein's office to build my own life and network of friends in San Francisco, I hadn't gotten very far. It wasn't that I wasn't trying. Making new friends in your thirties is harder than making it to work on time in your twenties. I frequently loitered after yoga class to chat with the instructors, but so far only movie-soundtrack enthusiast Roy remembered my name, and sometimes he called me Jill. I'd gone to a women-only empowerment retreat down the coast in Big Sur filled with karmic chanting, talking sticks, and intentional breathing. I'd enrolled in all kinds of other classes, including but not limited to knitting, ikebana (the Japanese art of flower arranging), pizza making, and even pickling (even though I worried Nick's ex-girlfriend would be the instructor). I struck up conversations with strangers in my Uber Pool. I'd gotten recommendations for a dentist, a landscaper, and a psychic, but no one who wanted to have wine with me on a Friday night.

I was set up on friend dates with friends of friends, one of whom got blind drunk, texted her ex-husband the entire night, and then tried to kiss me. I met people all the time who said, "Let's get dinner" or "Let's grab a drink." I promptly e-mailed or texted them with available times and possible locations.

Then, silence.

Why do people say they want to get dinner or drinks if they don't really mean it?

Things looked promising after a couple of girl dates with women I met through work. One of them was cool and shared my love of travel, food, and red wine. We had a good rapport. This was exactly what I'd been waiting for. But I got too eager. I hugged her too hard at the end of dinner. "Call me," I said in a desperate tone. She never called.

....

I didn't want to leave Naropil's house. I wanted to stay with these women a little bit longer to remember what it felt like to have a community of women around me, a lady squad. I could hear the others outside singing and laughing. Naropil squeezed my arm in a motherly way, as if she could tell what I was thinking. I realized that she might be younger than I was, even though it seemed like she'd lived a dozen lifetimes more. I wanted to tell her everything that was happening to me. *I'm scared. I'm sick. I'm lonely.* I hadn't told any of my friends these things, not even my news about my muscular dystrophy. It's a strange thing to say over text message, and no one gets on the phone anymore without exchanging at least a dozen text messages about when might be a good time to talk.

I could hardly make out Naropil's face in the dark room, but I could see her lips move into a smile as she prepared to say goodbye.

"You can always come back."

Four days later we left the Maasai Mara by a rickety four-seater plane for Samburuland in northern Kenya, arriving on an airstrip that was nothing more than a thin clearing of the shrubbery where a herd of zebra, unconcerned by the plane's engines, whinnied a welcome as we landed. I choked on the hot red dirt that spun like a top into the air when we stepped onto the runway. We were staying at a family-owned and -operated ranch called Ol Malo, where our hosts were a newly married couple named Andrew and Chyulu, white Africans who had both grown up in the bush. The couple lived with Piper, their ginger-haired toddler with a predilection for camel milk, and their five-hundred-pound pet pig named Sausage.

Nick and I slept in a tree house perched on a ridge looking down into a rocky valley that could have been Arizona if it hadn't been for the white-bellied zebras running below and the elephants that crashed into the vegetable garden. The equator ran right below us, and during the day the maroon-tinted earth was as hot as the surface of the sun.

Northern Kenya has been home to the Samburu people, who like the Maasai are nomadic cattle herders, for thousands of years. They are also polygamous, and men can have as many wives as they can financially support. Samburu marriage is also arranged based on factors that do not include love. The Samburu often maintain sexual relationships with their boyfriends and girlfriends after their marriage to another person. This is socially acceptable as long as no one gets pregnant. They ensure this using various techniques from the rhythm method to condoms to discreet forms of oral contraceptives.

And while the Samburu are technically patriarchal, the women are silent leaders. "They [the women] are the elephants. A herd of elephants is ruled by the women, and the Samburu women are matriarchs in their own way," Julia Francombe, the founder of the Samburu Trust, told me. "They are so strong. Their husbands beat them and they shake it off. They will do whatever it takes for their families and for their children. They help one another. They *really* help one another."

"We keep no secrets from each other," a Samburu woman my mother's age named Mama Bee said to me during a beading workshop Julia took me to in the Laikipia Highlands of northern Kenya.

Mama Bee sat higher than the other ladies, poised on a table with her long bare legs dangling below her a couple inches shy of the ground. The rest of the women sat on the floor, their bare feet stretched in front of them on cowskins. I was captivated by their feet. They were so different from my own. These feet did work. They walked more than twenty kilometers a day. They could withstand the prick of the sharp acacia needle. Their nails were hard and thick and had never seen a drop of paint. This was where the Samburu mamas gathered away from the Samburu men. Run by the Samburu Trust, the jewelry workshop was the hub of commerce and socialization for these women. This was where they traded beads, where they gossiped, where they borrowed money. They chattered away about their kids and their husbands and who had bought a new motorbike and where did he get the money for that motorbike and whose daughter was about to marry whose son and whether or not that was a good thing or a bad thing. When I arrived, the women couldn't stop talking about the girl who'd married a warrior they referred to as B.

"She's terrible," one woman said.

"Awful," another agreed.

"Mean and hateful."

"And ugly. So ugly."

"Why did he marry her?" I asked in disbelief.

I expected them to shake their heads in confusion and tell me they didn't know why B would marry someone so horrible, but Mama Bee knew the answer.

"She's so good at taking care of the goats."

The women make jewelry and trinkets and beadwork, really nice stuff, not the junk you find in the Nairobi airport. Children as small as a few weeks were quiet at their mothers' breasts. Older kids ran in circles, playing at being warriors.

With cool efficiency Mama Bee used a squat, short knife to cut through a band of leather to make beaded coasters for the tourists. "I share everything with these women." She swept her arms in a wide arc.

I stared at Mama Bee's beads. You can tell a Samburu woman's life story by reading her jewelry. When a warrior takes a wife, he doesn't give her a ring. He buys a chain from the local spear maker. She loops this chain through one of her many earrings and around her neck. She will wear it until her husband dies and then remove it forever.

The Samburu women brought Nick a chain to give to me and fashioned an earring for me out of a stray piece of copper.

Nick tried to place it in my ear but the women clucked and brushed him away. While the chain symbolized *our* marriage, these women felt it was their job to make sure I wore it properly.

"Now you have to slaughter a cow," one of the women said to my husband.

Nick was adamant that he did not want to slaughter a cow.

"It's okay, honey," I said to Nick. "You can go to the silly expensive organic grocery store in San Francisco and buy me some hormone-free grass-fed beef when we get home."

You can tell a woman is the mother of a warrior if she has two long strands of beads running down from the chain of one of her ears. You can tell she's the mother of twins if she is wearing cowrie shells in her large beaded collar. Different beads indicate if she has delivered a baby by a breech birth, if she's had a miscarriage, or if she's barren. You can even tell if a bull cow was properly slaughtered at her wedding. Other things are more personal. Beneath the decorative beads are strings of blue or green prayer beads, one for each of her children, each one holding a piece of her child's umbilical cord.

On her wedding day the bride wears a necklace, woven by the other women in the village from giraffe tails to symbolize joining her life with the rest of the tribe, particularly with the women.

"The women all take care of one another," Mama Bee said. "If I give birth, the other women take care of my children. They do my chores. They cook for me. They are there for me. I love these women."

"What about your husband?" I asked. "Do you love your husband?"

Mama Bee considered it.

"After you have babies you start to love your husband. You don't know him before that. Once you have the babies, you say, 'Okay, now I know you. Now I love you.'"

It made sense that these women would take their time learning to love their husband. I loved Nick now. I really did. But even though we'd chosen to marry each other, that love was still so brand-new that part of it had to be infatuation. It wasn't the good times that made me love Nick more; it was the hard times. It was the past few months that had turned our love into something different, something more real.

When a young Samburu wife is brought to her husband's village for the first time, she is handed a baby to take care of. It's someone else's baby, but she treats it like her own for a time and this helps her bond with her new community. "She goes directly from being the child of her mother to being a mother," Mama Bee said. She lives with that baby and her husband's mother, sometimes for as long as a year. In the Samburu tribes the mother-in-law decides when a new wife is ready to consummate her marriage.

Mama Bee grabbed me by the crook of my elbow to introduce me to a group of children playing in the dirt outside.

"All of them call all of us Mama." I raised my eyebrows in a question and she went on to explain. Once a Samburu woman gives birth, she takes on the name Mama, joined by the name of her firstborn. Mama Bee gets her name from her firstborn son, Beesus.

"All the women take care of all the children like their own," she said. This sounded idyllic in comparison to the $3,000 a month for daycare in San Francisco.

I told Mama Bee I liked her name. In fact, Bee was the name I wanted to give to a little girl if we ever had one, Bee, short for Beatrix, named after Nick's grandmother and Beatrice, the older sister in my favorite children's book, *Beezus and Ramona*.

"So if I have a daughter, then I will be Mama Bee too," I said.

"It's a good name," Mama Bee assured me as she bade the two of us good-bye.

I gazed at the toddlers. Five of my friends had given birth in the past six months, and I hadn't met a single one of the babies.

"I want to go home for a while," I said to Nick later that night. "Not home San Francisco. Home to New York. Just for a week or so. I want to be with my family and my friends."

If there was one thing our new marriage was lacking it was this—this kind of strong community, a support system to help brace it when things get tough.

"You know we can live wherever you want. We don't have to stay in San Francisco," Nick said.

I nodded. I knew. But we had bought a house and both our jobs were in San Francisco. Still, it was nice to know that we might not be there forever, that maybe once we did have kids, we'd go back to a place where we had more of a community to help us raise them. Sitting on the plane later that week, ready to make the thirty-six-hour journey home, I wrote an e-mail to my five closest girlfriends.

> Hey you and you and you and you and you.
>
> I suck. I'm sorry I've been so out of touch since I left. Planning a wedding, getting married, moving across the country, buying a house . . . it takes a lot out of you, but those aren't excuses.
>
> I miss you. I miss you guys so much.

And I need you.

Last month I found out I have the same gene for muscular dystrophy as my dad. Don't freak out. I'm OK and Nick is being amazing and we're going to figure this out. We don't know much, but we know there's no reason to worry right now.

Maybe I'm not OK, but I'm no longer curled up on the floor in a ball crying . . . baby steps.

I'm coming to terms with it, but it's scary and no matter what happens I want you to know about it, because I need you.

Love you,

Jo

P.S. I'm excited for all the new babies in our lives. Your kids are all welcome to call me Mama.

10

Holland

You Didn't Marry Your Job

> Things which matter most must never be at the mercy of things which matter least.
>
> —JOHANN WOLFGANG VON GOETHE

We were flying over the choppy and icy waters of the Arctic when Nick began watching a video clip of the comedian Chris Rock. The most important thing about being a husband, according to Rock, who was married for eighteen years before his 2014 divorce, is waking up every morning and making sure your wife is happy.

Of course, he said it in a much more elegant way.

> Fellas, when you wake up in the morning, you should look yourself in the mirror and say, "*Fuck you!* Fuck your hopes, fuck your dreams, fuck your plans. . . . Fuck everything you thought this life was going to bring to you. Now let's go out there and try to make this bitch happy."

Nick laughed loud enough to make the people around us uncomfortable, wiping tears from his eyes.

"You're distracting me," I muttered as I stared out the plane window at a particularly large cluster of icebergs. "I'm trying to spot a polar bear." If I squinted hard enough I was sure I could see them down there, each one on its own ice floe hunting for fish. I stared intently at white and blue nothingness and then closed the window.

"Do you feel that way?" I asked Nick after I leaned in for his second viewing of the Chris Rock video. "Do you feel like it's your job to make me happy?"

Nick hesitated. "Sometimes. Yeah. Sometimes making you happy feels like it is my full-time job."

....

I didn't feel much like laughing at Chris Rock. I didn't feel like laughing at anything. The truth was I was flailing, and nothing Nick did or could do was going to make it better. I'd become a very disagreeable person to live with, the kind of person you'd avoid on the street if given the choice because she was often frowning and muttering things to herself. But poor Nick didn't have any choice but to continue to wake up in bed next to me every day, and now we were stuck together on an airplane traveling to Holland for a conference. It was Nick's conference, not mine, but he'd wanted me there with him—an example, I know, of his efforts to make me happy.

In what the press described as a "bloodbath of layoffs," I'd been let go from my job at Yahoo! I first learned I was laid off over text message, which I supposed was better than a Post-it. The higher-ups said things like "I want you all to know this is for the good of the company," like we were Greenpeace laboring to save the whales from extinction rather than an old-school Internet behemoth laboring to please our shareholders. My only contact with the company postlayoff had been the delivery of a padded box in which I was supposed to mail back my phone and laptop computer.

Being out of work was daunting for many reasons. We'd just

bought our apartment, which completely drained my savings account. Nick and I had both been on my Yahoo! health insurance, and it was damn expensive and I had a weird genetic disease, which meant we should have damn expensive insurance. We'd procured newer and cheaper health insurance that had a $65 copay and a $10,000 deductible, which we soon learned didn't cover the kinds of specialists I would need going forward.

But more than that, I was a person who defined herself by her job. It was the thing I talked about when I met new people. Working was how I occupied most of my days. Since I'd met Nick, I'd been working eighty-five hours a week, which had come to seem normal. That's what the Internet has done to us. It's made us all feel as though we have to be "on call" all the time. Studies have even shown that more and more women are working themselves to death—literally. According to research from Ohio State and the Mayo Clinic, women who work more than forty hours per week are at much greater risk for things like heart disease, cancer, arthritis, and diabetes.

I slept clutching my phone and had a panic attack if I found myself somewhere without it, including the bathroom, which is just gross. This was the third company I had worked for that laid people off because it was going under. I couldn't help but wonder why I kept devoting myself to, killing myself for, companies where both I and the company were disposable. But now I was doing nothing, and I had no idea what to do next.

Everyone I told about my layoff said pretty much the same thing: "You're going to get a bigger job right away, a better job." Bigger and better meaning more money and more hours. I'd nod politely at them because they said it out of kindness and confidence in me. But no offers came in, and the truth was there weren't enough hours in a week for something bigger.

Nick wanted me to take a beat and think, really think, about what I wanted to do next.

"I'm a little thrilled about your layoff," he said and then backtracked. "For you. I'm thrilled for you in the long run. How much longer can you run on empty? I'd love to see you work less, relax, take bike rides, and learn to enjoy your life outside work a little more. Find something where you can have a better work/life balance." What the hell did that mean?

When it came to the concept of work/life balance, I had few good role models. Most of my friends dedicated their own lives to their careers, at least until they burned out. Many times, to the detriment of my health and past relationships, I'd worn my busyness and work title like badges of honor, believing if I didn't keep straining for that brass ring I'd be a failure.

As I sat around the house in my pajamas refreshing LinkedIn to see who looked at my profile, I Googled things like "work AND happiness AND fulfilled." Google's answer was the Netherlands.

Like Denmark, the Netherlands is a place that consistently ranks among the top five happiest countries in the world and where couples claim some of the most satisfying long-term relationships. The *New York Times* once reported that the "Dutch as a nation emerge close to the top of the world happiness rankings established by Ruut Veenhoven, professor of social conditions for human happiness at Erasmus University in Rotterdam. On a scale of 1 to 10, where 10 signals greatest life satisfaction, the Dutch score 7.5—beating 6.5 for the French and 6.2 for the Japanese. They also defeat Americans with 6.4, the British with 7.1, and the Italians and Spanish who each total 6.9."

I'd also heard from my Dutch friends that one of the causes of this elevated level of happiness was that Dutch women give zero fucks about other people thinking they have it all. They don't let their careers dictate their relationships or their family life. The majority of Dutch women, married or not, choose to work part-time in order to have more time for their marriage, their children, their hobbies, and their personal well-being. In 2011 nearly 75 percent of working Dutch women were employed part-time. Many of my Americans girlfriends scoffed at this. They'd never dream of working part-time. They'd call that giving up, or worse, failure. But, Dutch women call the decision liberating and they don't see their choice as bucking the feminist system.

"Every woman in Holland can do whatever she wants with her life," fifty-two-year-old Marie-Louise van Haeren explained in an interview with *Maclean's* magazine about how Dutch women got to be among the happiest people in the world.

Van Haeren described an idyllic existence filled with choices, where she rides her bike to work three days a week. She and almost all of her friends work part-time their entire careers in order "to have time to do things that matter to me, live the way I want. To stay mentally and physically healthy and happy. . . . Maybe this will turn out to be the fourth wave of feminism. Women protect the possibility that one day we'll wake up to realize that life is not all about acquiring more material wealth, power, status. Many Dutch women that I know want to stay sane, happy, relaxed."

It's worth pointing out that the Netherlands has a strong government safety net in place that helps to make things like health care, retirement, and child care more affordable. That makes it much easier for women to choose to work part-time. Many women in the United States still have no choice but to work at least one job, sometimes more, just to pay their bills, feed their families, and keep a roof over their heads.

But there are also plenty of women and men in the States who *choose* to allow our careers to dictate our lives—where we live, how we live, how often we see our spouse, how often we see our kids, and even how we define ourselves. This often happens after we've reached a certain level of career achievement or as a result of having been born with a certain level of privilege. Among my own friends, you were considered a failure if you didn't try to "have it all."

Because of our jobs we often come home late at night, moody and irritable. Because of our jobs we don't have enough time to work out or eat well, leading to chronic and costly health problems down the road. Because of our jobs we often live thousands of miles from our families and supportive communities.

The best decisions for our careers will often trump the best outcome for our marriages.

What if it didn't have to be that way? What if we could find space in our lives for ourselves, our marriages, and our careers?

....

Nick was pleased the moment we arrived in Amsterdam.

"I'm going to take you on a little date. It will be rainy, but it'll be nice. We could live here, Squeak. It's a very civilized country." Of course, Nick is wildly optimistic that we could live anywhere together, while I believe that if we permanently left New York or San Francisco we would die.

"They bike everywhere. Look at all those wind turbines. And the train system is excellent."

My first steps inside the city of Amsterdam brought me face to face with study-abroad stoners stumbling out of the city's many coffee shops (places to smoke weed that have nothing to do with coffee) and drunken hordes of men with beer bellies and bald heads screaming in the streets during their stag parties. I narrowly dodged a drunken bachelor Brit wearing a red thong bikini before he puked Heineken into the gutter, his mates cheering him on and filming him for posterity.

"You want sexy time?" a strange Turkish man said to lure us into a sex show where he promised topless women would do elaborate and confusing things with bananas. After our thirteen-hour overnight flight from San Francisco I couldn't imagine that I looked like the kind of person in search of sexy time, but what do I know?

"No, thanks! We're heading to the Anne Frank Museum," Nick said with polite cheer.

I did like Amsterdam. It was like Paris but smaller, cooler, and less pretentious. Once we'd escaped the main tourist zone for the classically Dutch streets farther from the train station, the ones with the impossible-to-pronounce names that all sounded like warm, delicious pastries, I couldn't help but begin to buy into the promise of

Dutch happiness. Nick and I took great pleasure in sounding out all of the words, with their excess of vowels and silent consonants. I liked that the walls were free from graffiti and that the city was clean—immaculate, in fact—save for that chap who vomited in the gutter. But even he was really polite about it.

Small signs of gender equality appear all over the city. The yellow "child crossing" signs on the street have a photo of a man holding a child's hand rather than a woman. All of the bathrooms, even the ones in very small restaurants, have a box of free tampons in them. If that doesn't scream, *We respect your equality and womanhood*, I don't know what does. A popular T-shirt shop was selling out of a shirt emblazoned with the words "He offered her the world. She said she had her own." Waiters handed me the check as often as they handed it to Nick.

Dutch women may not be the breadwinners, but they are often the decision makers in their relationships. Equality is less of a battle in Holland, where it is ingrained in the culture, than in the States. Women's rights are well established here, participation in the labor force is high, and there is a legal system in place to give women equal opportunities. It's a system that breeds independent women who are less dependent on the institution of marriage. But beneath the fierce independence is an even fiercer love of family and a sense of practicality focused on keeping the family unit strong. As in Denmark, there's a different value attached to the marriage contract in Holland than in a lot of countries, particularly in America. It's common for the Dutch to live together and have kids well before they actually get married. Like the Danish, they rarely throw a huge wedding or any kind of large to-do. When people do get married, they don't do it out of any sense of obligation. It's a very conscious decision, since it's as acceptable to cohabitate for twenty or thirty years without the pressure to make anything legally binding.

"We'd have a boat if we lived here," Nick said, bouncing up and down on his heels as we strolled along the canals. "A party boat with a grill and a bar, or—oooooo!—a houseboat. We could live on a boat." Dutch houseboats come in all shapes and sizes—tiny green and red ones no larger than a tugboat and elaborate floating mansions with sleek modern lines. Amsterdam's canals are storybook wonderful, like moats, really, winding around the four-hundred-year-old townhouses that lean at precarious angles from age and sinking soil. More bikes than cars cruised the streets. But these weren't the hardcore road bikers I'd grown used to in San Francisco. Dutch bikes are heavy and tall, allowing you to sit perfectly straight and poised. Dutch women look stunning while riding them, their long blond hair streaming behind them.

"They're all wearing sensible shoes." Nick admired the ladies commuting to and from work. "And see how lovely they look."

I rolled my eyes. "I can ride my bike in high heels," I said, which was partially true.

They do look lovely, though, and confident. And happy.

....

"Dutch women are terrifying," Alice, one of Nick's female colleagues who lives in the Netherlands, warned while we were out drinking blond beers in a bar along the Amstel River. Alice is half Dutch and half British and lives outside of Amsterdam in the nearby city of Haarlem. "I'm part Dutch so I can tell you that. They're bossy and determined and fiercely independent." They sounded like my kind of ladies.

And Nick's too. "I'm not intimidated at all," he said about the strong-minded Dutch women, ordering a second beer from a particularly bossy lady bartender. "I like assertive women. I want a woman who tells me how it is!" The bartender smirked.

I asked Alice if Dutch women's fierceness carried over into the workplace. She paused for a second to consider the question. Alice had a career as a very successful executive at a Dutch company.

"There aren't as many women executives here as there could be. I'd like to see more," she said. "But most women here value their life outside of work much more than they value a title or getting ahead in the workplace." Alice shrugged. She was divorced with two kids. "It's nice that women here can make that choice. But I worry that we aren't encouraging ambition enough."

Alice never once asked me what I did for work. We spent the rest of the night talking about my recent foray into planting seasonal vegetables, the upcoming American election, and whether hot yoga was better than regular yoga.

This was very different from the cocktail-party conversations I'd been having back home. Right before we left for Amsterdam, Nick and I attended an event for his company, where I learned that not having a job felt weird and even alienating in San Francisco.

"What do you *do*?" people asked me politely, since that is the first thing everyone asks you at an American party. I stumbled. I'd always relished talking about my fancy job. Now I didn't know what to say.

"I'm in between jobs, doing some writing, fixing up the house," I said in a small voice. Nick introduced me to one of the public-relations executives he worked with. She was a lot like the PR girls I knew back in New York, dressed entirely in black, with straight, shiny hair and a confident swagger. She was interested in planning a honeymoon to Africa, so I told her we could maybe have lunch and talk about it. She threw her head back and let out a cackle.

"Ha. Ha. You think I have time for lunch. Oh God, I never have time for lunch." I suddenly felt very sad for a woman who didn't have time for lunch. I remembered being that woman.

Spend a night out in the Netherlands, swing by a canal-side bar or a dinner party, and start talking to the Dutch. No one will ask you what you do. I don't think anyone asked me about my job the entire time I was in Holland, unless I was the one to bring it up first.

"The Dutch attach a slightly different value to their careers and money than British and American people. They are slightly less materialistic. They put much more of an emphasis on family and quality time, and they'll ask you about those things at parties. They don't care how you make money," Ben Coates, the author of the book *Why the Dutch Are Different*, told me. His book was selling like crazy when I arrived in Amsterdam, and I couldn't help but pluck one off the towering piles of them in the WHSmith in the Schiphol airport. Coates is originally from the UK, but he fell in love with a Dutch girl and never left.

When I mentioned to one Dutch woman that I used to work six days a week at my last job, and sometimes a few extra hours on Sunday, she looked at me with horror, her un-Botoxed brow furrowing in disbelief. "You Americans love talking about how busy you are with work. Does it make you feel important?" She said this without malice, with genuine curiosity. I'd grown used to the Dutch bluntness from the moment the woman who stamped my passport at the airport remarked that I was prettier as a blonde. "When do you have time to see your husband?" Then she added with greater gravitas, "Or do yoga?"

"They think we're crazy," I said to Nick later that night. Despite the fact that neither of us was particularly interested in smoking weed, curiosity had gotten the better of us and we'd decided to try smoking a legal joint in one of the city's coffee shops. Being a naturally anxious person, I was particular about which of the coffee shops we gave our business to. My ground rules were that it had to be clean, have nice lighting, have no photographs or paintings of Bob Marley on the walls, and not be decorated in the manner of an Eastern European youth hostel.

"Don't you think we're a little crazy?" Nick said, looking down at the menu, which offered five-euro individual joints and a seven-euro space cake. "Seventy-five percent of your stress and our arguments start because of something to do with work. Don't you think it makes more sense to actually create a work/life balance instead of just talking about it all the time?"

We smoked about half a joint, decided we might be too old for this shit, and walked back to our Airbnb rental, which was really an attic, up two flights of steep and narrow stairs that were really ladders. Our attic was so cold at night we had to curl into each other under two comforters to stay warm. I moved as close to Nick as humanly possible. The two of us talked about the concept of work/life balance for the next couple of hours, coming to the conclusion that Americans blather on a great deal about the topic but rarely take concrete actions to find better balance. We write and read articles about it, we buy books to help us try to rearrange our too-busy schedules, we fill our Sundays with dread and unhappiness over the prospect of Monday morning. But we rarely choose to do anything that actually solves the problem.

We agreed on the fact that both of us too often prioritized our jobs over our marriage.

The next day I chatted with a Dutch friend of a friend named Marieke. She's been married for fifteen years and has two beautiful daughters. When her girls were young, she and her husband figured out a system where they both worked four days a week.

"It was the most fantastic way of living. It allowed us to prioritize both our family and ourselves," Marieke told me. "Dutch men don't worry that if they aren't working for five days a week they aren't a good man. It is totally okay. In fact, it is better than okay. We know it's better for us to enjoy our lives. We may earn less money, but we figure that out and the rewards are much greater. We don't define ourselves by our jobs. We define ourselves by our relationships and what we do to feel fulfilled."

Now that her girls are a little bit older, Marieke works three and a half days a week and her husband works five, since his current job is less flexible.

"Now that I work less, I am the manager in the house. I oversee a lot of the housework and the children, but we still share most of those things. He is still doing much of the grocery shopping and the housecleaning. I picked my husband because he doesn't see men and women as any different. Together we will raise our girls as independent feminist women, and for me feminism means making the right choices for yourself and your family."

My best friend, Jackie, surprised me with her response to the Dutch. Jackie is one of the most ambitious women I know, a lawyer who was climbing the ranks of a prestigious law school when she was pregnant with her third child. A couple months shy of her due date, she asked her boss if they could work out an arrangement that would allow her to work from home a couple of days a week following her (very short) maternity leave.

"My boss made me feel bad for even asking," Jackie said. She quit on the spot. At eight months pregnant she launched her own legal recruiting business so she'd have the flexibility to work more convenient hours.

"I think I'd like Holland!" Jackie texted me while I was in Amsterdam. "We've been force-fed this notion that feminists work and achieve and impress other people with their job titles and accomplishments. Why can't feminism mean I have the freedom to prioritize what I want without the judgment of other (ambitious) ladies? What is ambition anyway? Can't I be ambitious with my kids and my marriage?"

I have another set of American friends who have gone a different direction in terms of careers and made it work for them. When she got pregnant she was a rising star in tech and he was in a corporate job he hated. He quit and stayed home to take care of the baby and work on a business plan for his start-up. About two years later, her company started going under and he got a great job offer. They traded places and career ambitions. She took care of their toddler and worked on a book. They've been going back and forth ever since, allowing one spouse time to follow a dream or take care of the family, while the other brings home a regular paycheck. I've heard this referred to as the stock and bond approach to the marital division of labor. One spouse has to be the bond, the one without risk, with a dependable payout. If that's the case, the other can be the stock, focusing on something that could pay off big in the long-term. Of course it's only fair if the partners keep switching who is the stock and who is the bond.

Dutch women *are* fierce, independent, and ambitious. They just use that ambition to craft a life rather than a career path. That did seem like a feminist choice to me.

There's so much talk about women trying to have it all. That "all" is ambiguous and ever shifting. It can include the perfect marriage, a successful *and* fulfilling career, a happy family, and a healthy mind and body to boot. It often includes children but doesn't have to.

There's less talk about how the hell to do it, how to juggle everything, and what trying to have it all can do to a marriage.

I had no idea what I was going to do next. It wouldn't be easy for our family to live on one salary; in fact, it would be nearly impossible. Plus, I didn't want to define myself as a wife. I love working. It's not that I wanted to check out of the workforce. I just wanted to reset. And if the time ever came, I wanted Nick to have that option too. The only thing I did know is that I didn't want my next job to dictate my life or my marriage. I'd said in Denmark that Nick and I had to stop existing like two business travelers who happened to wind up in the same place once in a while. I wanted a career that I loved without killing myself and my relationship to have it. There had to be a way to achieve something closer to the reality of a work/life balance.

"It's not your job to make me happy," I said to myself as much as to Nick as I picked at a plate of *frites* at a café along one of the canals. "At the most, it should be a pleasurable hobby, like fantasy football or orienteering."

Nick nodded in agreement. "You're right. Do you know what orienteering is?"

"No. But that isn't the point. I think it involves a compass and birds. Anyway, it *is* my job to make myself happy. I'm just trying to figure out what that means right now."

11

India

A Little Thanks Goes a Long Way

I am beginning to learn that it is the sweet, simple things of life which are the real ones after all.

—Laura Ingalls Wilder

Boondi, a petite and shriveled woman of indeterminate age with leathery skin the color of a ripe coconut, held both of my hands inside her tiny wrinkled ones.

"When my husband died, he said to me, 'Bye-bye. I am going. But I will come back again for you,'" Boondi said, grinning through lips stained orange from the betel nuts she chewed on all day long. She said "bye-bye" in a high-pitched singsong. Boondi married her husband when she was fifteen. When I met her she thought she was ninety, but she wasn't sure.

We stood on a muddy road in Boondi's rural village in northeastern India on the banks of the Brahmaputra River, and she wasn't going to let go of my hand. The touch was warm and comforting. The only thing that made me nervous was that the boat I'd taken to reach this remote location would float away in less than twenty minutes. I needed that boat to eventually find my way back to New Delhi. I'd been on my way back to the boat after sightseeing at the town's modest temple when Boondi provoked my fascination.

I'd been walking through rain, nudged every few steps by defiant cows crowding the streets, when Boondi's laugh caught my attention. It was a laugh too large for a such a small person, and it rippled through her belly, which played peekaboo from beneath her dark violet sari. I beckoned my translator to stop walking. Boondi and her two friends, both as old and stooped as she was, immediately wanted to take a selfie with me on my phone. Everyone in India wants to take selfies with white strangers. I obliged her and promised to send the picture through Facebook to her great-grandson. Boondi was very proud of her great-grandson and his prowess on social media. She asked if I was married, if I had children, if I wanted to have children, and if my husband was in India with me. I nodded yes, no, yes, and no. Then she told me about her own marriage.

Boondi spit the betel nut out of her mouth before continuing. "My husband and I were very happy. I was very happy because my husband loved me. He loved me and we had enough food and we had many children. We never had a bad moment. If you have a husband who loves you, then you need to be thankful for that. You need thanks to make a marriage work." Boondi was saying this through a double translation from the local Assamese language into Hindi and then into English, but I was pretty sure I was getting it right. When she smiled at me I noticed most of her teeth were missing and her gums shimmered, soft and pink like a baby's. Wrinkles carved canyons in a face burnished with the wisdom and heartache of age.

"When he came home every day, I made sure I fed him and I gave him massage when he was sore and tired. Do you massage your husband?"

I don't. I almost always ask Nick to rub my head or my shoulders when I'm cranky and tired. He knows exactly where to dig his thumb in between my shoulder blades to release all the tension from hunching over my laptop for hours at a time.

I made a mental note to learn how to give better shoulder massages.

"How'd you meet your husband?" I asked her.

She batted her eyelashes like it was a silly thing to ask. "My parents talked to his parents and we decided to get married." It was simple and straightforward. But Boondi was no dummy. She had a great-grandson who was a master of the Internet. Her village had satellite dishes on nearly every roof. She knew Americans could be skeptical about arranged marriages.

"I know what you're thinking," she said. "But I did love him very much. True love. The love of a good marriage always comes later, and I don't care what anyone else says."

Boondi squeezed my hand with determination. "You are young and strong and healthy. If you have a good husband and he has a good family, you should appreciate it. If you have these things, you must be thankful. To be thankful is most important. To say you are thankful and mean it. *Teekay*?" she asked. *Teekay* is the Indian equivalent of "okay" or "understand?" "*Teekay*," I responded. Nick and I had plenty of things to make us happy. We had a roof over our heads and food, and we loved each other very much. We should be thankful. We should be happy.

The old woman hugged me, clasping me firmly around my waist, the bottom of her head barely grazing my shoulders. I carefully hugged her back, afraid if I squeezed too tight I'd break her delicate bones.

"My husband and I were so happy!" She looked up at me and her light eyes, the color of the muddy Brahmaputra, sparkled. "You are happy too. I know it."

....

Did I need to go all the way to one of the least visited areas of India to understand how important gratitude is for my marriage? It felt kind of silly to travel thousands of miles from home, in cars, trains, planes, and boats, just to realize my life was already pretty goddamned sweet and that I should appreciate it.

It's not that I didn't hear about the many virtues of gratitude at home in San Francisco. I did. All the time. So often, in fact, that I was a little over the idea of gratitude. Not actual gratitude, but the unintentional abuse of the word. Sometime in the past ten years everyone in San Francisco started talking like a yoga instructor. You can hardly show up at a dinner party without the host heaving a belly sigh and announcing, "I want to begin this meal with gratitude." The checkout clerk who sold us our organic vegetables smiled with gratitude for the radishes we'd just purchased from him and my dog walker once left me a list of five reasons he was grateful for Lady Piazza. San Francisco is also a city where people will tell you without irony that sauerkraut changed their lives, so I don't take any of it too seriously, and after all, their hearts are in the right place. But I still wanted something that felt more genuine: showing gratitude instead of peacocking about it.

Researchers tell us gratitude—the practice of showing appreciation, saying thanks, sending a text that says, "What you did was amaze-balls"—is an integral part of any healthy relationship, especially as couples waltz further and further away from the honeymoon stage and into the slog of real life. Scientists at the University of Georgia once surveyed 468 married people and found that gratitude could consistently predict how happy someone was in their marriage. "Even if a couple is experiencing distress and difficulty in other areas, gratitude in the relationship can help promote positive marital outcomes," said the study's lead author, Allen Barton, a postdoctoral research associate at UGA's Center for Family Research. In another study Dr. Amie Gordon, a psychologist from UC Berkeley, asked fifty committed couples to fill out appreciation journals. The couples who were successful in conveying ongoing appreciation were less likely to break up in the next nine months. The researchers reported that a nourishing cycle of encouragement helped to develop more trust and respect.

Dr. Gordon found the "highly appreciative" couples were ones who openly expressed their gratitude, listened to each other actively, and touched each other appreciatively. She also found that having gratitude in a relationship isn't a static thing. It's not something you simply have or don't have. Gratitude is a skill that can be learned and cultivated.

Peter Pearson of the Couples Institute in Palo Alto gives his patients a thirty-day task called the Daily Double. It's simple. Each person has to say something that makes their partner feel good or improves their partner's life two times a day. These can be little things like "Honey, I appreciate when you take out the garbage" or "You look sexy in that gray T-shirt." They can be expressions of thanks or admiration, and they can come in person or over e-mail, Skype, or text. I asked if a thumbs-up kissy-face emoji could suffice. Pearson reluctantly said yes.

....

After nearly a year of marriage, I still loved most things about Nick Aster, but as we now struggled to make ends meet and shuttled among endless doctor's appointments, it was more and more difficult to keep that in perspective, to feel thankful on a daily basis.

The most recent doctor's appointment before I left for India had been particularly challenging. Nick and I met with a neurologist to figure out whether the muscular dystrophy had already started degrading my muscles.

"Can you whistle?" the doctor asked me.

"No. But I've never been able to whistle," I replied.

"Can you shut your eyes really tight and then open them quickly?"

"Yes."

Determining the severity of my disease required a battery of tests that mostly involved making strange faces.

"Because this kind of muscular dystrophy affects the facial muscles, people often have a hard time smiling, and so people often think they're unhappy," the neurologist said. "Do people often think you are unhappy?"

"So you're saying a symptom of this kind of muscular dystrophy is resting bitch face?" I asked. My posture collapsed, causing me to slump lower into my chair. Weren't strangers on the street always telling me to smile more? I should have known all along that something was gravely wrong with me, but I bit the inside of my cheek to keep my sarcasm at bay. Nick could tell I was agitated and cast me a look that said, *Bear with the guy and we'll get ice cream after this.* I shot him a look back that said, *We're gonna need a big spoon.*

"How's your arm strength?" the doctor asked.

"I can do a handstand. I did one in yoga yesterday, for about forty-five seconds. Okay, maybe thirty seconds," I volunteered eagerly, wanting to provide pieces of information that would make him jump up and exclaim, "By God, how could we all have been so wrong? If this woman can do a handstand for thirty seconds, then there's no way she has muscular dystrophy!"

The doctor scribbled silently on a notepad.

"But I suck at push-ups," I added. "Is that a symptom?" The night before I had dug out a twenty-pound weight from behind piles of boxes in our basement, gripped it with both hands, and lifted it over my head for twenty repetitions, grunting with the intensity of an MMA fighter. I made a mental pact with myself to do this every day. The day when I couldn't do it anymore, when lifting twenty pounds over my head twenty times was too much, would be the day I started to worry.

In the doctor's office Nick squeezed my leg, causing me to look down at my pants. Nick called them my backpacker pants. They were a thin cotton with intricate blue and white elephants on them, the kind that travelers pick up from run-down stalls in Thailand and India. We'd bought these in Africa, but they were probably made in China. Why had I decided to wear something that looked like pajamas to this important appointment? All of a sudden I felt very small and childish. I pinched my thigh above the knee . . . hard, my nails curling into my skin. I needed to feel it.

"I think that's a symptom of being a thirty-five-year-old woman who hates push-ups," Nick whispered to try to make me smile, but I could see the concern causing the skin around his eyes to wrinkle.

I pretended not to hear him. "Is there any concrete way of telling when the real symptoms will start affecting me?" I asked, needing tangible answers. "Will I be able to walk? Will I need a wheelchair? When will that happen? Will there be a lot of pain? Is there any way of knowing anything?"

"No," the doctor said. He had a strange look on his face. No one had ever looked at me this way before. The look was pity.

Frustrated with his inability to tell me anything definite about my disease, I clammed up.

"You're showing very early symptoms, but the best we can tell you is that you will experience most of the effects later in life, the way your dad did. And you're healthy now," the doctor continued. "We don't know anything else."

"What about our kids?"

"They have a fifty-fifty chance of getting it too. You can't screen for it in an embryo, so IVF is out of the question. You can test a fetus, but not until about twelve weeks, and then you have the option of terminating the pregnancy." The words "terminating the pregnancy" hung in the air like a violet storm cloud ready to burst any second.

On the New Year's Eve after we were married, Nick and I attended a grown-up dinner party, the kind where kids run loose, and parents get drunk before 8:00 p.m. We celebrated the New Year when the clock hit midnight in Canada's Maritime provinces so everyone could be in bed before ten. Each person went around the table and made predictions for the year ahead. Some were funny (Justin Bieber will end up in prison) and some were serious (Karen will quit her job to pursue her passions). Nick and I both threw out our own predictions that seemed unthinkable at the time (Trump will be president; we'll get a goat), but when we went to sleep that night, he whispered in my ear, "This year we'll have a baby. I just didn't want to say it in front of everyone else."

Something changed in me once we got married. Friends of my mom's and my really old aunts called it "baby fever," but it was more subtle than that. For most of my adult life children had been something I tried to avoid—both making them and spending time with them. But things were different now. I didn't hate crying babies on planes anymore. I wanted to stroke them and comfort them and cuddle them and smell their baby heads and put their baby feet in my mouth. I felt an intense heightening of all of my senses around them. I'd never pictured my own children until I met Nick, and then I couldn't stop thinking about them. I began conjuring a little girl with Nick's curiosity and mischievous eyes chasing Lady Piazza around our backyard with her face covered in dirt. She'd climb trees and sing loudly but off-key. I'd read her all of the original Nancy Drews and everything Laura Ingalls Wilder ever wrote. But recently the image of that little girl had grown blurry. I had a dream where she waved to me, but I didn't know if she was saying hello or good-bye.

Nick did everything he could to cheer me up, but I was exhausted by the uncertainty, and it made me snappy and irritable. I knew I should be grateful for the wonderful things I did have in my life—I was currently healthy and I had a wonderful husband—but I couldn't get there. Some days it was hard to muster even a thumbs-up kissy-face emoji.

Later that week I hunted for my passport in a shoe box shoved under Nick's side of the bed and came across a pair of small blue notebooks embossed with curly gold lettering: *Reasons I Want to Marry You.* I'd bought them at the BHLDN wedding dress shop when I picked up my wedding dress the previous summer. In the months before we got married, Nick and I wrote in those books every single night, no matter where we were in the world. Both of the books were completely filled, front and back.

I grabbed a bar of dark chocolate and poured a generous glass of red wine as I cracked open the pages.

MINE:

Because you make me believe we can do anything if we are together.

Because you cook me burritos when I am busy with work.

Because you are trying so hard to love Lady Piazza even though she is a bad dog.

Because staying home and making dinner with you is better than doing anything with anyone else.

Because you invent silly songs to make me laugh.

Because I am not afraid to cry in front of you.

By now I was in tears.

NICK'S:

Because we accomplish incredible things together.

Because you have a cute little belly button.

Because you took a bite out of the cheese and put it back in the fridge when you were drunk.

Because you humor me when I speak Spanish at the taqueria.

Because you snort when you laugh.

Because you have seemingly boundless energy.

Because you open my mind to new things.

Because even in the nitty gritty of life you calm me.

Because the little details of life are little and together we are learning to figure them out.

They were wonderful. I read them both cover to cover. It was like hitting rewind and watching the beginning of our relationship again in slow motion. Even though life seemed so perfect in the pages of these books, I knew that at the time we had thought things were difficult as we planned the wedding and I moved my entire life across the country. But the only thing that came across in those pages was how happy we were and how grateful we were to have found each other. I loved these books. I wanted to find a way to keep expressing how thankful we were for the rest of our marriage.

....

Gratitude may be trendy in San Francisco, but in India it's a way of life. The concept of gratitude weaves its way into almost every facet of Indian culture and relationships. This doesn't mean that Indians go around thanking everyone for everything all the time. Rather, the concept of gratitude, in many Indian traditions, is about giving earnest thanks, expressing humility, and letting go of your own ego in order to cultivate more bliss and joy for yourself and for others. It's about feeling grateful instead of talking about it.

When it comes to gratitude in a marriage, I think the Hindu monk Radhanath Swami put it best when he said: "I've seen small things like a thank-you save a marriage from total collapse . . . if it's consistent. It's a small thing but it makes a bigger difference than all the big things you've been working for."

Nick and I had both been invited by the Ministry of Tourism of India to visit the country as journalists, but a work emergency made Nick bail on the trip just three weeks before we were scheduled to leave.

"That means we'll be apart on your birthday. Your forty-second birthday!" I lamented after he called the airline to cancel his ticket. Nick's birthday was also the anniversary of our engagement.

Nick looked properly chastened. "I know, Honeypot. I'm bummed too. But it's too stressful and we'll celebrate my birthday and our engagement-versary in May. And can you please stop reminding me I'm forty-two."

I set off without him for three weeks, the longest time we'd been apart since we got married. Friends warned me that "India is different. Travelers either love it or hate it. There's no in-between." I was worried I'd hate it before I even left. The process of applying for an

Indian visa is long and labyrinthine and practically requires you promise them your firstborn baby, along with a blood sample and a list of everyone you've ever slept with. I watched a grown man burst into tears and flee the visa office in San Francisco.

"I can't take it," he screamed as he stormed out the door. "Screw India. I'm not going."

Once I'd endured the dozens of forms and questions from bureaucrats and flown the sixteen hours from San Francisco to New Delhi, where the temperatures topped 114 degrees, another two hours to Kolkata, and one more to the smaller village of Jorhat, I'd been prepared to feel as broken as the man who bawled in the visa office, but I didn't. As soon as I landed, I immediately fell in love with India's riot of colors and smells and her warm and welcoming people. Everything was brighter and more intense. It was hot and dirty and beautiful and exotic all at once.

I didn't have to look for it; talk about marriage was everywhere in India.

The Indian man next to me on my flight looked at my wedding ring and asked why I was traveling alone. "My husband is at home in the States." He looked at me sadly, as if to say, *What kind of man lets his woman travel so far by herself?*

"The difference between American marriage and Indian marriage is heaven and hell," he informed me (I hadn't asked). "In the U.S. the sex is free. In the U.S. you believe in divorce. Divorce for us is a big deal. You might think us primitive, but we have one man and one wife. That matters to us. We protect our marriage."

"So do we," I replied politely and unfolded my copy of the *Times of India* to conclude the conversation. What did he mean by that? *We protect our marriage.* Didn't we also believe that marriage was sacred, a big deal? My eye landed on the marriage advertisements in the newspaper. Indian mothers and fathers still regularly place traditional classified ads in the hopes of finding their adult child a suitable spouse. They're wildly specific, with requests broken down by caste, profession, religion, and language.

Very b'ful & qlfd MBA 32/5'7" girls family seeks alliance from well settled business professional background.

Established business family from Bhopal seeks alliance for their only son (MBA London). Smart. Handsome. Issueless. Divorcee. 5'10" 25 ½ associated in well established family business looking for beautiful well-educated girl (suitable height).

The best marriage classified ad I've ever seen from India was specific and honest and perfect in a way you'd never see on a Match.com or OkCupid profile.

27/6'1" MBA/Engineering graduate with a good job based in Mumbai looking for a Tamil Brahmin bride. Had epileptic seizures 5 years back. Lost one testicle in accident. Doctors certify above conditions normal now and will not impact marriage.

It's always wedding season in India, and since weddings stretch over many days, you can stumble onto a wedding celebration any night of the week. Later that evening, as I checked into my hotel, I admired the intricate henna designs on the hands of a woman in the lobby. She informed me, in perfect English, that she'd just come from the *mehndi* ceremony of her cousin. The *mehndi* is one of a multitude of rituals that happen during the weeklong Indian wedding festivities. During the *mehndi* the women, sometimes hundreds at a time, gather with the bride to have their hands and feet painted with henna mud. Some believe that the darker the color the *mehndi* stains the hands of the bride, the more she will be loved by her husband and mother-in-law. Others believe the longer the *mehndi* remains on the hands, the longer the couple is allowed to enjoy the honeymoon period after their wedding ceremony. Traditional healers in India told me the herbs in the *mehndi* sink into the nerve endings of the hands and feet, helping to calm the bride's prewedding jitters.

Who would have expected my offhand compliment to turn into

an invitation to the wedding? But this was India! The cousins and aunties of the bride insisted I join them for the *mehndi* and wanted me to cancel my plans for the next week so that I could attend the entire wedding. “It’s fine. What do you have to do?” the sister of the groom asked me plaintively. “You’ll stay as our guest. You’ll come.” This isn’t so out of the ordinary. Indian families of all socioeconomic levels will often invite their entire village to a wedding celebration, sometimes up to a thousand people.

I smiled at her nervously. “Let’s start with the *mehndi*,” I said. She led me to the conference room of the hotel. The chairs and tables had been pushed off to the side, and the space was filled with women sitting cross-legged on the floor, their arms outstretched on pillows while artists illustrated intricate flowers, suns, peacocks, and butterflies on their hands and feet. Because it takes several hours for the *mehndi* to dry, the event brings female family members from both sides together for long talks, teasing, and advice for the wife-to-be.

I was introduced to the bride as I waited for my own *mehndi* to dry. “Are you excited?” I asked her.

She nodded but whispered, “I have some prewedding jitters.”

I smiled back. “So normal,” I assured her. “I had to have two, maybe two and a half, glasses of champagne just to get down the aisle. Just breathe and enjoy it. And don’t let your mother-in-law boss you around too much on the big day.” She let loose a girlish giggle. Some things were universal.

All the women in the room wanted to know everything about me. After we took many selfies, I explained I was recently married. An older woman in an intricately beaded Pepto pink sari insisted I call her Auntie and pinched my hip fat, her bangles jingling against my side, and shook her head. “Too skinny.” The older generations in India believe a fat bride is a happy bride. God bless them. “Do you feed your husband?” she asked in a mixture of English and Hindi, reminding me of the old Israeli women on the shore of the Dead Sea.

I nodded. “Too much,” and I made the motion of a circle extending from my belly region. “I’m making him fat.” This pleased them.

"Do you have a good *biryani* recipe? I can give you one. Make sure your husband is happy and fat and strong," they told me. "Make your home pleasant."

"Our home looks rad. Throw pillows everywhere! The Danes helped with that," I said to confused stares.

At most of these suggestions the younger women rolled their eyes. Marriage is undergoing a sea change in India. The Indian subcontinent has long been a universe where women were subservient to their fathers and their husbands. Both female infanticide (the killing of girl children in favor of boys) and bride burning (disfiguring a woman in order to obtain a new wife with a higher dowry) have been realities for centuries. Until as recently as 1988, distraught widows would hurl themselves on their husband's funeral pyres in a suicide mission called *sati*, which translates in ancient Hindu texts to "good wife." The rationale behind this is that the life of a woman without a husband is not worth living, so she may as well die with him. The practice is outlawed, but some of that sentiment remains: that a woman cannot be truly fulfilled unless she has a husband.

Almost all of the older aunties in the room had had arranged marriages. India maintains one of the lowest divorce rates in the world, and studies have shown that Indian arranged marriages based on community ties, caste, education, business connections, and potential compatibility often receive high marks in the satisfaction department in the long run.

"It's better when the family is involved," one of the aunties told me.

"We're looking out for your best interests," another chimed in.

"You young people focus too much on love. Love is not rational. When your family chooses a husband, we choose him based on his character," the first said.

But what if you don't want to have sex with his character? I thought, though I bit my tongue to keep from saying it out loud. My expression must have given me away, because all of the older women laughed in unison.

"The parents work hard to find someone you'll enjoy being with," one of them told me. It was similar to what I'd heard from the Maasai. An arranged marriage was a partnership between two families where the bride and groom were assigned the roles of husband and wife. In searching for partners, the elders took into consideration character, family bonds, education, and compatibility, things that are often overlooked in the throes of early romantic love. This careful consideration, the older generation assured me, was what made so many arranged marriages stick. It may also have something to do with expectations and choice. There's plenty of research on consumer behavior (and in Western cultures finding a partner is often like shopping for a new car) that claims having too many options can lead to dissatisfaction with the final decision, even if someone has made a good choice. "Psychologists and business academics alike have largely ignored another outcome of choice: More of it requires increased time and effort and can lead to anxiety, regret, excessively high expectations, and self-blame if the choices don't work out," writes Barry Schwartz, a professor of psychology at Swarthmore College in Pennsylvania and the author of *The Paradox of Choice: Why More Is Less*. It goes back to the lettuce experiment. When expectations are lower, as they often are with an arranged marriage, satisfaction is often higher.

Still, I didn't meet a single woman my age who was having an arranged marriage. That didn't mean their parents weren't trying. I heard one tale of a single woman whose mother and local priest were desperate to find her a match. She gave them the benefit of the doubt when they found a college-educated man from Mumbai now working abroad. He claimed to be a Secret Service agent for President Obama here in the United States. The pair corresponded over e-mail for three months before she learned that it was all a lie. He was an ordinary IT consultant who'd only ever seen Obama on CNN. The cover story was created by the suitor and his mother to make him seem more attractive to Indian women back home.

"Women are more independent now," my friend Narayani, an

editor for the *Times of India* newspaper in New Delhi, told me. Narayani has raised two daughters. She's divorced and happily travels the world with her own two sisters. "The deterrent for divorce here hasn't just been the cultural stigma. It's been financial insecurity. Now more women are working, and that means they don't have to stay in an unhappy marriage. It means they can postpone marriage. They can choose a love match or even choose not to marry at all."

My other friend Sunitta Hedau, who met up with me in India for this trip, is the perfect embodiment of the evolution of marriage for young Indian women. Sunitta is sassy and Bollywood beautiful, with dark hair reaching halfway down her back and the longest eyelashes you've seen on a human being. She was born in Mumbai, the youngest of four girls in a conservative family. Longing to travel and see the world, she moved to London and then the United States as a successful luxury travel adviser and finally started her own business, Kora Journeys. For years her conservative mother tried to set her up with a nice Indian boy back home, parading eligible but unsatisfactory bachelors in front of her when she returned to Mumbai for the holidays.

"At first she wanted me to marry a boy from the same caste. Then she relented and said to marry a nice boy born in India. A few years later she said I could marry an American as long as he was also Indian. Now she's given up and just told me to marry whoever makes me happy," Sunitta told me and tasked me with helping to find her a suitable love match.

Diana Hayden, a former Miss India, recently had a baby from a frozen egg at age forty-two. "A career woman need not think about her biological clock and get pressured into getting married earlier than she wants to or have a baby when she isn't ready," Hayden said after she gave birth.

And during my visit to the subcontinent, everyone was buzzing about a new Bollywood movie, *Ki & Ka*, where the main female protagonist has a successful career while her husband stays at home and attends to the housework. All over the cities you see billboards marketing big-ticket items to women—cars, motorbikes, and even houses. One advertisement even targets women for home loans: "Home loans for the ones who make the HOME."

At first I assumed this liberation from the traditional marriage system would be confined to the modern urban centers in Mumbai, Delhi, and Kolkata, the places most influenced by Western media, where newly engaged women wear diamond engagement rings and trade their brightly colored wedding saris for white wedding dresses. I began to wonder what I would find if I left the cities for the rural villages and tribal areas.

And so later that week (I was sorry to skip the rest of the wedding festivities), I traveled to the state of Assam in the northeast, one of the wildest, unspoiled, and least visited parts of the country, to find out.

Sunitta and I were welcomed into a traditional home of a woman who belonged to the Mishing tribe, an Assamese farming and fishing village where the houses stood on tall stilts to keep them safe from the frequent floods. It's not uncommon for entire towns on the banks of the river to be completely washed away during monsoon season. This was a place where women depended on having a husband to survive the harsh realities of monsoons, fires, animal attacks, and famine. The privilege of independence was not an option. The men farmed and fished and went off in search of odd jobs in neighboring towns while the women often stayed home taking care of the animals and the children.

Hens and pigs made their homes beneath the huts, and when I arrived piglets scurried to meet me with squeals of delight. The children were more reserved, hiding behind their mothers' legs. One little boy in particular caught my eye. He was missing his two front teeth and wore a T-shirt, clearly a donation from somewhere in the West, that proclaimed: "Be a good person, but don't try to prove it."

I stumbled, trying to climb the narrow ladder that led into the raised hut, using a long bamboo rod for balance. The simple room was meticulously neat, saris carefully folded on a shelf over the bed, pots and pans precisely stacked in the corner. There was no clutter, no mess. This single room was home to six people. Like the Maasai and Samburu, this was a tribe of women who took care of the other women. All of the jewelry and silks in the village are community property and there's no concept of ownership. They pass the pretty things along to whoever is celebrating a wedding or special occasion.

Lae, a forty-five-year-old woman with small eyes and a broad face, offered me tea. A group of women introduced themselves to Sunitta and me. We laughed and clapped as we learned the youngest of the women present was also named Sunitta. The pair of Sunittas immediately hugged and took a selfie together.

Sunitta was twenty and had left the Mishing village to attend college. She had just gotten married two months earlier to a boy she had chosen.

"I found him and I brought him home to my parents and I said this is the boy I want to marry," she told me. "My mother was angry. She beat me."

Her mother rolled her eyes and then beamed with pride at her daughter's boldness. "It was not so bad. I got used to the idea. I'm happy for her. I want her to be happy."

"But what does it mean to be happily married?" I pressed.

Lae squinted at me. "You Westerners make marriage too complicated. Be happy for the things marriage gives you. We have our husbands. I trust my husband. We have our pigs and our goats. We have our children. We are happy. You want too much. Be thankful, because you never know what tomorrow will bring." Those were strong words coming from a woman living on the banks of a river that regularly sweeps away entire villages in the blink of an eye.

I flashed my friend Sunitta a sheepish smile and thought about all of the things we expect our marriages to give us—great sex, perfect companionship, best friendship.

We enter marriage thinking our spouse is going to solve all our problems and fill all our voids. We too often take all of our unmet needs and desires and gift wrap them in a pretty dress and tuxedo and present them to our spouse at the altar.

Not only do we want someone who can guess our feelings before we know them ourselves, but we also need that person to replace the empty toilet paper roll. We want them to be selfless, nurturing, and endlessly entertaining while they tell us we look beautiful in our skinny jeans.

The women in the Mishing village had simple expectations for marriage, unsullied by a lifetime of movies starring Meg Ryan and women's magazine articles, the ones that provide a litany of things we "deserve" from a relationship. The role of the husband in this village was not the role of savior, life coach, cheerleader, or best friend. It was husband, plain and simple.

Maybe we do ask for too much.

Americanized Sunitta was fired up. "It's so true, don't you think? We're such brats! In America we cry over the things we don't have rather than cherishing the things we do have in our relationships."

I thought about my friend Raakhee then. For as long as she could remember, Raakhee had envisioned her family in a very certain way: a husband, three kids, a life filled with laughter and travel and a summer beach house. Then when her first daughter, Satya, was just ten months old, she was diagnosed with stage 1 neuroblastoma, cancer. It required two surgeries and months filled with hospital stays and uncertainty. It was a nightmare, but Satya came out of it a healthy, happy, badass toddler who adores leopard print pants. Raakhee later said that the nightmare became an opportunity to think about everything they had to be grateful for. "It's not just that we appreciate what we have together—although, trust me, it's hard to get pissed about potty training or being on a school wait list when your kid's résumé already includes 'cancer survivor.' Getting through cancer was like obtaining a master's degree in gratitude. Agan and

I are grateful for her life; we are grateful for our life together. . . . I want, finally, to slow things down. Savor them. Take stock of what we have rather than continue to visualize what we want."

And, on the advice of a friend, Raakhee keeps a gratitude journal of three things she's grateful for each day. "The first entry, every single day, is Satya's health. It seems cliché and simple, but I need to remember never to take it for granted." Now, I've known Raakhee for a long time, and she isn't the kind of person who throws "gratitude" around lightly. She gets that it's hard to be grateful. But she promised me that it helped her marriage. "Marriage can be annoying, overwhelming, and stifling. But like with most difficult situations, those feelings are often fleeting. Mostly marriage is lovely, a guarantee that you always have someone in your corner. Someone who doesn't just love you but will face the world and all of its bullshit with you. So gratitude is important to work through the little annoying shit so it doesn't fester, grow, and start to infect all the good stuff. It helps me to see Agan for the man that he is to me, to the world, and to Satya, as opposed to the asshole who didn't empty the dishwasher," Raakhee told me.

Raakhee's story reminded me that I should find ways to be grateful, to never take my life with Nick for granted, even as we faced a situation we didn't plan for.

"How do I show I'm thankful?" I asked Lae back in the Mishing village.

She looked at me as though she didn't understand the question, and I repeated it for the translator. Lae gave a small shake of her head. "You just feel it."

....

The women I met in Assam kept telling me I had to seek a blessing for my new marriage and offer thanks for my husband at the Kamakhya Devi temple in Guwahati, a sacred place of pilgrimage for India's 830 million Hindus, particularly for women. One of its more playful nicknames, one never used around men, is the Temple of Menstruation. In Hindu mythology Lord Shiva, the god of transformation, was so distraught when his wife Sati, also known as Parvati, committed suicide that he distributed 108 parts of her body around the world to be worshipped in different temples. Kamakhya is the place where her *yoni,* or vagina, fell, and some Hindus believe the temple actually bleeds. It's one of the few temples in India where animal sacrifice is still allowed. Men, women, and entire families visit the temple to seek blessings, but I'm told that many Hindu women come here specifically to ask for a long and successful marriage and fertility. In return for asking for these blessings they also give thanks for their husbands and for their families. It was early in the morning when Sunitta and I began our walk to the temple, perched high on a hill. We passed women in brightly colored saris walking to work, beggars lying prone and naked in the streets, and boys playing cricket in the gutter with a stick and deflated tennis ball. Street dogs with peculiar poise and confidence pushed their way past us as if they had somewhere very important to be, and everywhere the holy cows took up as much space as possible, batting their beautiful eyelashes at passersby. An astrologer with Hindi tarot cards squatted shirtless on the ground next to three green parakeets chirping from their cage. Closer to the temple pilgrims grasped live white pigeons by their wings and new brides with beautifully *mehndi*ed hands and arms led scruffy black goats covered in garlands of marigolds up the formidable stairs. The sacrificial goats pranced delicately up each new step, oblivious to the fate that awaited them past the temple gates.

Priests at Kamakhya wear red robes instead of the usual white or saffron to represent the blood of the temple. Crimson handprints and fingerprints cover every available surface, part vermilion powder, part blood. No shoes are allowed in the temple, and the bottoms of my feet would be stained red until long after I returned home to America.

Hindus bring presents to offer the gods and goddesses when they visit a temple. Because I was praying to Parvati, a female goddess, I was told to purchase pieces of gold and red fabric for her sari, kohl for her eye makeup, betel nuts for her lipstick, and plenty of bangle bracelets. Bangles, more than a ring, show that a woman is married in India, and only married women are allowed to offer the bracelets to the goddess.

I asked one of the temple priests, Nilambar, a bald, spectacled man with a calming demeanor, what most women asked the goddess for. Were they very specific? Did they ask for a bigger house, a better job, a smaller waist, a more attentive husband, a vacation somewhere warm and sandy?

"You can ask the goddess for whatever you want," he said with a wide smile, stooping to pat a doomed baby goat on the head. "Most ask for a long and prosperous marriage."

"That's it?"

He laughed. "What else do you need?"

To make my blessing I was also given two small terra-cotta pots with candles in them and two sticks of incense. It was imperative, the priest told me, that I light two candles, one for Nick and one for myself. The sickly sweet smell of animal blood and smoke overwhelmed me. It was so dark inside the temple that I needed to use my bare toes to grasp the edge of the next stair to keep from falling. I didn't realize until that moment that my hands had begun to shake. I wanted to get this right. I wanted to truly give thanks for all of the wonderful things in my life. I wanted to mean it. I felt a tugging in my stomach and a stinging behind my eyes as though I'd burst into tears at any moment. A baby goat nuzzled at my foot; I stumbled and dropped one of my candles, watching as the terra-cotta shattered onto the hard stone floor. A woman behind me clapped her hand on my shoulder and stuttered in broken English. "No. You cannot use that. No. Bad." I didn't know what to do. "I just doomed my marriage," I whispered to Sunitta. She shook her head. "Don't be ridiculous." She looked behind her. "The gods are pretty forgiving. They're cool. I promise." I squinted through the darkness and the smoke at the priest, who appeared to be suppressing a laugh. "Light one and think of two," he whispered.

Closing my eyes, I steadied myself. *Light one and think of two. Light one and think of two. Light one and think of two.* I thought about all of the times Nick had taken off work to come with me to my doctor appointments. I thought about the long nights when he had held me as I cried, scared about how long I'd stay healthy. Sometimes things don't turn out as you imagined them, and no marriage is without its flaws, but in the grand scheme of things mine was pretty good.

As I moved the single flame closer to the inner sanctum, the hairs on my arms stood on end and the single wick broke apart. It became two tiny flames flickering around each other.

12

Meghalaya (the Border of India and Bangladesh)

Money, Money, Money

In marriage do thou be wise: prefer the person before money.

—William Penn

India is an onion, one of those juicy ones you get from upscale farmers' markets. Just when I thought I'd peeled away all the layers, there was yet another one below, and then one below that, until I realized I would never fully understand the country.

I would have missed out on one of the most interesting models for marriage and partnership in India if I hadn't started talking marriage with this *tuk-tuk* driver outside the Kamakhya temple. A *tuk-tuk* is essentially a bicycle with a cart on the back where passengers can sit. In India's overcrowded cities it's by far the best way to get around. But even the *tuk-tuks* hit traffic jams (typically caused by the holy cows). As we waited for five minutes and then ten, I chatted with our driver, Chittesh.

"You can't leave without going to Meghalaya," he insisted. At this point I was used to being told I couldn't leave India without seeing at least one thing, be it the Taj Mahal or the new Taco Bell in Delhi.

"What's special in Meghalaya?"

"It's the place where the women are in charge. They're the heads of the family," he explained. That was all he had to say. I changed my plans.

That's how I ended up in Shillong, the capital of the northeastern state of Meghalaya, so close to the border with Bangladesh that the two cultures spill into each other, a melting pot of Muslims, Hindus, and Christians with dark skin and wide-set features.

The Khasi and Jaintia hill tribes of Meghalaya are matrilineal. Property and assets are passed down through the youngest daughter in a family. All of the children take the mother's name instead of the father's. The husband moves into his wife's home, often bringing with him just a single suitcase of his things—a few changes of clothes, maybe his guitar or his cricket bat. It's the women who run the households and are largely in control of the finances and the major financial decisions. The men work, but they often hand their money over to their wives.

Meghalayan tribes have been matrilineal as long as anyone who lives there remembers, since long before the British came, back when all of what we now call India was just a medley of tribes linked by geography. No one could tell me for certain where the matrilineal tradition originated. It's as old as the oldest stories they talk about. There are theories, of course. Local men told me it came from a time when so many men were off fighting wars that it became necessary for names and property to be passed down through the women. Others claimed the tradition began in premonogamous times, when the Khasi had multiple partners, making maternity easier to discern than paternity.

I'd traveled to more than thirty countries in the past two years and never been anywhere, including the States, where women were institutionally favored above men.

"How incredible is it, this matrilineal thing?" I said to Nick over a spotty Skype connection before I met with the women of Meghalaya. It was morning for me and very late at night for him. His eyes drooped as I poured myself a second mug of coffee and readied for an enthusiastic discussion with my husband about cultural gender norms.

"What makes you think that things will be better there just because they're matrilineal, because the women control the property and money? Why is that naturally a better way to live?" Nick yawned. He didn't say it, but I know he was crabby because I'd missed his birthday to be in India. He'd spent it with friends in LA who dragged him to a beach party with strangers that looked fun in pictures but was exhausting and awkward in real life. "I presume there will be both good and bad things. I wouldn't be so quick to judge them as awesome just because of the woman thing. Take some time to get to know them first."

"Oh, honey," I said. "Don't you remember what happened in *Lord of the Flies*? That wouldn't have happened if there were little girls on that plane." Nick had heard my *Lord of the Flies* argument too many times to count when I lobbied for more women running more countries and companies.

"Keep an open mind," he said and turned off his light. He began snoring before the Skype connection could fizzle out.

....

The way the women in Meghalaya control the money and the property made me think of my own marriage and the dynamic between money and power. When Nick and I first met, I earned the higher salary, which made me feel like I had the right to manage our finances and make major decisions. In America I was definitely in the minority. In 1970, only 4 percent of husbands had wives who brought home more income than they did. In 2016, only 24 percent of straight women earned more than their significant other, according to a study from the website Refinery29.

There is plenty of evidence that suggests there's greater conflict in a marriage when the woman earns more. Research from the University of Chicago found that unequal earning, particularly when the woman earns more than the man, could contribute to higher rates of divorce because it often makes both parties unhappy. The man can resent the woman for her financial success, and the woman can often feel like her husband is a slacker.

Let's be honest, the relationship between power and money is an issue no matter how you live, where you live, or how wealthy you are. I talked about it with Wednesday Martin, an author and social researcher who studied a very different tribe of women for her book *Primates of Park Avenue*—the elegant, (very) wealthy "wife tribe" that makes its habitat on the Upper East Side of Manhattan.

"I've seen this often when the women I studied on the Upper East Side go back to work right around when their kids are settled in school full-time. A fair number of them have reported seismic shifts in their marriages. Sometimes for the good, but some got divorced afterward," Wednesday said. She recounted one tale of a stay-at-home mom who felt like she had no power and no control in her relationship. Having four kids kept her at home full-time for a long while. When they were finally all in school she went back to work. Her husband was skeptical at first, but then she closed a big deal and he came around.

"He was nicer to her, consulted her on more financial decisions," Wednesday said.

But soon after the economic downturn she began making more money than him. That's when he wanted her to quit her job.

"Her husband was a good guy, a committed guy, but his ego was fragile. She said, 'No way in hell am I going back to the way things were,'" Wednesday told me. "All marriage is about power, and money gives that power."

The conflation of money with power is a difficult thing to shake off. Now that I made much less than my husband, I felt a complete loss of control. I worried constantly that I wasn't contributing enough, and that made me feel even more powerless.

I wasn't sure how the recent changes in my earning power would shift the dynamic of our marriage.

We didn't have a joint checking account, not yet. Both of our names were on the mortgage and we both paid it each month with a transfer from our own separate bank accounts. My bank account was even in my maiden name. I didn't need my therapist to tell me what my refusal to merge our finances meant. My checking account felt like the last thing that belonged only to me. It didn't matter that the balance was now inching down to zero without being replenished each month. I would cling to it like spandex on a Kardashian until it went into overdraft.

Extensive research shows that issues surrounding finances are often the main cause of conflict in a marriage. According to one study conducted by Utah State University, couples who disagreed about their finances once a week were 30 percent more likely to get divorced than couples who disagreed about them once a month. The National Institutes of Health has done research that determined "compared to non-money issues, marital conflicts about money were more pervasive, problematic, and recurrent, and remained unresolved."

There's even a growing field called "financial therapy," which is exactly what it sounds like, therapy that helps a couple work on their financial issues, as opposed to their emotional ones.

The key, according to financial advisers, therapists, and marriage experts, is to have a constant dialogue about money, to talk about the good things that money can do and the stresses that not having enough money can cause. It's important to make sure that money doesn't become some kind of weird taboo topic in your marriage. It should be an ongoing conversation to make sure that money doesn't create a wedge between a couple.

The only time I could bring myself to talk about money was after I'd had a third glass of wine, which is never a good time to talk about anything except whether you should adopt another dog.

Money conversations in a marriage are most productive when

they aren't spontaneous, or fueled by Chianti. I learned this from Jean Chatzky, a financial journalist and the money guru who gives practical financial advice on the *Today* show while wearing smart dresses and the perfect shade of nude lipstick. First she counseled me to set up times to talk about money with Nick when we were both sober. She wanted me to make an actual appointment and put it on the calendar.

"My husband and I set ground rules before we start talking about money, so that we won't fight," Jean told me. "This isn't fun for anyone! It also helps to come in with a list of questions, because when you get in the thick of it, you can never remember what you wanted to talk about."

"But what if one person is making way more of the money?" I pressed her. "Doesn't that make everything weird?"

Jean didn't mince words.

"Money definitely gives you power in a relationship. And that's why it's important to keep talking about it on a regular basis and come to an understanding about how where the money is coming from impacts your relationship. Open the floodgates! Don't be afraid to talk about it."

....

When the British first came to Meghalaya in the early nineteenth century, they nicknamed the area the Scotland of the East for its heavy rainfall, stately pines, gurgling brooks, and lush green rolling hills. While most of India has remained Hindi and the nearby Bangladeshi villages are Muslim, during the British colonization of the country, many members of the Meghalayan tribes converted to Christianity.

Today, statues of Jesus and Mary dot the undulating hills. Brightly colored homes painted yellow, orange, red, green, and robin's egg blue are terraced along the palm trees, bamboo, lush green jackfruit, and red hyacinth bushes. Sal trees, which produce some of the hardest wood in the world, so tough you can't put a nail through it, stretch their branches high into the sky. These hardy trees reminded me of the women who lived here—tough as nails.

I drove into the bustling capital, where I was supposed to meet up with a translator named Sukher, a petite, soft-spoken, and meek man in his twenties. His shoulders curled into his body in a way that made him take up even less space.

"Of course the men just accept that the women have power here. That's just the way it is," he told me very matter-of-factly in a voice as low as a whisper. "It's important to listen to my wife. She makes good decisions." His wife is the second daughter in the family, but not the youngest. This means that she doesn't stand to inherit any of the family's property. I kept asking why it was the youngest and not the eldest daughter who inherited. The answer makes a lot of sense. The youngest daughter will be around the longest, so she'll be able to use the family property and money to take care of her parents and then the older siblings as they age.

Sukher had recently moved into his wife's ancestral home in a neighboring village called Mawlynnong and he commuted into Shillong each day to work as a translator and tour guide. He and his wife had been arguing because Sukher wanted to move closer to the city to make his commute for work easier, but his wife was adamant about not leaving their village. In the end, she won.

Sukher dutifully led me into Shillong's Khasi market, which was tucked down a dank, narrow alleyway, past a series of winding side streets, dark tea shops, and counters for placing bets on professional archery. They love professional archery in Shillong, and skilled archers are the equivalent of NFL football players in the United States or soccer stars in Europe. The Khasi market is a series of neverending stalls where the women sell everything from betel nuts and banana leaves to tobacco and fancy dresses for less than five American dollars. Elsewhere in India the men control the markets, but here the women do the buying and the selling. The only men I saw sat quietly in the backs of the shops, sometimes making change, feeding a baby, or running an errand for their female boss.

I struck up a conversation with a young woman from the Jaintia tribe named Daphi, the proprietor of a small dress shop. The shop had been passed down through the women of her family for three generations. A photograph of her deceased mother hung above the counter, gazing down at her daughter with pride. Her mother's younger sister owned the dress shop across the way, and they teased one another about which stall had the prettier dresses and better deals.

"My mother made all of the decisions for our family herself," Daphi told me. "When I get married, I will be the one to make the big decisions. This is just the way our culture is." Daphi was the youngest daughter in a family of two girls, which meant that ownership of the store went to her when her mother passed. "It's a lot of responsibility," she explained. "But I hope to find a husband to share it with me."

"To share it with me" was an interesting choice of words. I asked Daphi if she thought that being the owner of her shop would present problems in her future relationship.

"I don't think so. I think that I will always consult my husband and we will have discussions about all of our decisions. I saw my mother do that and my female relatives do that. We involve the men. Why wouldn't we?"

I thanked Daphi for being so honest and bought two colorful Indian nightgowns from her and one fancy child's dress from her aunt across the street.

Down the alleyway I ran into a woman named Diana standing barefoot in front of tall bins of betel nuts, wearing the traditional Khasi checked *kyrshah*, or apron. Her hair was pulled back in a tight ponytail revealing a high, regal forehead.

She told me she was forty-two years old and that she'd been married for more than twenty years. She and her husband had three boys. She'd love to have a girl who could inherit, but she was too tired to keep trying. Instead, her sons would be the heirs when she and her husband passed away.

Diana laughed when I asked about the merits of living in a matrilineal society.

"This is the best place in the world to live. In other places it is hard to be a woman," she told me, her positive pride in her culture evident in her thrown-back shoulders and expanded chest. "We are a very special people, you know." Her eyes danced with mischief. "Obviously it's the women who have the power. Doesn't that make sense?" she said and smiled, flecks of betel nut caught in her teeth. "I never do anything at home. My husband does the cooking, the cleaning, everything. But he does that because he likes to do that. You have to have an understanding in marriage. Marriage is a compromise. If he needs help, then I help him." She leaned in close to me. "You have to give the men some understanding. You work hard to understand each other, but the men, they need it more."

The Khasi and Jaintia women control the money and the property, and yet every woman I met talked about understanding and compromise. They told me it wasn't their place to force their husband to do things. They stressed that no matter who controls a family's wealth, the most important thing in a marriage is an understanding of equality between the two partners, compromise.

Of course, this matrilineal world wasn't a utopia. The women of Meghalaya had their own special breed of marital woes.

I soon learned that many in the younger generation of both men and women no longer consider their matrilineal customs to be as sacrosanct as they've been for centuries.

Even my guide, Sukher, wasn't sure if he would carry on the traditions of inheritance. "I hope that we have one girl and one boy child and we will split their inheritance between them equally," he told me. He did add: "As long as that's what my wife wants to do."

There are other, more serious, downsides.

"Can you imagine the shock of leaving your family home and suddenly becoming a nobody in your mother-in-law's house?" Kaith Pariat, a Khasi male suffragist, said in an interview with the *Guardian* in 2011. "She gives the orders and you become a good-for-nothing servant. Men are not even entitled to take part in family gatherings. The husband is up against a whole clan of people: his wife, his mother-in-law, and his children." Pariat may have been exaggerating to prove his point, or maybe conditions for men have improved in the five years since he spoke to the newspaper. During my time in Shillong, I didn't meet any men who were particularly abused or women who treated them like dogs. The men I met had jobs outside of the home, and their wives seemed to treat them with kindness and fairness. Even Diana, who told me that her husband did all of the housework, claimed he did it only because he liked doing it.

One of the biggest problems for the Khasi and Jaintia matrilineal tradition is modern mass communication. Exposure to the Internet and satellite television has shown the Khasi and Jaintian men that in other parts of the world the men are not considered second-class citizens, in fact just the opposite. They've realized that men rule most of the world. Why should they stay in the one place where women are valued more highly than men?

"The men have stopped sticking around," Patricia Mukhim, one of the top editors at the daily newspaper the *Shillong Times* and an outspoken researcher of matrilineal societies, explained when I visited her in her busy office high in the hills. Patricia has three children from three different men.

"They say they feel like they are just breeding bulls with no claim on their own children, and it makes it easier for them to leave. They leave their wives and their children and they never come back."

Nick was right, as usual. This matrilineal society was not as idyllic as I'd imagined. But if I'd learned anything from talking about marriage around the world, from experiencing the ups and downs of my own first year of matrimony, it was that no one system for long-term partnership offers all of the answers.

Yet even though the matrilineal tribes of Meghalaya had their problems, it was the women's insistence on the importance of fairness and understanding in a marriage that stuck with me on my long journey back to California. Women in America have been fighting for equality for more than a century. We've come a long way from the housewives of my grandma's generation. But here was a society where women were born not only equal but with *more* privileges than men, and the system was still flawed. The women wanted to involve their husbands in the decision making. They seemed to crave compromise and fairness, and yet some of the men still wanted out.

My biggest takeaway from Meghalaya was that my issues with money and control were exactly that—my issues. Nick never made me feel less important because I stopped making as much money. I did that to myself, and it was time to get over it.

We were partners in this marriage and money was going to come and go. How we handled that together would be the only constant.

I placed a betel nut in my mouth. I'd bought a sack of them from Diana, and I still wasn't used to the way the nut's bitterness clung to the sides of my tongue, but I liked the way it stained my lips a reddish orange. As I rolled it between my lips, trying to soften the tough meat in my mouth, I mulled this one question over in my mind: Was a true marriage of equals, a sharing of both power and responsibility, a possibility anywhere in the world?

13

Sweden

Bending Gender Roles

We've begun to raise daughters more like sons . . . but few have the courage to raise our sons more like our daughters.

—Gloria Steinem

"Excuse me. Pardon me. Excuse me. Pardon me." I maintained an unfailingly polite tone as I searched for Nick in a coed Scandinavian sauna filled with old naked Swedish men.

"So sorry. Didn't mean to touch you. Oh, thank you for clearing a space for me." Once seated on the end of a warm cedar bench, I searched the crowd for my husband's face without focusing too hard on any one part of any body in particular.

Meeting in a coed sauna seemed like such a good idea twenty minutes earlier, when Nick and I parted ways at the entrance of the Ribersborgs bathhouse in Malmö, a vibrant city on the southern coast of Sweden. The plan was to take separate swims in the freezing near-arctic waters of the Øresund, the strait in between the Baltic and North Seas, then meet here in the sauna, the one place in the bathhouse where men and women were allowed to hang out together.

On the women's side the bathing decks had been filled with naked women of all shapes, sizes, and ages, reading, laughing, solving sudoku puzzles. One woman sloppily ate an ice cream sandwich, the vanilla dribbling down her fleshy belly. I couldn't help but stare. How often do Americans see normal women's naked bodies out in the open? There were giant breasts and tiny breasts, gumdrop nipples and flat nipples with the circumference of ripe plums. There were taut bellies and big bellies and bellies that could balance a martini (yes, I saw a woman with a martini on her belly).

I'd forced myself to dive into the icy sea, howling as I hit the water. It poured into my mouth and tasted like rusted pennies.

Be a polar bear. You're a fucking polar bear, I'd lied to myself as I lost feeling all along the left side of my body.

I fled the sea for the warmth of the sauna, assuming Nick would do the same. But each time the door on the men's side opened, another naked human who was not my husband strode into the room, forcing the bathers seated on the sauna's narrow blond-wood benches to grow even more familiar.

The Swedes could tell I was American, not by my accent or lack of pubic hair but because of how I strategically covered my body with my towel as I walked around the bathhouse and from the way I curled my elbows inward to protect my breasts and nipples. I struck up a conversation with the only other women in the sauna, two Swedes about my age who giggled at my shyness. I told them I was meeting my husband in the sauna. They informed me, with no small amount of glee, that they'd left their husbands at home with their babies.

"It's nice of them to babysit," I said. The pair gave me a strange look. I repeated it more slowly and apologized that I tended to speak English too quickly, but they shook their heads.

"Babysit?" the first one said. "He isn't babysitting. He's just . . . How do I say it in English? Being a father. Parenting."

The second chimed in. "My husband is used to it. He's the one who stays home with our kids. I went back to work right away." The two women proceeded to explain their country's parental leave policies to me. In Sweden the government pays for both men and women to take parental leave after having a child. Men are even applauded for taking time off in lieu of their wives.

Before I could ask too many questions, Nick strode into the sauna, towel-less, confident, invigorated. He was keenly self-assured as he cut through the scrum of pasty flesh.

"Where were you?" I whispered. "I've been in here for half an hour. I'm quite pruney."

"Didn't you jump in the water?" he said, confused about why I'd been there so long.

I nodded. "Of course I did. As quickly as possible."

"Didn't you swim all the way to the buoy?" he asked. "It gets really choppy out there but it feels incredible. How freeing is this? No one cares that you're naked. No one even looks at you. I could do this every day. Maybe we could live here."

This was the fifth country Nick had thought we could happily settle in. "Not the worst idea. It would be a damn good place to have a baby, that's for sure," I said, still shivering, disappointed with myself for not being more polar bear–like.

Nick surveyed the crowd in the sauna, which was mainly composed of my new girlfriends and very old men talking about the weather. He lowered his voice.

"I don't think this is *that kind* of bathhouse."

....

What I was trying to say in the sauna is that Sweden is a great place to raise a baby, for both men and women, in stark contrast to the States, where it is becoming more and more difficult and expensive for most couples to raise children.

Nick and I had been going back and forth with my team of doctors about our options for having kids. None of them saw any reason we shouldn't try to have kids naturally. They assured us that if the child carried the muscular dystrophy gene (and there was a 50 percent chance of that), he or she wouldn't show symptoms until midlife. Like me. There was no chance of childhood muscular dystrophy or any other complications associated with muscular dystrophy.

Still, as a mother you want your child to come into the world with every possible advantage. Why would you choose to start their life at a disadvantage? But how do you stack the odds in your kid's favor? We could use a donor egg. We could adopt. None of these options came without their own risks. There are so many things that can go wrong when you decide to have a child. In our case, we just happened to know one possibility.

I loved everything about my life, even the shitty parts of it. I'd lived an incredible thirty-five years with my messed-up genes. Yes, the future was scary, but it was also promising and filled with the possibility of medical advances that could halt the progress of my own disease and eradicate it in a child.

Toward the end of my trip in India I'd visited an ayurvedic doctor at the Ananda wellness center in the foothills of the Himalayas.

I told him about the muscular dystrophy and he laughed.

"There are no genetic conditions until they appear. Live your life, girl," he counseled in the same breath in which he told me to stop eating spicy foods, dairy and to try to get more sleep. All I could do was nod and ignore the fact that he was talking to me like he was Beyoncé.

But it wasn't just my genetics that had me worried about having a baby. There was everything else—the tumultuous world we live in, one plagued by terror attacks, overpopulation, economic uncertainty, and reality television.

There was also the fact that having a baby would effectively end our marriage as we knew it.

I'd recently read in the *Wall Street Journal* that "a couple's satisfaction with their marriage takes a nose dive after the first child is born. Sleepless nights and fights over whose turn it is to change diapers can leach the fun out of a relationship. . . . About two-thirds of couples see the quality of their relationship drop within three years of the birth of a child, according to data from the Relationship Research Institute in Seattle. . . . A key source of conflict among new parents is dividing up—and keeping score of—who does what for the baby and the household."

A few weeks earlier, back in the States, I'd had this conversation with a girlfriend who recently went on maternity leave:

"Want to blow up your life? Do you want to throw a grenade into your marriage and fucking blow it up?" I briefly wondered if she knew this was a reference to a line from Nora Ephron's *Heartburn* or if every new mother likened procreation to armed conflict.

"No. I don't." I was afraid of her at this point. It didn't matter. She was going to tell me.

"Have kids," she said and took a slug of wine that was actually more of a gulp that finished the glass.

"I don't care how good your marriage is. Having a kid will change everything," she cackled and motioned for the waiter to bring one more glass of wine and the check at the same time so she could get back to her husband who insisted both that his time with their children be called babysitting and that he receive a blow job in return for his sacrifice.

I've always considered Nick and myself equal partners in our marriage. He does laundry better than I do and sweeps the floors every single day. He doesn't mind running errands and even loves visiting Target, where he's wildly amused by the contraption that wheels the shopping carts up the escalator.

Nick does the so-called manly things too, changing tires and building things. The last time I'd been out of town he'd built me two new bookshelves and erected a hummingbird platform outside of our bedroom window so I could watch the birds eat their breakfast when I woke up in the morning. We both pay bills and take the car to be serviced and go grocery shopping. If one of us cooks, the other does the dishes. It's just the way things are with us. I knew this was a good thing, a really good thing. It can even lead to a better sex life. According to a 2016 study in the *Journal of Marriage and Family*, heterosexual couples who split up the housework equally said they had more sex than couples who didn't share chores. "When couples share similar tasks rather than different, gender-stereotyped ones, this seems to deepen desire," the study claimed.

But I was warned by friends and marriage experts alike that all of this could change once we had kids. Another study published in the *Journal of Personality and Social Psychology* followed 218 couples over eight years and found the vast majority were less happy with their marriages after becoming parents. Only 15 percent of fathers and 7 percent of mothers were more satisfied with their marriage after having a child.

In the past five years more and more married friends have told me they've decided to forgo children altogether. Many of them proudly announced, "We're child free by choice!!!" Others were more subtle about it.

"Neither of us ever wanted kids. We like them in theory, but we like our dogs more. We want to travel and have nice things and keep our hard-earned money instead of paying for college," our friend Jess explained.

The choice was more complicated for the Megs, two of my closest and oldest friends, the beloved gifters of sensible Patagonia hiking underwear.

"Lesbians are lucky that getting pregnant doesn't happen without a miracle of modern science and financing, so we have to be very sure we want them before we do it," Little Meg said to me. Together both Megs talked about having kids for years before deciding that it wasn't right for them. They're fantastic aunties to a dozen kids by now and they spoil them rotten, but they also fly off to the wine country at a moment's notice without worrying about much more than where to board their aging pug, Turbo.

"Be conscious. Don't just do things because they are the next step," Big Meg said. "Really talk about it. Know what you're getting into."

....

Visiting Sweden was part of learning what we were getting into, figuring out if we could find an archetype for parenting that would keep our marriage in a good place.

As I learned in the coed, naked sauna, there are few better models for equality between parents than Sweden. The Scandinavian birthplace of the BabyBjörn, IKEA, and ABBA has been dubbed the "Land of the Stay-at-Home-Dad" due to its government-funded parental leave policies, which are so generous they should make the American government feel ashamed.

Swedish "dad leave" has enjoyed a highly publicized and colorful history. In 1974, when the country became the first in the world to introduce federally funded paid paternity leave, the government began running an incredibly effective ad campaign starring the beefy heavyweight wrestling star Lennart "Hoa-Hoa" Dahlgren posing with an equally beefy baby in his arms. It would be the equivalent of one of our NFL football players taking off a season to change diapers and then posing in commercials for Pampers. In 2009 twenty-six-year-old economics student and new dad Ragnar Bengtsson may have taken things too far when he attempted to breast-feed, saying that it "could prove very important for men's ability to get much closer to their children at an early stage." After months of trying to pump his nipples, Bengtsson proved unable to produce a biological miracle. Today most Swedish men opt for the easier path of sharing parental leave duties with their partner.

Here's how it works: New moms and dads in Sweden are allowed to split fourteen months of parental leave between them. During this time, 80 percent of their salaries are paid by the government. If fathers don't spend at least two months at home with the baby on their own, the couple forfeits those two months. Around 85 percent of Swedish fathers take this "daddy leave." Some fathers even take on the entire parental leave, allowing their wives to go right back to working full-time after they have a child.

How does this compare to America? The Department of Labor supports paternity leave . . . in theory. "Paternity leave—and especially longer leaves of several weeks or months—can promote parent-child bonding, improve outcomes for children, and even increase gender equity at home and at the workplace. Empowering more dads with paid parental leave means they can achieve their professional goals and be supportive, nurturing fathers and partners," the department explained in a policy briefing from 2015.

But in the States the burden of making sure that dads are still paid while on paternity leave falls on employers. The government really likes the idea but won't pay a dime in support of it. And most companies remain stingy about any kind of parental leave. A 2012 Department of Labor study found that "only 13 percent of men who took parental leave received pay compared with 21 percent for women."

The singer John Legend made headlines in 2016 when he announced he was taking paternity leave after the birth of his daughter Luna. It's easier to afford paternity leave when you're a multimillionaire performing artist or an employee of a fancy and progressive tech company like Facebook, Google, or Twitter, all of which offer some paid paternity leave. Most of our friends who took paternity leaves were unpaid, and even then they only took off a week or two tops. My friend Alice's husband was posted overseas in Europe working for the State Department. He scheduled his vacation time around her due date. We had friends without paid vacation time who counted their blessings that their baby was born on a Friday so they would be able to be with their wife and new child for two days over the weekend.

It may be this lack of government and private-sector support that's making couples with children less happy than couples without children.

Researchers recently looked at the happiness levels of parents versus nonparents in twenty-two countries. In places like Sweden, Norway, and Hungary, countries with more flexible work options, generous parental leave policies, and subsidies for day care, parents tended to be happier than nonparents.

Not so in the United States.

"The bad news is that of the 22 countries we studied, the U.S. has the largest happiness shortfall among parents compared to nonparents, significantly larger than the gap found in Great Britain and Australia," wrote Jennifer Glass, a sociology professor at the University of Texas at Austin and coauthor of the study. "What we found was astonishing. The negative effects of parenthood on happiness were entirely explained by the presence or absence of social policies allowing parents to better combine paid work with family obligations. And this was true for both mothers and fathers."

....

"I'm married to a modern man and not a dinosaur! Of course he took care of our baby after she was born," Birgitta Ohlsson, a member of the Swedish parliament, told Nick and me over a coffee in Stockholm. "Gender equality is one of the cornerstones of Swedish society. It truly contributes to keeping happy families together."

Nick and I met Birgitta over a *fika* in the Swedish parliament building in the Gamla Stan neighborhood of Stockholm, the small medieval heart of the city filled with tourists buying elk hides, lingonberry jams, and mugs in the shape of moose. Birgitta had invited us to meet her to chat about Sweden's wonderful parental leave policies and why they helped contribute to stronger marriages. Before arriving at the Swedish parliament, I'd been picturing a severe and serious building filled with Viking legislators dressed in sharply cut suits. I thought we'd meet Birgitta in a dark wood–paneled office and shake hands formally. I wasn't expecting this cheery coffee lounge with peach-colored carpet and an excellent flaky-pastry selection.

Fika, a wondrous invention, could be compared to teatime

in England, except with coffee instead of tea and *fikabröd*, sweet Swedish pastries, instead of British wafers with the consistency of cardboard. During our time in Sweden I'd grown partial to the *chokladbiskvi*, an almond biscuit topped with chocolate mousse and coated with crunchy chocolate, and the *kardemummabulle*, a rosette-shaped bun coated in butter, sugar, cinnamon, and cardamom. The Swedes take *fika* very seriously as a break from their workdays and will sometimes schedule at least two of them in a single day.

Birgitta Ohlsson's schedule that day was harried, as a colleague had recently quit to become the ambassador to Jordan to help deal with the current refugee crisis, and we were lucky to get her for a single *fika*. I had wanted to meet her since I saw her quoted in the *Times* extolling the virtues of her country's paid parental leave, saying: "Now men can have it all—a successful career and being a responsible daddy." Birgitta has long been an advocate for both feminism and equality in Sweden, but she became a part of the paternity leave story when she was appointed to be Sweden's new European Union minister while pregnant with her first child.

The Swedish media were upset that Birgitta might not take enough time off. She stood strong in her decision to accept the EU post and told the press that her husband, a law professor, could handle the new baby as well as she could.

Ohlsson was as cool and fierce as I'd expected her to be, but more casual and inviting than the American politicians I'd met face to face. But then, most American politicians would never invite a random foreigner to pop into the Senate for a latte and a pastry. She wore a vaguely sparkly top and sensible but chic black patent-leather flats. Before digging into the meat of Swedish policy, we meandered through the obligatory small talk about the horrors of the current American political season. Her observations about American politics were intensely astute in a way that made me embarrassed that I still wasn't sure of the names of Sweden's political parties. But she wasn't critical of the American political system. She was kind when she explained that Sweden had also taken a long time to evolve toward government-supported equality.

"Among my parents' generation it wasn't common that fathers were home with their kids. It was an odd situation back then. Among my generation it's almost standard that fathers are active in taking care of their children," Ohlsson explained. "Bad parental leave policies mean that brilliant women tend to stay at home, which is bad for society. We can't afford to have the best-educated housewives in the world."

I cringed and thought about all of the highly educated women I knew back home in the States who had to drop out of the workforce because of the astronomical cost of child care, their companies' poor parental leave policies, and the lack of opportunities for flexible work schedules.

Ohlsson continued. "When the men stay at home, they develop a special sense for their kids and they also become much more active in the household chores. It makes for a happier marriage. Look around Stockholm. It's so normal here to see dads out and active with their kids."

She nodded over toward the corner of the room, where a father was diligently tapping away at his laptop with one hand and rocking a baby carriage back and forth with the other.

Nick, always a business journalist keen for economic proof that a policy has been successful, leaned in toward Birgitta.

"But how do you know this works? Are there statistics that say footing the bill for parental leave pays off for society in some way down the road? How do you know it's the right thing to do?"

She gave him a strange look before she replied matter-of-factly. "It's just better."

....

It was true. Everywhere else we went in Stockholm we saw dads pushing the strollers. We saw them on the island of Djurgården when Nick agreed to visit the ABBA museum, an entire institution dedicated to the Swedish pop group that brought the world "Dancing Queen" and "Mamma Mia." We saw them in the hair salons that dotted each and every block. There were more salons in Sweden than coffee shops. I assumed it was because everyone, men, women, and babies, was getting confusing yet flattering asymmetrical haircuts at least once a week. There was a daddy/baby carriage traffic jam in the chicest store in the chicest neighborhood in the city. *Vogue* had recently knighted Södermalm one of the "world's coolest neighborhoods" and praised the store Grandpa as a top-notch boutique for both men's and women's clothes. It's one of those stores where you know right away that everyone in it is more interesting than you are. Yet I could hardly move a few feet without running into a stroller containing an adorable Swedish baby pushed by a handsome dad wearing suspenders without irony, rad sneakers, and acid-washed jeans.

I was alone that afternoon. Nick had run off to a meeting, so I needed this gang of Swedish dads to help me decide which rad Swedish sneakers to purchase. They took the job quite seriously, lining the carriages up against a wall and paying close attention as I tried on one pair after another.

"Too boring," they frowned to a simple black pair with an elevated platform bottom.

"Too flashy" to the sleek electric blue ones.

"*Underbar!*" they exclaimed, which means "wonderful, magnificent, and lovely" in Swedish, to a pair of kicks with an intricate basket-weave pattern and thick black soles.

The excitement woke the babies, and suddenly my supporters were busy with bottle preparation, funny-face making, and nappy changing.

In another shop I found a series of greeting cards to give to new moms and dads on the occasion of their parental leave. "Happy Mommy Leave," read a card showing two women enjoying a coffee with a baby carriage in the background. "Happy Daddy Leave," read another of a man with a similar carriage drinking a beer at a bar. A third card in the series just said "Swede," with an illustration of a man and woman each holding one handle of a woman's purse.

"The Swedish dads helped me pick out these sneakers," I told Nick as I modeled them in our hotel room that night. I was pleased with myself for buying "sensible shoes." He was stressed about finishing up an important presentation for work.

"Why do the Swedish dads shop for sneakers all the time?" he snapped.

"The store had shirts and pants too. They're enjoying their daddy leave," I said defensively.

"I don't think parental leave is going to be all shopping and having fun," he replied tersely.

"Neither do I." I carefully packed my new sneakers and mommy-leave greeting cards into our suitcase.

Nick sighed and rubbed his temples. "I get nervous," he said. "It *is* going to change everything. Having kids." I don't know why I wasn't as scared as Nick. I probably should have been as scared as Nick. For some reason I had this intense, if maybe naive, faith that I had chosen the right partner to have kids with and that would make all the difference. Nick was the right partner. Everything was going to be OK. Right?

During our time in Sweden I kept thinking back to a conversation I'd had with Jessica Valenti, the founder of the blog *Feministing* and author of the best seller *Sex Object*. Jessica had been married for six years when I talked to her about my own search for a template for marital equality. She told me that she and her husband felt like they had to make it up as they went along, even more so after the birth of their first child.

"We did it by the seat of our pants," Jessica told me. "But as feminist as you are, it is easy to fall into traditional gender roles. We both take care of the kid in equal numbers, but somehow only one of us is making doctors' appointments or buying clothes. And we had to have a conversation about that. For us it's about having a constant conversation and keeping that conversation open and being as proactive as possible."

....

If you're ever looking to dive deep into a rabbit hole of stay-at-home-Swedish-dad porn on a hungover or overcast Sunday afternoon, I highly recommend taking a look at photographer Johan Bävman's photo book *Swedish Dads.*

When Johan, a freelance photographer, had his first son, he took advantage of the country's leave policies and traded off staying at home with his wife, who also works full-time as a writer. Johan quickly felt isolated as a new parent, particularly as a new dad.

"All of a sudden I was responsible for another life, and I was lacking in role models. I needed to find other men that I could relate to as a new father, men like me," Johan told Nick and me over lunch in his hometown of Malmö shortly after our dip in the sea. I'd been trying to interview Johan over Skype for months, but he was constantly on dad duty with a toddler and newborn at home. Calls were canceled to deal with sick babies, a wife heading out of town for work, and the general exhaustion from parenting two small humans.

"On TV you see these superdads who can do everything. They can make the perfect cupcakes and get all of the vacuuming done and put the baby to bed and the house looks wonderful and they seem like they don't feel any stress or frustrations," Johan continued. *What the what?* I thought. When was the last time you heard an American dad lamenting his inability to make the perfect cupcakes? On American TV we typically see plenty of supermoms, but the fathers are either the bumbling dad who puts the diaper in the garbage disposal or the cool dad who dons a BabyBjörn while drinking a sixer at his weekly poker game.

Johan continued: "I felt a lot of frustration. I was worried I wasn't being a good parent. I needed to find other dads who I could relate to."

So Johan plastered ads all over town looking for willing subjects.

He'd even recruit other dads he met at the playground. The objective was to find out why the fathers elected to stay home with their kids, and how it changed their relationships with both their children and their partners.

"That's why I'm writing this book," I interrupted him. "I was worried I didn't know how to be a good married person, and I needed to find other married people I could relate to." Nick patted my leg to indicate I was being rude. "Sorry. Go on."

"It was a really personal thing for me at first as I tried to figure out how to be a dad," Johan continued. "But at the end of it I wanted it to inspire other men to think about what it really means to get to spend that extra time with your baby at home," he said. "I wanted my son to come to me as easily as my wife. I want to be there for him, and I think it's important that he knew that from the very beginning."

The photos in Johan's resulting book are raw and mesmerizing, and not just because Swedish men are so damn photogenic. In one, Urban Nordh, a thirty-three-year-old infrastructure consultant sporting a hipster brown Adidas track jacket, holds his recalcitrant toddler over a toilet with little success. In another forty-one-year-old Ola Larsson carries his son Gustav in a pack on his back while gracefully vacuuming the living room floor. Loui Kuhlau, a twenty-eight-year-old artist who took a full year of leave with his son Eiling, said he had a hard time understanding why anyone would not want to be at home with their kid. "I think I've learned a lot about myself during my time at home with Eiling, including how much I'm capable of—despite the sleep deprivation. But the biggest benefit is experiencing the joy of being at home with my child."

One of the ancillary benefits of Sweden's dad leave is helping to open up the nation to the idea that men can do all of the things women do.

"I'm hoping I can change how people perceive masculinity," Johan said. "I'm hoping that I can show this can be the norm, men taking care of children and showing their emotions."

The other thing that being a stay-at-home dad taught Johan was that staying at home is a real job.

"It's not just about raising the children. It's about learning how to do all of the unpaid work in the home. It's about getting a better understanding of what women have traditionally been doing for the last several thousand years, all of that work that has been taken for granted." I wanted to grab Johan's hand and stand up on the table in the middle of the café and have a Sally Field–in–*Norma Rae* moment. "We each share the work of the house and of the children, and it isn't about asking for credit. She doesn't have to tell me how good I am and I don't have to tell her how good she is. We both know it."

"And you would never call what you do babysitting?" I asked, just to drive the point home.

Johan burst out laughing and stood to excuse himself.

"I have to pick my son up from day care."

....

"Do you have kids yet?" Leffe Lindh, the owner of a Swedish moose farm, asked us.

"Soon. Someday. We're working on it." Nick let out a low, deep chuckle and gave a sideways glance in my direction to make sure it was the right thing to say to a stranger. I gave a slight nod.

"It's a lot of fun to work on it." I plastered a smile on my face. That was what people wanted to hear. It was easier than talking about how un-fun making a baby can actually be. From the day we got engaged, the occupancy of my uterus became fair game for discussion among friends, family, and complete strangers.

"When, when, when will you have a baby?" asked my aunts, our dog sitter, and the checkout clerk at Trader Joe's. No one wants to hear "Well, it's complicated for us. . . ."

Leffe clapped his hands and pulled a plush gray moose toy off the shelf and handed it to me. "For when you're done working on it." He laughed with a jovial snort. We'd driven two hours outside of Stockholm to visit this farm, a place where humans can get up close and personal with Sweden's most famous animal. Since we'd arrived in the country we'd been eating at restaurants with names like the Flying Elk (a Swedish term for moose) and the Moosehead. We'd eaten moose meatballs (which were delicious), moose burgers (which were pretty mediocre), moose milk (better than camel milk), and moose jerky (too salty). All I wanted to do was see a moose.

"It's like Minnesota out here," Nick observed during our drive to Leffe's moose farm as we passed bright red barns and tall evergreen forests, winding our way through towns with names like Skogstibble.

"Now, that's how you name a town," Nick remarked. "Skogstibble. That's a town begging for a drink to be named after it."

Just twenty minutes past Skogstibble we came upon the farm and Leffe, who greeted us with a boisterous hug, a coffee, and a waffle over which he told us his own life story. Leffe Lindh's path to owning a moose park involved the breakup of his first marriage. Nearly twenty years ago he was given his first moose to take care of, a baby whose mother had been killed by a car. Leffe, who was then a hunter, worked day and night to nurse her back to health, but in the end the baby moose didn't make it.

"I cried when she died," he told me. "But from then I got it in my head that I would start a moose park. I said that to all of my friends. They told me I was crazy. My wife called me crazy."

And so he divorced his wife. A couple of years later he began dating a new woman, Ilona. Two weeks into their courtship he grabbed her hands and looked into her eyes and told her: "I want to marry you and start a moose park with you."

Some women wouldn't know what to say to that. Ilona said yes.

The couple bought two moose babies in 2006 and built a twenty-five-acre farm. Ilona and Leffe had two of their own human children and now take care of thirty moose. They run two businesses together, the moose park and an apartment rental company, as equal partners. The year before we visited, when one of the female moose rejected her baby, Leffe convinced Ilona to let the calf live in the house with them, like a pet. Olivia, the moose, ate with the family at the breakfast table, and to this day she remains fond of buttered toast.

Leffe rose to a moderate level of Internet fame as the man who kisses the moose on the lips. He shows off by doing this in front of all of the visitors to the farm with a large male moose named Holger.

I tentatively approached Holger to pet his massive antlers. I leaned over and smelled him, expecting something horsey, but he smelled sweet, like oats.

"She wants to kiss your moose," Nick laughed to Leffe. "Trust me. I can tell."

Leffe held his head while I gave Holger a peck on the snout. In return he licked my cheek.

"Sometimes I say he kisses better than my wife," Leffe laughed. But he got serious when I asked him about why his second marriage has thrived and his first one didn't. It was more than the fact that Ilona agreed to open the moose park.

"We share everything. You have to share everything. It's hard, but you figure it out. Everyone chips in. Work, pain, stress, joy, happiness, you share all of the things," Leffe said. "Together. We're partners. We split it, but it's not always equal. Sometimes I'm there 90 percent and sometimes she does 90 percent. My best advice is don't keep track."

Nick and I stayed quiet most of the drive back to Stockholm, but I could see Nick working something out in his head, talking silently to himself, his hands moving, like a mild schizophrenic.

"You're really nervous about having kids, aren't you?" I liked playing voodoo mind reader when he talked to himself. I was usually right.

"I'm just thinking, Squeak."

"About what?" I nibbled on a gummy moose candy Leffe had given me before we left. ("Like Swedish fish. But moose," he said.)

"About everything."

"Everything, like what?"

"Yeah, I'm nervous about having kids. It's a big step. Are we ready?"

I raised an eyebrow.

"I mean it. Are we ready. Do we need more time?"

I didn't want to snap back at him that I didn't have a whole lot of time. I was thirty-five. Three of my friends had had miscarriages in the past year and one had delivered a stillborn baby. When you walk into a doctor's office at thirty-five and say you want to have a baby, they give you a withering look and refer to you as an "older" mother.

"Actually, the term is 'geriatric mother,'" my geneticist had said during one of my appointments.

"That's not funny at all," I responded.

His expression didn't change. "It's just what we call it."

"What are you so nervous about?" I pressed Nick in the car. My hopelessly optimistic husband was never nervous about anything. He's the one who calmed me, who urged me to have faith that everything would work out the way it should. Why this one thing? I knew the answer. It was because it was something he wanted to be good at, to be completely ready for. Having kids *is* a big deal. It can be the grenade that blows up your relationship. Having kids for us was an even bigger deal, since we still weren't sure how we wanted to go about having kids. But no matter what we decided—trying to have our own kids, using a donor egg, adoption—it would all take an investment of time, energy, and money. My head began to hurt. I'd been buoyed by Leffe's enthusiasm for teamwork. *Husband and wife facing the harsh reality of life as a team of equals.* Now I felt deflated that Nick wasn't as excited about facing the next step as I was.

"It's just . . . Sometimes it takes over. . . . Sometimes it's all we talk about and it dominates every conversation. And I feel left out," Nick said. "I want to feel more involved."

When had he said that before? When I'd sidestepped him in our house auction. He was right. I'm a planner. When I decide I want to do something, I go after it. I had been talking a lot about pregnancy and having babies. And it felt like Nick was floating away from the conversation. When it's your body that has to get pregnant, it can become a very self-involved choice.

Nick went on.

"And sometimes I worry it's too soon. Have we been through enough things together? Have we done enough? Have we done everything we wanted to do before we have kids?"

I had my own fears about kids, but Nick's doubts made me feel even more scared than my own.

"I love you, baby girl. Maybe I'm being ridiculous," he said and pulled the car to the side of the road so he could hold my hand and look at me. I blinked back the tears.

"No, I get it," I said. "There is one more thing we could do."

14

Tanzania

Conquer the World Together

> When it's over, I want to say: all my life I was a bride married to amazement. I was the bridegroom, taking the world in my arms.
>
> —MARY OLIVER

Before Nick and I left San Francisco to climb Mt. Kilimanjaro in Tanzania, I wrote out a list of things I wanted us to accomplish during the trip:

Be together
Be happy
Don't die
Maybe pet a baby elephant

We also made a pact. If one of us couldn't make it up the mountain for any reason, the other would keep going.

"Seriously," I said to Nick. "If I get tired or hurt or sick or if I see a kitten or a small monkey that I think I need to rescue, you keep going." I knew if anyone was going to fail to make it to the top of the mountain, it would be me.

"We're not getting another pet. We've talked about this," Nick said. "And if I can't make it to the top, if I fail, then you keep going too." Nick wasn't going to fail. He doesn't fail at anything.

At 19,341 feet, Kilimanjaro is a very, very tall mountain. And while the climb to the top isn't technically difficult (you don't need an ice ax or ropes or anything), it's a strenuous four-day challenge that is incredibly taxing on the body. About 25,000 people climb the mountain every year, and of those only 40 percent make it to the summit. High-altitude pulmonary edema, where your lungs begin to take on potentially fatal fluid, is a real threat when humans venture that high. The effect the altitude has on the body is unpredictable and it doesn't matter what shape you're in. In 2010 Grand Slam tennis champion Martina Navratilova was brought down the mountain by a crew of porters before reaching the summit after becoming deathly ill. The woman whom *Tennis* magazine chose as the greatest female tennis player for the years 1965 through 2005 had to be evacuated from the mountain!

Almost everyone experiences some form of altitude sickness—intense muscle pain, nausea, an inability to breathe, dizziness, insomnia, or mind-altering headaches.

Why were we doing this again?

My dad takes seventeen different kinds of medications a day to treat his muscular dystrophy. He can no longer breathe on his own, and without the aid of an oxygen machine he would suffocate. He's frequently nauseated and stricken by intense bouts of pain and headaches. It wasn't lost on me that the symptoms of altitude sickness that I could experience on Mt. Kilimanjaro mirrored his daily existence.

"You're not him," my mom told me during one of our many conversations about my muscular dystrophy diagnosis.

About a month before we left for Africa my mom started getting better. She went into a behavioral therapy program and had her medication calibrated. She was like a whole new person, bright, cheery, and optimistic. She was my cheerleader again. She texted both Nick and me several times a day to tell us how much she loved both of us and how happy she was doing cardio and yoga with her new trainer.

It would have been overwhelming, if it wasn't such a huge relief. Her happiness even let some lightness into her relationship with my dad. She was more content, less angry. As I watched her massive transformation, I thought back to Chana's advice: Take care of yourself first.

"Seriously," my mom repeated to me. "Your future won't look anything like Dad's. We waited until it was much too late to be proactive against this. You're doing everything you can to fight it before it even begins."

I also did everything possible to ensure against failure on the mountain. My friend Mikey Sadowski works for one of the top-rated Kilimanjaro climbing companies, Intrepid Travel. Before I booked the trip with them, I talked to Mikey for hours about the best routes and guides. "Is there a guide who can carry me if I need to be carried?" I inquired. Apparently I wasn't the only one who asked this question. The answer was no.

Before leaving for Africa, Nick and I took iron pills and drank non-FDA-approved chlorophyll drops that supposedly increase the body's ability to take in oxygen. We got a prescription for Diamox, a drug that promises to decrease the potential for altitude sickness despite causing intense and painful tingling in the limbs, dizziness, ringing in the ears, and blurred vision. It forces you to pee every twenty minutes and makes beer taste like rusted copper.

"The side effects of this have to be worse than altitude sickness," I complained to Nick when we tested the drug back home and I walked straight into a wall. Both my hands and feet stung with pins and needles for an hour.

"Nope," he said with confidence. "Altitude sickness makes you feel like you're going to die."

....

To reach Mt. Kilimanjaro from San Francisco you take an eleven-hour flight to Amsterdam, an eight-hour flight to Nairobi, a one-hour flight to Kilimanjaro Airport, and then a two-hour drive to Marangu, a village nestled in the jungle at the foot of the mountain.

It was rainy and cold when we finally arrived at the Kibo Hotel in Marangu. The ramshackle German-built lodge appeared abandoned. A stooped man named Isaac, who couldn't have been younger than 110, heaved our two enormous duffel bags out of the car. I worried he'd collapse under the weight, but he excitedly ushered us into the shelter of the lobby.

"I'm starving!" I pleaded with Isaac.

"Do you want French fries?"

I almost kissed him. "That's all I want in the entire world."

A sign above the front door of the hotel proudly welcomed Jimmy Carter.

"Do you think Jimmy Carter is here?" I whispered to Nick.

"Mr. Carter, the president of the United States, was here in 1988," Isaac interrupted proudly. That sign had hung above the door for twenty-eight years.

"Well, if Jimmy and Rosalynn can climb this mountain, then I shouldn't have a problem," I said. "They don't exactly strike me as mountaineers!"

"Mr. Carter, the president of the United States, climbed it by helicopter," Isaac said and shuffled into the kitchen to fry the potatoes. Isaac was a one-man operation.

Threadbare lime green sheets with hot pink giraffes covered the two single beds in our room. I'd never seen an electric shower before, but Nick was very excited by the one in our bathroom. It looked like a showerhead from a postapocalyptic future, held together with thick rubber bands and fraying wires sticking out in every direction.

"I haven't seen one of these in years! Not since I backpacked

South America. This will shock the fuck out of you," Nick said with nervous excitement as he inspected the unraveling wires. "Seriously! Do not touch anything metal while you're wet. God, this is cool! I'll bet I could build one of these."

We squeezed into one of the very small beds and stared at the ceiling and the flickering single fluorescent bulb hanging from it.

"It's a little tight, don't you think?" I didn't want to give up on the romance or anything, but the two of us didn't fit in a single bed.

"It's good practice," Nick replied.

"For what?"

"In case we ever sleep on a submarine."

We'd both finally turned off our phones. There'd be no Wi-Fi or cell service on the mountain. The last time I had "unplugged," or not had both Internet and cell service for longer than twenty-four hours, was when we'd met in the Galápagos. I remembered the last moments I had cell service on that trip. With a small glimmer of a signal left, I frantically e-mailed everyone I knew to tell them I would not be available for eight days. In the midst of it, this straw-haired California dude reached over the seat on our bus to shake my hand.

"Hi. I'm Nick," he said. His eyes were an honest shade of blue.

"Yeah. Hi. You know we won't have Internet this whole trip?"

"I know. Devils! But I've made peace with it," he said, leaning back comfortably into his seat.

"Good for you! I haven't . . . so can you just let me finish a couple of things here? I'm busy." Without the Internet the course of my life was forever diverted.

I smiled at the memory. It helped keep my trepidation about the days to come at bay.

"I'm nervous," I finally said. "I'm scared I'm not in good enough shape to make it up the mountain." I wasn't worried about Nick. At age forty-two Nick was still able to drink a six-pack of beer at night, rise the next morning, and then run a half marathon without training.

I couldn't see his face, but I knew my husband was drifting off to sleep. He wrapped his arm around me and just murmured, "I'll carry you if I have to."

....

Rural Tanzania smells different—the way the planet smelled before humans went everywhere wearing Axe body spray and coated in Purell—a sweet mixture of burning earth and animals and human sweat and life that's real and comforting. We were just two hundred miles below the equator, but the air at the foot of Kilimanjaro was cool and crisp.

We set out early on a Sunday morning, the sounds of the village slowly fading into the distance. Other climbers stretched and fueled up with bananas and energy bars while I gnawed cautiously on a Cadbury chocolate bar.

The concept of actually climbing Kilimanjaro and not just talking about it didn't become real until we stood at the base of the mountain.

"It's much bigger than it looks on postcards," I said, gazing at the vast cloud-covered mass of earth looming in front of us, so tall we could only see a small portion of it.

One of the mountain guides, named Jos, tried to assure me that people in much worse shape than I had made it to the summit.

"The Russians, they drink the vodka all the way to the top," he said. "They fine."

I told him vodka makes me do funny things too.

"And another man, Helmut was his name. I think he was Austrian. He was seventy-two. He drank gin all the way up the mountain. At five thousand meters he pulled out a bottle of the Johnnie Walker. He drank it and collapsed and then he died. His wife just started laughing. She told me we must go on and call someone to get his body. 'He wanted to die on Kili,' she said. But she made it to the summit and she was very old."

"That's a terrible story, Jos."

"But she made it," he insisted.

Our main climbing guide was Justaz, pronounced like "justice," who looked like a more fit and more approachable version of Jamie Foxx and had climbed Kili more than 250 times. Even though he was younger than both Nick and me, he was married with four kids.

Justaz warned me he'd seen more than twenty couples break up while trying to summit the mountain, most memorably a pair on their honeymoon. The new wife felt crappy, with headaches and a chill, when they set out for the mountain. By the end of the first day her husband had stridden to the front of their hiking group while she lagged behind. The tension between the two was so high that on the third day he threw her things out of their shared tent, telling her he was sick of her whining.

The woman sat on the ground and cried. Justaz tried to comfort her.

"Do you know how to sing?" she asked him. He nodded.

"Can you sing anything in English?" He nodded with less confidence and hummed a tune from the British pop band Westlife.

When they reached base camp for the summit at just over fifteen thousand feet, the husband demanded that he be allowed to summit the mountain without his wife. He scurried to the top with a guide and hightailed it back to Marangu. She went up later with the rest of the group.

"He just left her?" Nick asked in disbelief.

"I thought we'd see him when we got all the way down the mountain," Justaz recalled as he held pace next to me. "But he changed his flight and left her there."

I think he sensed the story was getting me down.

"But I've also organized a wedding on the summit. We were at 5,895 meters with a priest, best man, maid of honor, bridesmaids, and twelve other guests!" he said to lighten the mood.

"Climbing the mountain is actually a good metaphor for succeeding in marriage," he said to us. "What you have to remember is that both the mountain and a marriage can be completely different in the afternoon from what it was like in the morning. You can't try to predict what any day will bring. Trying to predict it will only bring grief. You have to try to enjoy the parts that are wonderful."

Butterflies the size of my hand flew just inches from my face—some speckled periwinkle blue, others black with perfect white polka dots. Violet monkeys the size of large dogs bolted into the path and let out bloodcurdling shrieks at the sight of us.

"Monks on the run!" Nick shouted and chased after them to take a picture.

Giant tree roots and moss-covered boulders obstructed our path. We wandered through a dead volcanic crater filled with willowy waist-high elephant grass. Glacial streams rushed over boulders, winding their way through beds of red mountain gladiolus.

Looking ahead at the steep and rocky inclines made me anxious, and when I concentrated on those, I became convinced I'd never get over the next ridge. Instead I looked down at my feet, just putting one in front of the other. There were stretches of the mountain where I didn't think at all and bits where my monkey mind leaped from branch to branch. When my body started to hurt I chanted a personal mantra softly: "Your body is strong. Your body is strong. Your body is strong. Thank you for being able to climb this mountain. Thank you. Thank you. Thank you." I'd frequently stop and pretend to take pictures on my phone just to catch my breath.

I began to appreciate the flat bits—the simple sections, relaxed and smooth. It was nice for things to be easy. These reminded me of the parts of a marriage you might call boring—the long stretches where you settle into a daily routine, grocery-shop, do the laundry, binge-watch *The Wire*, go to sleep at a reasonable hour every night, and wake up and do it all over again the next day. For so long I'd considered this kind of monotony to be boring. I wanted the hills, the roller coaster, the constant adrenaline rush of newness. For too many years I had relished the things that were hard. I wanted to conquer the most difficult jobs, explore the furthest reaches of the world, tame the men everyone else said couldn't be tamed. Now I wanted to just appreciate the flat bits of my life and marriage.

Nick outpaced me, often leading our small group up the mountain. I wanted to call up to him, but I was reluctant to slow him down. Was I becoming the woman who was ditched on her honeymoon?

On the mountain you lose all concept of time. Hikers on their way down from the summit trudged past us through the rocks and dirt like zombies, refusing to meet our eyes. They'd likely finished their ascent to the summit less than twenty-four hours earlier. The last day of any Kilimanjaro climb has been described by serious trekkers as "hell on earth," and "the most painful thing I've ever done." Even Arctic trekkers who have experienced temperatures of –30 degrees say they have never experienced cold like the bitter chill on the way to the top of Kilimanjaro. On the final day of the climb, the ascent to the final peak begins just after midnight, on about three hours of sleep. When you ask the guides why they do this gonzo thing in the dark, they tell you that it's better for you psychologically if you can't see the steepness and distance involved in reaching the summit. The rocky scree coating the ground at that altitude turns all climbers into Sisyphus. Two steps forward are rewarded with at least one step back. The trail is littered with climbers who have passed out or are experiencing debilitating nausea from altitude sickness. Throughout the hike, the thought of that last day constantly festers in the back of your brain.

Hiking the mountain is difficult, but sleeping on it is impossible. There's no fire or heat in the A-frame sleeping huts stationed along the trail, just wooden walls to protect you from the intense wind. Ravens perch on top of them and howl, as if warning you to turn back toward the comfort of the Kibo Hotel, Isaac, and French fries. The huts sleep five, with three sleeping pads on the floor and two bunked. The only warmth came from my sleeping bag, a rented four-season down bag that alleged it would protect me to –22 degrees Celsius.

I couldn't sleep after an endless first day of hiking. I was freezing and the door to our hut would stay closed only with three pairs of boots piled in front of it. My feet had been torn to shreds that day by boots just a touch too tight. My breathing was labored from the altitude and a dull ache had formed just behind my eyes. I couldn't imagine how I would endure three more days of this. The damn Diamox made me need to pee worse than I'd ever needed to pee in my entire life, but outside of our hut a tree hyrax, a chubby rodentlike creature that resembles a cross between a muskrat and a raccoon, made a noise like it was killing a Japanese tourist. I turned my headlight on low and read the graffiti former climbers had etched into the hut's walls.

I made it to the top but it was so fucking hard.

It's cold and long and endless. We smell like shit, look like shit and really need to take a bath.

The mountain kicked our asses but it was worth it.

Don't do it. Stay here. I wanted to die.

I climbed unsteadily down from my bunk and sat on the floor, stroking Nick's forehead to wake him up. His skin was warm under my cold hand.

"I can't sleep," I whispered. "Can I climb into your sleeping bag?"

"There isn't room, Platypus."

"There is. It will be practice. For a submarine."

"Squeeze my hand," Nick whispered, his face lit softly by a small sliver of moon coming through the hut's solitary window. "Squeeze it hard. Like you mean it." I squeezed as I crouched there, staring through the window at some of the most magnificent stars I'd ever seen. Nick unwrapped himself from his own warm sleeping bag and led me back to mine, making sure it was properly zipped.

"Scooch all the way to the bottom to get all of the air out of it. Okay. Now we need to pull this all the way up and over your head."

"I'll be smothered!"

"You won't be smothered. I will never let a sleeping bag smother you."

....

Justaz was spot on about the mercurial moods of the mountain. The next morning was sunny and clear, so much so that we could see across the vast expanse of Tanzania for miles, all the way to the plains of the Serengeti. Climbers set out early each morning just as the sun cleaves the horizon because it's the only time the mountain is free of clouds. You can see just far enough ahead to be comfortable with the next steps and so, for a small window of time, the future feels as safe as the past.

The afternoon is another matter entirely. It can unexpectedly pour buckets in the afternoon, even if it's not supposed to be rainy season yet. And as in a marriage, if you begin your day with too many expectations, the mountain will throw them back in your face with glee. But that's part of the fun of it, really—the unknown and the slight terror that accompanies it. The day before will never prepare you for what happens the next, and yesterday is forgotten the second your tired body lies down. And yet each day on the mountain does make you stronger and more open to the uncertainty.

As I continued to hike, I thought about all the time I spent worrying and whether that worry had yielded anything productive. The locals have a phrase in Kiswahili, *Hakuna matata*, that literally translates to "No worries." I'd thought it was something Elton John made up for Disney's *The Lion King* soundtrack, but it isn't. The phrase began to resonate even though altitude sickness was constantly on my mind.

When it came to altitude sickness, Justaz was the Dalai Lama. He wouldn't allow any members of our group to discuss their symptoms with one another. "Much of it be in your head, and then those symptoms become contagious throughout the group," he advised. "You be positive and you probably will not have it. When I trek and I feel a little headache, I switch off my brain and it goes away. I feel a little nauseous. I tell my brain this is not happening."

"You could make a fortune as a mindfulness coach in New York City," I said to him.

"But Jo, then how would I climb the mountain?"

I slept better, but not great, that second night, a night even colder than the first. The secret to my intermittent slumber was the Ambien I'd stashed inside my bottle of Advil. I'd promised myself I'd be careful with the pill, since I had no idea what it would do to my body at a high altitude. But I couldn't bear another sleepless night, and so I nibbled just a half before scrunching into my sleeping bag.

I woke feeling like my entire body had been rolled in broken glass from the arduous treks of the two previous days. Even though he felt fine, Nick made sure to slow down with me. He carried some of the weight from my pack and stole a salt shaker from the mess hut so I would stay hydrated as well as napkins from the other trekkers so I'd never run out of toilet paper.

There are no rest stops along the trail. When you gotta go, you find a place in the bush.

"We call it an LWV, a loo with a view!" Justaz said.

"*Pole-pole*," Nick insisted to the guides. It meant "My wife needs to go slow" in Kiswahili. Picture the movements of an arthritic septuagenarian; that was the pace my body preferred. It had nothing to do with my weird genetic condition and everything to do with the fact that climbing this mountain was really hard. We fell in step with a group of Japanese wearing ski goggles and face masks and a ninety-year-old dentist from Germany who wore hiking pants and a Bavarian-style sweater cut off at the midriff to stay both warm and cool on the trail.

On the path Nick invented a whimsical song to keep me going. It made no sense but had a rhythm that worked well with the click, click of my walking sticks.

"Oregano, oregano. Gotta keep it moving. Gotta keep it moving.

Oregano, oregano. Oh yeah. All right." I didn't have to say anything to Nick. We both knew this was what teamwork should feel like.

By the close of day three, going *pole-pole*, I felt a mixture of adrenaline and pride. We'd ascended thousands of feet, slowly but surely, to land at an altitude higher than I'd ever been. I'd even become immune to the weird side effects of the Diamox.

The highest summit of Kilimanjaro is called Uhuru, which translates to "freedom." On the fourth day of our climb it was plainly in sight, so close we felt like we could reach out and touch it. I ran toward it, spreading my arms and doing a silly dance through a grove of giant groundsels, alien-looking trees found only on Kilimanjaro above fourteen thousand feet. They resemble Joshua trees mixed with cactus and pineapple. These would be the last substantial plant life we'd see before entering Kilimanjaro's alpine desert, a harsh, dry landscape consisting mainly of rock and ice. Nick thumbed through my phone and played the Toto song "Africa" and joined me, both of us waving our arms in the air, making the guides giggle.

Taking a thousand photos of the peak distracted me from the fact that my husband was slowing down.

We were in the alpine desert, so close to the final ascent, when Nick felt the effects of the altitude in new and severe ways. It began when he hallucinated that he saw a fish smiling at him from on top of a very large boulder.

"He's laughing at me." He pointed. I brushed it off as another of his attempts to make me laugh in an uncomfortable situation.

Next his head began to throb and his stomach heaved.

"I don't feel good," he whispered reluctantly. "It's getting worse and worse."

I sat in the sand and pulled Nick down beside me. I was conscious of the fact that I could smell myself and wondered if he could too. We hadn't showered in four days and the sweat on our bodies had frozen, unfrozen, and refrozen over and over again.

"I have to go down," he said.

"You don't. You're fine. We'll wait it out. Oregano, oregano. Gotta keep it moving. Gotta keep it moving." I handed him the salt shaker from my pocket.

"Eat this."

As we sat there, four guides silently wheeled a metal stretcher past us. Lying down on it was a lumpy, vaguely human form, sheathed in a sleeping bag cocoon, an oxygen tank clanging against the rusted metal of the stretcher.

"Is he dead?" I asked Justaz.

"No."

I couldn't tell if he was fibbing to keep us calm. "Are you sure?"

Justaz looked down the path where the stretcher had disappeared around a bend and remained silent.

Nick looked at me. His face was transformed, contorted. His eyes, usually curious and alert, were dulled and his jaw was tense and tight. "I need to go down."

I placed my hand on Nick's arm. "Are you sure?" I looked at him. So strong, so handsome, and for the first time since we'd met, so vulnerable.

"You can keep going," he said. "You're doing great. Keep going."

I could have kept going. Thanks to Nick's slowing down, carrying my pack, and sneaking me extra food, I finally felt strong enough to make it up the mountain. My ego wanted me to keep going, if only to post an Instagram from the summit. But I didn't need to. And I wasn't about to abandon my sick husband on the side of a mountain in a foreign country, scared and alone. "I feel like a chump," Nick said, wincing from the pain and closing his eyes.

"I've known a lot of chumps and you're the best one I know," I said and stroked his back. For the first time since we'd been married I realized that part of my role as a wife was taking care of my husband the same way he took care of me. I echoed the words he'd said to me before we got married.

"I want to take care of you," I said. I meant it. "Please let me take care of you."

Nick nodded.

"We'll do it again sometime," he said.

"When we're old and retired and comfortable enough with ourselves to wear sweaters cut off as crop tops," I answered. Not for a second did I catch myself and think, *Maybe I won't be able to do it when we're older. Maybe this is my last chance.*

I got more out of that mountain than I ever thought I would. I was certain of something now: No matter how my disease progressed, I had faith that if we wanted to climb that mountain again, I'd be able to do it with Nick by my side. I trusted my body and I trusted my husband. Sitting at nearly fifteen thousand feet in the air, I pulled a deep breath into my belly and let it rush out in a single sigh. I felt no pain, no anxiety, and no urge to do anything but hold Nick's hand. I didn't want to live my life with limitations or let fear govern what I would or wouldn't, could or couldn't do.

I also realized marriage means lifting up the other person when they can't do it themselves. How many times had Nick already done that for me? Too many to even count. He innately understood this about our commitment. It took climbing a very tall mountain thousands of miles away from home for me to grasp it. There would be days when I was stronger than Nick, when I needed to be the one to carry him.

"Thanks for taking care of me, Squeak," Nick said as we turned around and began our descent, his symptoms abating as soon as we went down another thousand feet.

I was quiet for a beat. "That's my job."

That night the nightmares would stop for good. My legs had proven they were strong, carrying me up over fifteen thousand feet. I was able to breathe, even in a place where the air is thin and cold and deprived of oxygen—a place where human beings shouldn't be able to breathe.

We didn't die on the mountain.

Before we left Africa I did pet a baby elephant at the David Sheldrick Elephant Orphanage. His name was Mwashoti and he held my hand with his trunk.

We'd been together.

We were happy.

15

Scotland

Good Decisions—Lessons from Year One

"This is going to be like *Brigadoon* meets *Thelma and Louise*," I said to Glynnis as she maneuvered our small black rental car onto the wrong side of the road away from the Edinburgh airport.

"But without the murder or getting lost in a mythical village," she said.

"But with the red lipstick."

With my first wedding anniversary a couple weeks away, I'd flown across the country and over the Atlantic Ocean to the Scottish Highlands, an assignment for Alaska Airlines that became a week-long trip with Glynnis. She flew in from Paris, where she was finishing her own book, to meet me for the week.

I can hear the wheels turning in your head. You're not ending the book with Nick? Is everything OK?

Everything is better than OK. But, after twelve months of being married and researching what marriage and partnership mean in the twenty-first century, I learned a few truths. Yes, I can tell you all about teamwork and communication and divvying up chores and duties and date nights and going to bed angry, or not angry, but one of the most important things I learned was to maintain my own life outside my marriage. I needed to make sure I still felt like me.

And so Scotland. With Glynnis.

"Life doesn't get much better than driving through the Scottish countryside while eating Cadbury chocolate," Glynnis said, reaching into a plastic bag filled with Twirls, Flakes, Crunchies, and Dairy Milks that we'd picked up at the local Tesco.

"I can't believe Cadbury hasn't asked us to make a commercial yet," I added.

"It's a real oversight on their part."

Glynnis was the one who drove me into my first year of marriage, literally thousands of miles across the country in a tiny yellow car that smelled like potato chips and giant dog and metaphorically by being the officiant at our wedding. Now she'd be the one to drive me, in a tiny black car with a stick shift, on the wrong side of the road, out of the first twelve months. That meant a lot to me. Getting married doesn't mean you leave the support systems that existed before the marriage behind you, or that they become less necessary. We create families for ourselves well before we get married, intricate webs of relationships that aren't recognized by law, but are no less important, valuable, and meaningful. Maintaining those is a crucial part of making any relationship work. Your spouse can't be your everything. Amazing friends can still feed your heart and soul in a different way, a way that ultimately supports the health of your partnership.

In researching the history of male-female relationships I also learned that it is much too easy for today's modern, independent ladies to forget that a married woman's freedom to travel without her spouse is a relatively new phenomenon. For most of human history a woman rarely traveled outside the boundaries of her hometown unless accompanied by her husband or her father. I planned to make the most of this privilege.

It isn't just a privilege in the sense that getting to see the world on your own or with your girlfriends is a wonderful treat, it's that the time away puts your relationship with your spouse in perspective. The moment I landed in Scotland, I realized two things. The first was that I'd missed traveling on my own, where I was forced to take care of myself. When Nick is around to handle things, it's easy to complain, to be a pain in the ass. It's easier than I ever expected to enjoy being taken care of. Nick has grown so good at noticing when I am cold or hungry or about to be crabby that sometimes I forget to anticipate my own needs. It's a pretty big difference from the girl who wouldn't let her husband help her off the devils' chairlift in Chile. It was nice to be that girl again. But the more important thing I realized was that I missed Nick like crazy and I began to appreciate all those small things he does for me without my ever having to ask for them.

When you wake up next to someone every day, pick their hair out of the drain, clean up their dirty dishes, socks, and underwear, listen to them bitch about their job and tell the same stories and jokes over and over again, it's nice to be reminded of what it's like when they're not around—and to realize things are better when they are.

I often think about what Bobby Klein said to Nick and me in the Mexican jungle: "People come to me right after they get married and they say, 'Now we're one.' That's bullshit. And it's a problem. You're not one. Becoming one is impossible." The intensity and newness of marriage compelled Nick and me to be together as much as we possibly could during year one. But as I learned from Chana in Israel, moving apart is also an excellent way to come back together stronger and happier.

....

"So has it sunk in yet? Being married?" Glynnis teased me as we drove through rolling green hills dotted with fluffy clouds of sheep. She had asked me this a year earlier when nothing had sunk in, when I was terrified about failing as a partner and giving up my independence in favor of an entirely new and uncertain future. And she already knew the answer. Hardly a week went by when we didn't text each other from halfway around the world about big things and little things—sick parents, failed pregnancy tests, work drama, a bad haircut, a creepy Uber driver, and weird doctors' visits.

"I don't know if it ever really sinks in," I said, stretching my legs out over the dashboard, my toes making smudges on the windshield.

"It's one year later, we're in a different country, you're married, and I'm driving you on the wrong side of the road. There's got to be a metaphor for marriage in that," Glynnis said, nipping at her Twirl bar.

I just shook my head. "I'm so done with metaphors for marriage."

There were 365 days in the first year of our marriage, our wet-cement year, and I still remember each and every one. Not just the long, lazy ones in Paris or the panicked ones faxing mortgage documents or being carried through a mud pit in Maine, but the "boring" ones where we sat on the orange couch and read different sections of the newspaper, or stood side by side in the kitchen chopping vegetables. These memories would fade soon and be replaced by new ones, milestones and ordinary moments alike, but for now I held these close rather than think about what lay ahead.

I started this book believing that somewhere someone has figured out the secret to the perfect marriage. Now I know everyone, no matter how good their relationship, struggles to make it work.

If you visited my Instagram in my first year of our marriage, you'd see a cute couple with a ridiculously good-looking dog traveling to exotic locations together, climbing mountains, strolling along Dutch canals, eating too much delicious food. You'd have no idea that I lost my job, that I had a shitty medical diagnosis, that the doctors told me my dad was close to dying three times, or that my mother had a nervous breakdown. You wouldn't know about all the times I fought with my husband or drank too much wine and cried myself to sleep, confused about whether I'd made any of the right decisions in my life. I hope this book showed some of that. Because that's what's real. That's what the first year of marriage is really like.

There were times during our first year of marriage when I wondered if Nick and I would still be together if we hadn't actually gotten married. In a single day I could wake up in the morning thinking, *I'm the luckiest girl alive for finding this wonderful, handsome man*, and by noon, with little to no provocation, wonder, *How I can possibly be with this person for the rest of my life?* But by bedtime it would all change again. And then there were weeks when I didn't think about my marriage at all, where it was all routine and simple like the flat bits on Mt. Kilimanjaro.

Glynnis and I planned to camp in a run-down little cabin in the Cairngorm mountains, the highest mountains in the UK (which isn't saying a lot), a tundralike wilderness filled with dense groves of ancient Caledonian pines reminiscent of fairytale forests. Nick is the camper in our family, but I did OK preparing for Glynnis and my overnight survival by packing ample provisions of chocolate and Scotch whiskey. It took a few hours of driving to make it to Aviemore, the sleepy village from where we'd set out on a three-mile hike up the mountain where we'd sleep for the evening.

"Do you know where we're going?" Glyn asked me.

"I think so," I said with false certainty once we began walking. "I studied the maps. It should be a straight shot. There will be a lake, a curve in the road, and then we should be there."

We walked in silence for a beat, letting our bodies adjust to the rhythm of the hike.

"So what have you learned?" Glynnis asked as we huffed our way up the slope. "Are you a marriage guru now?"

I laughed. "Not even a little bit."

I could tell her, and you, that Nick and I immediately took to heart and implemented all the advice in the book, but that would be a lie.

It takes time for things to sink in, and old habits are hard to break. Every time I tell someone that I wrote a book about marriage, they ask me for the best thing I've learned. I don't have a quick and easy answer to that question. The best advice has nothing to do with instant gratification or measurable results. Different advice is helpful at different times. There are some things, like the Five Minutes exercise, that we practice almost every week, and others, like building a strong community around us, that will take time. I have made three new friends in San Francisco, ones who call me back and actually meet me when we make plans. The hardest advice to integrate into our lives has been figuring out a positive work/life balance and articulating our feelings about money, how much we need, how much we can spend, and what both of us are willing to sacrifice to meet our shared goals. It's an ongoing conversation.

In her 2005 book *Marriage, a History,* the researcher and author Stephanie Coontz wrote that "Leo Tolstoy once remarked that all happy families are alike, while every unhappy family is unhappy in its own way. But the more I study the history of marriage, the more I think the opposite is true. Most unhappy marriages in history share common patterns, leaving their tear-stained—and sometimes bloodstained—records across the ages. But each happy, successful marriage seems to be happy in its own way."

That's true. There are no right or wrong answers. Nick and I are happy in our own way. Our society has a narrow definition of a "successful" marriage. My parents stayed married and slept in the same bed for forty years, but they couldn't stand each other. Still, in many people's eyes, their marriage is a success because they stuck it out. I also talked about this with Katherine Woodward Thomas, the author of *Conscious Uncoupling: 5 Steps to Living Happily Even After.* Her phrase "conscious uncoupling" made headlines when the actress Gwyneth Paltrow used it to speak about her split from husband Chris Martin. Woodward Thomas agreed with me that our paradigm for assessing marital success is ridiculously skewed. "We go to this automatic assumption that a relationship has failed if it ends before one or both people die. We're judging the relationship according to how long it lasts rather than by the quality of the connection. Yet, the reality of our time is that most people will not meet and mate with one person for life. 'Happily ever after' is an antiquated model from four hundred years ago, when the life span was under forty years of age. Rather than judge the value of a union according to how long it lasts, we may want to begin looking for the growth that happened for both people in that relationship, and the amazing things that union created, no matter how long they were together." That advice was a good lesson for me to resist passing judgment on anyone's marriage or divorce and to stop automatically thinking about the end of any marriage as a failure. Just staying married isn't my goal for Nick and me. The goals are constantly moving and shifting, but they include things like being fulfilled, growing together, and making a positive impact in our little corner of the world. Just sticking it out, that's not enough for us. I keep going back to Erica Jong's challenge that we create a new kind of marriage. It is up to us to figure out what the modern marriage looks like. It's scary, but it's also exciting and inspiring.

Even though I'm loath to single out any advice as the key to how to be married, there are insights that have stuck with us, words that ring with wisdom when times get tough, and they're worth mentioning again.

Don't let your job dictate your marriage.

Nick and I don't know where we'll be living five years from now. We could be in our cozy (so *hygge*) apartment in San Francisco, we could go back to Philadelphia or Milwaukee to take care of our parents, or we could give it all up to live in Madagascar. The one thing we know is that we don't want our jobs to make that decision for our family. We don't want work to decide where we live or how often we get to see each other. We want to make those choices. This is what a work/life balance means to us.

Go easy on yourselves.

We both learned a lot about taking care of ourselves in the midst of taking care of our marriage. Every day won't be perfect or easy, or even good, and that has to be okay. We talk about the imperfections and the hurts. We don't beat ourselves up, because we're in this for the long run. It's a marathon and not a sprint. Although some days do feel like an obstacle course where you carry your spouse up a mountain and through a pit of mud.

Obsessing over whether you have a good marriage, whether you're doing everything right, is a great way to set yourself up for failure.

There are no steps.

This advice from the Megs is something we tell ourselves often. Don't make the next move (buying a house, having a baby, having another baby, buying a second house) because it feels like the next step. There are no steps. Just enjoy each other. Let the marriage unfold the way it's supposed to rather than looking for the next big step.

It's okay to go to bed angry.

Everything looks better and less scary after a good night's sleep. It's okay to not like each other once in a while, even when that once in a while is after midnight.

Don't pee with the door open.

There's something to the French notion about maintaining a little bit of mystery in your marriage, just a little. Our small bathroom dictates that sometimes I do still pee with the door open, but I try to maintain mystery in other ways. Sometime in the middle of our first year I stopped texting Nick a play-by-play of my entire day. It's nice to leave a little something new to talk about at the end of the day.

Lose your expectations.

If twelve months of traveling taught us anything, it was that it's a waste of time to be disappointed when things don't work out exactly the way you expected. Smaller indignities like canceled flights, food poisoning, and altitude sickness teach you the value of being flexible in both life and your relationship, helping prepare you for the big stuff. Both of us can honestly say that learning to travel well together, which included compromising on the road, letting the other person lead, and knowing when to take charge, helped us get through some of the very difficult things we've faced.

Getting married doesn't turn you into a grown-up.

In fact, some of the most childish people I've ever met have been married for longer than I've been alive. Being married doesn't turn you into anything new except for a married person. We're still a mess in a lot of ways. We fight and go to bed angry. Our spare bedroom is filled with crap—a vortex of unfolded laundry, a guitar Nick will never play, still-packed boxes, and an eerily accurate watercolor portrait of Lady Piazza someone gave us as a wedding gift. One day a baby will live in there. But not just yet.

You're in the driver's seat.

The people you love and whose opinions you value may still not want the same kind of marriage as you. You're in charge of your happily ever after. You and your partner are in control of making the marriage you want. The institution of marriage carries a lot of baggage, but it doesn't mean that you have to keep it.

Modern marriage in America is about choice. We've broken free of antiquated traditions and been given the freedom to craft our own kind of partnership.

Nick and I gathered different ingredients from around the world. We stirred them together to create our perfect marriage cocktail, to design a life well-lived by how we love. Sheryl Sandberg told women how important it was to marry well. How well you are married is up to you.

Say thanks.

Call it gratitude, call it appreciation. Call it whatever you want. Just do it. It's truly the easiest thing you can do to make each day together a little bit better.

Equality isn't fifty-fifty all the time.

When I first got married, I worried that my feminist card would be revoked if my husband and I didn't split things right down the middle. Now I realize how ridiculous that notion is. There are days, weeks even, when I do all of the housework (laundry, cooking, bed-making) because Nick is swamped with work. Then we switch. Sometimes I nest, sometimes he nests. While I was in Scotland Nick completely transformed our house by wallpapering the bathroom, installing shelves in the kitchen, and buying new picture frames for our bedroom. Our responsibilities change on a daily basis and we try to be outspoken when one of us feels overwhelmed. It's still a constant conversation. After one month of cooking dinner every single night I got a little agitated and brought up the fact that I felt relegated to the kitchen. Nick was surprised. "I thought you were just getting into cooking," he said. The truth is we fell into a rut, we discovered it, and switched things up the next week. And to be honest, I *do* like cooking, I just didn't like the idea of it automatically falling to me. Balance in a marriage isn't about a spreadsheet, it's about both partners feeling supported. Our motto is: "If you see something do something. Don't say something. Why are you talking about it? Just do it." This goes for everything from making the bed to feeding the dog to paying unexpected tax bills. No one should expect praise or a medal for helping make both our lives run more smoothly. The balance of who does what will ebb and flow and the most important thing is to be conscious of how it changes.

Keep talking.

It's easier than you think to stop talking. I have entire conversations in my head that I believe I had with Nick, but I never said any of it out loud. For us it isn't about setting up a regimented schedule for serious conversations, it's more about keeping the floodgates open and not being afraid to speak up. The second anything feels off, or strange, we try to talk about it. It's something we're both still getting used to.

Money doesn't equal power.

Don't let money rule your relationship. It's easy to fall into the trap of believing that earning power determines who has a bigger say in marital decisions. Both partners have to let that go. While who does what in a marriage will ebb and flow, big decisions need to be made by consensus, or it will lead to resentment down the road.

Never stop adventuring.

This doesn't mean climbing Mt. Kilimanjaro once a year. Adventuring can be as simple as trying a new restaurant together.

The anthropologist and relationship guru Dr. Helen Fisher put it best when she explained that "Research shows that novelty—taking risks or trying something new—can trigger the release of dopamine in the brain. I'm not just talking about novelty in the bedroom (although that would be a good start). You can get the same effect from sampling a new type of cuisine together or riding the roller coaster at an amusement park."

Relationships thrive on newness and the ability to keep learning and growing together. And if you ever get the chance to sign up for a wife-carrying race, take it. We'll buy you a beer.

....

I think a lot about how I've changed in the past year. I'm still surprised by the fact that I'm now a person who always has stamps in the house, and cloth napkins, and very *hygge* napkin rings. I learned to fix the garbage disposal on my own and I've managed to keep the houseplants alive.

Nick and I have dinner together at the dinner table at least three nights a week, and we use the cloth napkins and the napkin rings. I no longer sleep with my phone. Nick has stopped being such a snob about artisanal slow-drip coffee. We do ride our bikes most everywhere in the city, but Nick has agreed that taxis, Ubers, and Lyfts make better sense in inclement weather and when we don't know where the hell we're going. We've learned the value of teamwork and compromise and what it actually means to tough it out through sickness and health, good times and bad. We've learned that marriage is work. It's getting up every single day and saying, "I choose you and I choose us. Let's do this!"

Nick makes my life better. He provides the warmth, comfort, and security I've craved since childhood. When we got engaged so quickly, friends wondered whether we knew each other well enough to get married. I know without a doubt that I know him better than I've known anyone in my entire life.

....

The sun had nearly sunk behind the mountains and Glynnis and I were lost. Nick would know what to do, I thought. He'd know where to go. Shit! The straightforward trail veered off into a half dozen tributaries, leaving us to guess at the direction of the shelter. I glanced over at Glynnis, who was wearing a rabbit fur sweater that wouldn't keep her warm much longer.

"Is this the right way?" she asked me.

"It feels like the right way," I said in a voice I hoped was reassuring.

"At least there are no predators in Scotland! The last wolf was killed here in the seventeenth century. I Googled it. There's a plaque to commemorate it," she said. Between the two of us we had about half of the wilderness and camping knowledge of Nick Aster. It would have to be enough.

I chose a path and hoped it was the one that would lead us to shelter.

We continued our walk up and over rolling hills blanketed in royal purple heather, leaping over gurgling mountain brooks and skirting a loch so green it had to be a home for fairies. The still-damp air smelled vaguely of peat and something smoky, like the aftertaste of Scotch whiskey. We ascended yet another hill and went around a bend, nearly tripping on tree roots that cracked up through the rocky path. And then we saw it—a small stone structure so tiny and quaint, it was likely inhabited by a hobbit. Our shelter for the night.

"We did it!" I exclaimed. "I got us here!" It was such a small thing, but there was something powerful about doing this without Nick.

Of course we had remembered to bring the chocolate and the whiskey, but had only packed a total of two matches.

"If we use one match to light the end of this *Us Weekly* then we can use it to light the other candles," I said, feeling like Bear Grylls.

We managed to light a small fire that kept us warm through the night.

Glynnis fell right to sleep, but I stayed awake, staring out the window at the black hills. I rolled over and dug my phone out of the bottom of my backpack. It had maybe a bar of service. I texted Nick.

"Are you sad that this is over? The first year? That our adventure is ending?" I wrote. After this trip, we had no more plane tickets booked, no trips planned.

I closed my eyes and waited to see if the message would send.

His reply came just as I drifted off to sleep.

"Baby girl . . ." he texted back. "This adventure is just beginning!"

Bibliography

1. San Francisco: After Happily Ever After

Coontz, Stephanie. *Marriage, a History: How Love Conquered Marriage.* New York: Penguin Books, 2006.

Friedan, Betty. *The Feminine Mystique.* New York: W. W. Norton, 2013.

Shaw, George Bernard. *Getting Married.* 1st World Library—Literary Society, 2007.

Syfers, Judy. "Why I Want a Wife." Originally published in *Ms.* magazine. N.d. Web, accessed October 5, 2016, cwluherstory.org/why-i-want-a-wife.html.

U.S. Travel Association. Valentine's Survey Finds Traveling Together Strengthens Relationships, Makes Sex Better. Web. October 5, 2016.

2. Chile: Surrender?

Brown, William M. et al. "Dance Reveals Symmetry Especially in Young Men." *Nature.* December 22, 2005. Web.

Cury, James Oliver. *The Playboy Guide to Bachelor Parties: Everything You Need to Know About Planning the Groom's Rite of Passage—From Simple to Sinful.* New York: Simon & Schuster, 2003.

Finkel, Eli J. "The All-or-Nothing Marriage." *New York Times.* Web.

February 14, 2014, nytimes.com/2014/02/15/opinion/sunday/the-all-or-nothing-marriage.html.

Reece, Gabrielle. *My Foot Is Too Big for the Glass Slipper.* New York: Scribner, 2014.

"Salsa Your Way out of the Blues." BBC News. BBC, January 8, 2007. Web, accessed October 5, 2016, news.bbc.co.uk/2/hi/uk_news/england/derbyshire/6239269.stm.

Zabell, Samantha. "The Rise of the Man-Gagement Ring." *The Atlantic,* February 14, 2014. Web, accessed October 5, 2016. theatlantic.com/national/archive/2014/02/the-rise-of-the-man-gagement-ring/283827/.

3. Mexico: Never Stop Talking

Grunwald, Lisa. *The Marriage Book: Centuries of Advice, Inspiration, and Cautionary Tales from Adam and Eve to Zoloft.* New York: Simon & Schuster, 2015.

Levy, John. *The Happy Family.* New York: Alfred A. Knopf, 1938.

Nietzsche, Friedrich. *Human, All Too Human.* Lincoln: University of Nebraska Press, 1984.

4. Maine: We're a Team?

Gottlieb, Lori. *Marry Him: The Case for Settling for Mr. Good Enough.* New York: Dutton, 2010.

Parker-Pope, Tara. "Reinventing Date Night for Long-Married Couples." *New York Times,* February 12, 2008.

Sonkajärven Eukonkanto Oy. "How to Become a Master in Wife Carrying—Sonkajärven Eukonkanto." Web. October 5, 2016, www.eukonkanto.fi/en/How+to+Become+a+Master+in+Wife+Carrying.html.

5. Denmark: Make Your House a Home

Alexander, Jessica Joelle, and Iben Dissing Sandahl. *The Danish Way of Parenting: What the Happiest People in the World Know About Raising Confident, Capable Kids.* Copenhagen: Ehrhorn Hummerston, 2015.

Baylor University. "Baylor Study: Cellphones Can Damage Romantic Relationships, Lead to Depression." EurekAlert! Web. October 5, 2016, eurekalert.org/pub_releases/2015-09/bu-bsc092915.php.

Ephron, Nora. *Crazy Salad and Scribble Scribble: Some Things About Women and Notes on Media.* New York: Vintage, 2012.

Rainie, Lee, and Kathryn Zickhur. "Americans' View on Mobile Etiquette."

European Communication Council Report E-Merging Media (n.d.): 15–17. Pew Research Center. Web. August 26, 2015, pewinternet.org/files/2015/08/2015-08-26_mobile-etiquette_FINAL.pdf.

Russell, Helen. *The Year of Living Danishly: Uncovering the Secrets of the World's Happiest Country*. London: Icon Books, 2015.

Turkle, Sherry. "Stop Googling. Let's Talk." Web, nytimes.com/2015/09/27/opinion/sunday/stop-googling-lets-talk.html.

6. France: Be Your Husband's Mistress

Berest, Anne et al. *How to Be Parisian Wherever You Are: Love, Style, and Bad Habits*. New York: Doubleday, 2014.

Ollivier, Debra. *What French Women Know: About Love, Sex and Other Matters of the Heart and Mind*. New York: Putnam, 2009.

Wike, Richard. "French More Accepting of Infidelity than People in Other Countries." Pew Research Center RSS. January 14, 2014. Web, accessed October 5, 2016, pewresearch.org/fact-tank/2014/01/14/french-more-accepting-of-infidelity-than-people-in-other-countries/.

10. Holland: You Didn't Marry Your Job

Brothers, Caroline. "Why Dutch Women Don't Get Depressed." Web, nytimes.com/2007/06/06/arts/06iht-happy.1.6024209.html.

Coates, Ben. *Why the Dutch Are Different: A Journey into the Hidden Heart of the Netherlands*. London: Nicholas Brealey, 2015.

Rock, Chris. *Never Scared*. HBO. 2004. Television.

Ward, Claire. "How Dutch Women Got to Be the Happiest in the World." *Maclean's*. Web. August 19, 2011.

11. India: A Little Thanks Goes a Long Way

Berg, Molly. "The Power of Thank You." Discover UGA. University of Georgia, n.d. Web, discover.uga.edu/index.php?/article/best15-thankyou.

Gordon, Amie M. et al. "To Have and to Hold: Gratitude Promotes Relationship Maintenance in Intimate Bonds." *Journal of Personality and Social Psychology* 103 (2012): 257–74. PsycARTICLES. Web.

Iyer, Malathy. "Ex–Miss World Gives Birth from Egg Frozen for 8 Years—Times of India." *Times of India*, January 12, 2016. Web. October 5, 2016, timesofindia.indiatimes.com/india/Ex-Miss-World-gives-birth-from-egg-frozen-for-8-years/articleshow/50554334.cms.

Mirchandani, Raakhee. "Stop Telling Me to Have More Kids." *Elle*. August 3, 2016. Web, accessed October 5, 2016, elle.com/life-love/a37837/daughter-survived-cancer-one-kid/.

Schwartz, Barry. "More Isn't Always Better." *Harvard Business Review.* July 31, 2014. Web, accessed October 5, 2016, hbr.org/2006/06/more-isnt-always-better.

Schwartz, Barry. *The Paradox of Choice: Why More Is Less.* New York: Ecco, 2004.

12. Meghalaya (the Border of India and Bangladesh): Money, Money, Money

Allen, Timothy. "Meghalaya, India: Where Women Rule, and Men Are Suffragettes." BBC News. Web, bbc.com/news/magazine-16592633.

Bouissou, Julien. "Where Women of India Rule the Roost and Men Demand Gender Equality." *Guardian.* January 18, 2011. Web, accessed October 5, 2016, theguardian.com/world/2011/jan/18/india-khasi-women-politics-bouissou.

Chou, Jessica. "My Husband Makes $240,000—& I Make $36,000." Gender Wage Gap. Web, refinery29.com/gender-pay-gap-husband-wife.

Martin, Wednesday. *Primates of Park Avenue.* New York: Simon & Schuster, 2015.

13. Sweden: Bending Gender Roles

Bävman, Johan. *Swedish Dads.* Malmö: Self-published, 2015.

Carlson, Daniel L. "The Gendered Division of Housework and Couples' Sexual Relationships: A Reexamination." *The Journal of Marriage and Family.* Wiley Online Library, May 25, 2016. Web, accessed October 5, 2016, onlinelibrary.wiley.com/doi/10.1111/jomf.12313/abstract.

Doss, Brian D. "The Effect of the Transition to Parenthood on Relationship Quality: An 8-Year Prospective Study." *Journal of Personality and Social Psychology* 96 (2009): 601–19. PsycARTICLES. Web.

Glass, Jennifer. "CCF BRIEF: Parenting and Happiness in 22 Countries." Council on Contemporary Families. June 16, 2016. Web, accessed October 5, 2016, contemporaryfamilies.org/brief-parenting-happiness/.

O'Mahony, Paul. "Swedish Dad in Bid for Breast Milk." *The Local.* September 2, 2009. Web, thelocal.se/20090902/21842.

Petersen, Andrea. "Here Comes Baby, There Goes the Marriage." *Wall Street Journal.* Wsj.com, April 27, 2011. Web, accessed October 5, 2016. wsj.com/articles/SB10001424052748704099704576288954011675900.

14. Tanzania: Conquer the World Together

Pole, Warren. "Martina Navratilova Describes Her Rescue from Kilimanjaro." *Telegraph*. Web, accessed October 5, 2016, telegraph.co.uk/news/worldnews/africaandindianocean/tanzania/8212080/Martina-Navratilova-describes-her-rescue-from-Kilimanjaro.html.

Thomas, Katherine Woodward. *Conscious Uncoupling: 5 Steps to Living Happily Even After*. New York: Harmony, 2015.

Acknowledgments

Thank you, Glynnis, for delivering Nick and me into the great unknown of marriage in so many ways, for being the Thelma to my Louise and the Louise to my Thelma.

Donna Loffredo went above and beyond to usher this book to its conclusion and Heather Jackson had the vision to help me start its journey. Thank you both for your wisdom, patience, brilliance, wit, and understanding.

It takes a village to make a marriage work and to write a good book, and I couldn't have done it without the help of Jaclyn Boschetti, Danielle Antalfly, Megan Hall, Megan Bramlette (The Megs), Ben Widdicombe, Dan Wakeford, Leah Ginsberg, Kim Rittberg, Micaela English, Sheryl Connelly, Jackie Cascarano, Lisa Belkin, Amy Benziger, Annie Daly, Raakhee Mirchandani, Kavita Daswani, Rebecca Prusinowski, George Rush, Joanna Molloy, Daisy Noe, Ruth Ann Harnisch, Sara Dunn, Laura Begley Bloom, and Leah "my mana" Chernikoff. Thanks to Mikey Sadowski and Justaz Leonidas for getting us almost to the top of Mt. Kilimanjaro. Thanks to Sunitta

Hedau for being my ever-faithful translator and guide through the wilds of India. I plan to find you a husband yet.

Thank you to John and Tracey Piazza and Dick and Patsy Aster for making Nick and me both humans who thought getting married before thirty was a ridiculous idea (although Nick was really pushing it at forty). Thanks to Geoff Aster for keeping me company in the Galápagos while Nick climbed volcanoes and stalked marine iguanas.

I have the greatest agent in the world. I couldn't write books without Alexandra Machinist, who is never afraid to tell me when I'm not living up to my potential and was kind enough to tell me I could turn this into a book idea after I'd had several glasses of wine. Here's to a lifetime of eating good food and writing good books together.

Nick. This book wouldn't exist without you. No one would read a memoir about a girl and her big gross dog. On second thought . . . maybe they would. Thank you for being my teammate, my partner, my companion, and my husband. Thanks for showing me that with a lot of hard work, cheese, and frequent-flier miles, happily ever after might just be possible.